The Forest City Lynching of 1900

CONTRIBUTIONS TO SOUTHERN APPALACHIAN STUDIES

1. *Memoirs of Grassy Creek:*
Growing Up in the Mountains on the Virginia–North Carolina Line.
Zetta Barker Hamby. 1997

2. *The Pond Mountain Chronicle:*
Self-Portrait of a Southern Appalachian Community.
Leland R. Cooper and Mary Lee Cooper. 1997

3. *Traditional Musicians of the Central Blue Ridge:*
Old Time, Early Country, Folk and
Bluegrass Label Recording Artists, with Discographies.
Marty McGee. 2000

4. *W.R. Trivett, Appalachian Pictureman:*
Photographs of a Bygone Time.
Ralph E. Lentz. 2001

5. *The People of the New River:*
Oral Histories from the Ashe, Alleghany and
Watauga Counties of North Carolina.
Leland R. Cooper and Mary Lee Cooper. 2001

6. *John Fox, Jr., Appalachian Author.*
Bill York. 2003

7. *The Thistle and the Brier:*
Historical Links and Cultural Parallels Between Scotland and Appalachia.
Richard Blaustein. 2003

8. *Tales from Sacred Wind:*
Coming of Age in Appalachia. The Cratis Williams Chronicles.
Cratis D. Williams. 2003

9. *Willard Gayheart, Appalachian Artist.*
Willard Gayheart and Donia S. Eley. 2003

10. *The Forest City Lynching of 1900:*
Populism, Racism, and White Supremacy in Rutherford County, North Carolina.
J. Timothy Cole. 2003

The Forest City Lynching of 1900

Populism, Racism, and White Supremacy in Rutherford County, North Carolina

J. TIMOTHY COLE

CONTRIBUTIONS TO SOUTHERN APPALACHIAN STUDIES, 10

McFarland & Company, Inc., Publishers
Jefferson, North Carolina, and London

LIBRARY OF CONGRESS CATALOGUING-IN-PUBLICATION DATA

Cole, J. Timothy, 1959–
　　The Forest City lynching of 1900 : populism, racism, and white supremacy in Rutherford County, North Carolina / J. Timothy Cole.
　　　　p.　　cm.—(Contributions to southern Appalachian studies ; 10)
　　Includes bibliographical references and index.

　　ISBN 0-7864-1623-8 (softcover : 50# alkaline paper) ∞

　　1. Lynching—North Carolina—Forest City.　2. Murder—North Carolina—Forest City.　3. Rutherford County (N.C.)—Race relations. 4. Mills, Avery, d. 1900.　5. Flack, Mills Higgins.　I. Title.　II. Series.
HV6465.N8C65　　2003
364.1'34—dc21　　　　　　　　　　　　　　　　　　　　　　　　2003014406

British Library cataloguing data are available

©2003 J. Timothy Cole. All rights reserved

No part of this book may be reproduced or transmitted in any form or by any means, electronic or mechanical, including photocopying or recording, or by any information storage and retrieval system, without permission in writing from the publisher.

Cover photographs: Uptown Forest City, early 1900s *(courtesy of Helen Flack Cole);* Otho Remus Flack, ca. 1900 *(courtesy of Nelda Wilson Maxwell). Background image ©2003 Clipart.com*

Manufactured in the United States of America

McFarland & Company, Inc., Publishers
　Box 611, Jefferson, North Carolina 28640
　　www.mcfarlandpub.com

Acknowledgments

The research presented herein was conducted at the following: Davis Library and the North Carolina and Southern Historical Collections in Wilson Library, The University of North Carolina, Chapel Hill, NC; The North Carolina Office of Archives and History, Raleigh, NC; The Baptist Historical Collection, Wake Forest University, Winston-Salem, NC; The Old Tryon Room, Isothermal Community College, Spindale, NC; the library of The Genealogical Society of Old Tryon County, Forest City, NC; the Register of Deeds, Rutherford County Courthouse, Rutherfordton, NC; Charlotte-Mecklenburg Public Library, Charlotte, NC; Rowan County Public Library, Salisbury, NC; High Point Public Library, High Point, NC; Forsyth County Public Library, Winston-Salem, NC; Greensboro Public Library, Greensboro, NC; and the Greensboro Historical Museum Archives, Greensboro, NC.

Valuable assistance was provided by Nelda Wilson Maxwell, granddaughter of Mills Higgins Flack, and Flack's great-granddaughter and my mother, Helen Flack Cole, who, as always, was very supportive throughout this project. I wish to thank both of them for sharing family photographs and what they knew of the lynching. I would also like to thank Stephen Massengill of the North Carolina Office of Archives and History, who showed me a hitherto unknown biographical source for Mills Flack, helped identify what I believe is the only known photograph of John Baxter Eaves, and located many of the other photographs used herein; the Southern Historical Collection at the University of North Carolina at Chapel Hill for permission to use materials in the Marion Butler, Zebulon B. Vance, David Schenck and Robert Wilson Papers; the University of North Carolina Press for permission to use the photograph of William S.O'B. Robinson; Sarah Morgan, church clerk, Mountain Creek Baptist Church, Gilkey, NC, for searching extant records of her church for information on the Flacks; James M. Beeby, West Virginia Wesleyan College, for his kind willingness to read and comment upon the manuscript; and Marianne Heckles of the Lancaster County (PA) Historical Society for the genealogical research she did on the Flacks.

Finally, let me add a special thanks to all my colleagues in the Information Services Department at Greensboro Public Library. Without their encouragement and support I could never have completed this project.

Two notes on manuscript/public document sources: First, where citations for the Ralph R. Flack Papers are followed by the abbreviation HFC, they are among those papers still owned by Ms. Helen Flack Cole. However, much of this material is duplicated in the Flack Papers at Isothermal Community College (ICC). Secondly, if a note or bibliographic entry for manuscripts or public documents is followed by the term "microform," the materials are likely available in more than one collection or could be obtained through purchase or inter-library loan. In most cases where an entry is followed by the name of an institution (e.g., the Southern Historical Collection), the materials must be used there.

Table of Contents

Acknowledgments v
Preface 1
Introduction 5

1 Mills Higgins Flack and the Agrarian Revolt in Rutherford   23
2 The Fusion Era and White Supremacy in Rutherford   42
3 The Forest City Lynching and Its Aftermath   62
4 Epilog: The Silence of Dishonor   82

*Appendix I. A Partial List of Members (Chiefly Officers) of the Farmers'
   Alliance in Rutherford*   89
Appendix II. Populist Candidates in Rutherford (1892–1898)   93
Appendix III. The Charlotte Daily Observer *Article of 29 August 1900*   95
Appendix IV. The Charlotte Daily Observer *Article of 31 August 1900*   98
*Appendix V. Affidavit Submitted by Raney Mills to Rutherford County
   Superior Court, Fall 1900, and the Order of Judge Shaw, Etc.*   100
*Appendix VI. Research on the Origins and Revolutionary Services of
   the Flacks of Guilford and Rutherford Counties*   103
*Appendix VII. Plato Durham, John Baxter Eaves and the Ku Klux
   Conspiracy in Rutherford*   118
Notes   145
Bibliography   179
Index   189

And our iniquities, like the wind,
have taken us away.
Isaiah 64:6

Preface

MY MATERNAL GRANDFATHER WAS Ralph R. Flack (1884–1969), a sixth generation Rutherford Countian. He was for many years manager of the Grace Cotton Mill, served a term as Mayor of Rutherfordton (1931–33), was a leader in the First Baptist Church of the same town and spent much of his retirement immersed in the study of genealogy and local history.

Some of the fondest memories of my childhood are of my Grandfather Flack's rambling home on Main Street in Rutherfordton. I spent many hours there during my parents frequent Sunday visits in the 1960s, usually on my own, exploring the house and grounds: the faintly musty smells of the porch and rooms; the great painting of a moose which dominated the parlor wall; and the Scuppernong vine, which my grandfather grew and nurtured for many years.

My grandfather died when I was only ten, so these are faint memories for me now. But immediately after he died, my mother, Helen Flack Cole, became the caretaker of the genealogical research he compiled during the last two decades of his life — a large collection of photographs and notebooks, much of which our family still retains and I occasionally peruse. In the early 1970s, as my Mother began preparing some publications based on his work, I was exposed to the names and faces of my Flack ancestors for the first time.

As vivid as any memory I recounted above is that which I recall upon being told that my great-great grandfather, Mills Higgins Flack (1838–1900), was slain by a Negro. I was astonished that a member of my family could have been murdered, and I am certain that my first thought was of a shootout in a dusty, small town street of the old West, no doubt influenced by the television fare of that day.

My mother could add little in the way of substantial facts, other than that the alleged assassin had been lynched. Even though *my* grandfather would have been fifteen years of age at the time, and would certainly have remembered the death of *his* grandfather, it seems that he spoke little on the subject — which is all the more extraordinary, given his interest in family history.

However, in the years after Ralph Flack's death, his brother, Charles Z. Flack, Sr. (1893–1991), a prominent Forest City realtor, former mayor of Forest City, and an enthusiastic genealogist in his own right, did make some inquiries into the death of Mills H. Flack.

I am told by his son, Charles Z. Flack, Jr., that a friend of the younger Flack once chanced upon some ephemera associated with the Ku Klux Klan which included a photograph of the "murderer" of Flack — a black man named Avery Mills. Charles Jr. presented this photograph to his father, and the elder Flack sent a copy to my mother some years ago, along with the following note:

> This is a picture of Avery Mills who was a tenant on the eighty acre farm of my grandfather, Mills Higgins Flack. This farm is located just east of Flack Road in Forest City. On August 28, 1900, Avery Mills murdered Mills Higgins Flack on this farm.
>
> Avery Mills was arrested and on the way to jail in Rutherfordton, the County seat, he was taken from the officers and on Ledbetter Road, later known as the Prison Camp Road, into the woods and lynched. Unfortunately, lynching was very common in the South following the Civil War and the years of Reconstruction.
>
> So far as I know, no arrests were ever made in the above connection. Warrants were issued, according to my information, but those for whom warrants were issued skipped the County for several months and the matter was then somewhat forgotten.

The photograph of Avery Mills' corpse shows a rather muscular, light-skinned black man lying flat upon his back beneath a tree, arms spread-eagle, dressed in a shirt and trousers. He stares vacantly upward and blood seems to trickle from the right corner of his mouth. To his right is a blanket which had apparently been used to cover his battered body.

This was for many years all I knew about the demise of Mills Flack. In life, I knew he was distinguished as our family's most prominent political figure — though I knew little else other than that he had served in the State House in 1895. Then, about five or six years ago, browsing in an antiquarian book shop, I found a curious propagandistic political pamphlet about the very assembly in which Flack had served. I quickly thumbed it in search of his name. I found it only once: he was listed among those who had voted against the erection of a Confederate monument on the Capital grounds in

Raleigh. His party affiliation was identified as Populist.[1] I found all this very strange because I also knew Flack had served with the Home Guard in the War, and, as his descendants had been Democrats, I had always assumed that he had been one as well.

I think it was at this point that I finally resolved to investigate the Forest City lynching and the political career of Mills Flack. It has been hard work. I have scanned microfilm until I was dizzy; sacrificed weekends, vacations and full-time employment to write; and I *even* gave up my morning paper to read scholarly dissertations on Fusion and Populism. *Why* I cannot really say — or at least I can give no rational explanation. While both of my parents were born in Rutherford County, and I have deep roots there which extend back to the 18th century, I have never lived there and know few people in the County today.

I prefer a more unorthodox explanation for my deep immersion in my great-great grandfather's past. Call it mysticism if you like, but I have come to believe, as one of my colleagues once said to me (in my public "persona," as a librarian), that the ancestors *speak* to us. Or perhaps they speak *through* us. For the depth psychologist Carl Jung once said that the mind itself "consists of the sum of the ancestral minds, the 'unseen fathers' whose authority is born anew with the child."[2] And when I wander through graveyards and find the memorials to Rutherford's long dead public men of another era — not just Mills Flack, but also men like M.O. Dickerson, O.C. Erwin, J.B. Eaves, M.H. Justice and A.D'K. Wallace — I feel I am meeting old friends. They have all become "unseen fathers" for me. Put another way, perhaps this project merely has been my way of coming home.

However, I must confess that the work (this "echoing of the ancestors") has at times been depressing, for it has led me to confront a *dark* side that we may not wish to acknowledge. I know now that these same "unseen fathers" whom I venerate committed *sins*— sins of power, sins of hate, even sins against their own laws. And this leads me to another question: Are not these sins part of our inheritance also? Does not the relationship between power and race dwell in *our* "psyches"— especially Southern psyches—just as it must have dwelt in the minds of our great-great grandfathers? For white Southerners with deep roots, the ancestors plainly do *not* speak as "many voices"— as today's exponents of "multiculturalism" and "diversity" would say — but as one; and to hear the voice of racial hatred and understand it, we must listen *again* to this "God within"— or demon — of "the fathers." It is perhaps ultimately to *this* understanding that *The Forest City Lynching* aspires.

To this work I have appended two other studies which I hope may be of some interest. Appendix VI is a compilation of research on the ancestry of Mills H. Flack. Though the central problem of Flack genealogy (i.e., just where John Flack of Rutherford came from) remains unsolved, I believe readers will find in my use of collateral family sources intriguing evidence for connections between the Flacks of Rutherford and those of Guilford County, NC, and Lancaster County, PA. The final appendix addresses the Ku Klux conspiracy in Rutherford (1870-71) within the broader framework of a dual portrait of two of the section's most outstanding public men of that era: staunch Cleveland County Conservative and Klansman, Plato Durham, and Rutherford Republican leader, John Baxter Eaves. Therein, I challenge the largely held view that Rutherford's Ku Klux raids manifested from a leaderless neighborhood feud, but little motivated by political or racial purposes. Instead, I emphasize the unifying role of ex–Confederate leadership. This appendix also provides background for Republican strength in late 19th century Rutherford (which underpinned the success of Fusion).

> J. Timothy Cole
> *Greensboro, June 2003*

Introduction

MILLS FLACK'S HOME PLACE, ON the farm where he was killed, was located just inside the city limits of present-day Forest City near the intersection of West Main and Vance streets, and has long since vanished. On this spot one will now find the Dollar General Store and the Cool Springs School Gymnasium. Ledbetter Road, the site of the lynching, is three miles or so to the northwest. It is difficult to imagine an August morning over one hundred years ago when on these same streets an angry lynch mob was in hot pursuit of its victim, a black man named Avery Mills—apparently the only racially motivated lynching ever to occur in Rutherford County.

Forest City developed at a crossroads where the Shelby-Rutherfordton road intersected with another which ran north to south and branched off to Spartanburg. The place was first named Burnt Chimney after the burnt-out remains of the old McArthur house, which stood near the junction, and seems best remembered in local lore as the location of the old militia muster grounds. It was here that the local militia drilled, and that CSA units raised in Cool Springs Township, such as Co. D, 16th NC Rgmt., were assembled before marching to the bloody combats of Northern Virginia. After the War, the crossroads community grew into a village, and in 1877 Burnt Chimney was incorporated. The name was officially changed to Forest City in 1887.[1]

During the 1880s and 1890s, Rutherford County and the rest of the rural South was shaken by an agricultural crisis—steadily lowering crop prices, indebtedness, inability to obtain credit and a short money supply—which profoundly affected the farmer. Essentially, the farmers were caught in the transition between the agricultural economy of the old South and the developing industrial economy of the new. For the South's new men of industry,

Uptown Forest City as it appeared in the early 1900s. (Helen Flack Cole)

the panacea for this crisis would be the cotton mill — at once offering hope to the agricultural masses and opportunities for capitalist entrepreneurs. Thus would rise from the ashes of the old a "New South," yet reforms addressing the problems of the farmer would be few.

The rapid development of Forest City during this period — from a tiny village to a thriving town — must be understood in the context of the industrialists' vision of the new South. In 1880, its population was only 110, but by 1900 Forest City was the largest town in Rutherford County with a population of 1,090 people.[2] This dramatic growth was due primarily to the developing textile industry, which was in full bloom in Rutherford, largely through the efforts of Raleigh Rutherford Haynes and Simpson Bobo Tanner.[3] The agricultural crisis of the 1890s had affected the County economically and politically, but by 1900 the emerging textile industry was fueling an economic resurgence and offering landless and yeoman white farmers a way out of the economic crunch. When the Florence Mill opened in Forest City in 1897,[4] men and women were needed to run the mill and they came in droves.

However, for those who continued to wrest a living from the land — and many did — times were very tough. The toll taken on the farmers knew no racial or class boundaries. Black and white, tenant, yeoman and large landholder, all felt the effects of declining prices, over production and the currency crisis. Especially for poor blacks—such as Avery Mills—there was often little alternative to the relentless cycle of sharecropping, the furnishing merchant and debt peonage. Three of five Negro farmers in the County were sharecroppers, and the number of tenant farms in Rutherford would in fact continue to increase. In 1900, there were 1,419 tenant farms in Rutherford County; by 1910, there were 1,589.[5]

Agricultural decline had resulted in the creation of the National Farmers' Alliance and Industrial Union in 1888—a sort of "labor union" for the farmer, built upon old Grange and Greenbacker traditions—which for a time seemed agriculture's last and best hope. This organization became the institutional basis for a mass agrarian movement, and through its various state and local appendages, Southern farmers, in the main Democrats, lobbied their party for reform. Black farmers had their own Colored Alliance,[6] but it was the far-reaching effects of the agricultural crisis upon the self-sufficiency of *landholding* farmers (chiefly white men) which was really instrumental to the growth of the movement and the power it would wield.[7] Few of these men could justify the exchange of their farms and independence for the slavish toil of the mills—only for the landless or the small holder could the mill seem a better alternative.

Theirs thus seemed a class under assault. The independent farmer, so long at the center of the Southern universe, had been asked to give way to the rising sun of industrialization. As Edward Ayers writes, "Landholding farmers occupied an anomalous class position in Gilded Age America. In an era increasingly concerned with appearances, the farmers fell behind ... [and] became identified with makeshift and awkward clothes, unpolished language, and red necks."[8] Helen Edmonds also notes the loss in social prestige to the farmers "because they were no longer [as in the antebellum period] the dominant class."[9] But the landed farmer would not forego his cherished independence without a fight. Through the Alliance, he would re-assert the nobility of the *producer*,[10] all too forgotten by the bankers, railroad men and lawyers who dominated the political process. Moreover, these same men of property would lead Alliancemen to direct political action when it became clear that the farmers' lobby had failed and reforms sufficient to ease the agricultural crisis would not be forthcoming. Awkward or no, landholding farmers would form the backbone of an impressive third party movement,[11] and, in North Carolina, lead it briefly to the corridors of power. Mills Flack belonged to this class, and he would emerge as a leader of the movement in Rutherford County.

But while the farmers' revolt was led by men of property, it was also a genuine grassroots phenomenon. Through the Alliance's myriad sub-alliance organizations, an elaborate lecturing system and newspapers such as the

Progressive Farmer, Flack and other farmers met regularly, made their problems intelligible, educated and indoctrinated each other upon "monopolies" and "plutocrats," and rapidly became "true believers"—or, in the jargon of the farmers, "mid-roaders" or "radicals." And they were indeed radical, for the ideas they entertained were often innovative and even revolutionary ones (ideas on cooperatives, government ownership and bi-metallic currency) intended to re-establish the farmer-producer as the political, moral and fiscal axis upon which America would turn.

Millions joined the movement and it had varying success throughout the South and Midwest between 1888 and 1892—perhaps most notably the breaking of the so-called "jute-bag trust" in 1889.[12] But, by 1892, having witnessed the collapse of many of their fledgling cooperatives and failed in efforts to persuade the politicians on the cherished idea of a "subtreasury" system,[13] the farmers formed their own political party, known as the People's Alliance or Populist Party, and fielded state, local and national candidates. In North Carolina, the Populists had little success in the 1892 election, but, by forming a "Fusion" coalition with Republicans in 1894 (i.e., running "cooperative" tickets), they stunned "the Democracy" by taking the State legislature—and would remain in power for the next four years.

The Fusionists likewise would control local offices in Rutherford from 1894 to 1898. Among the Populist candidates for state office in 1892 and 1894 was Mills Flack, nominated in both those years for Rutherford's seat in the legislature. Running as a straight Populist in 1892, he was easily defeated, but, as the County's Fusion candidate in 1894, he was victorious, and thus the Rutherford farmer would serve in the so-called "Fusion legislature" of 1895. The triumph was an impressive one both for Flack and the agrarian movement; as Lawrence Goodwyn puts it, "North Carolina Alliancemen ... had achieved, momentarily at least, a stunning victory on what appeared to be *socially radical terms*."[14]

It was indeed Populist cooperation with Republicans which had produced this victory, yet Fusion meant more than cooperative tickets. For it also embraced the "socially radical terms" referred to by Goodwyn—in other words, *interracial cooperation*, an essential element, the *lynch*pin, as it were, of the story that follows. Fusion victory in North Carolina would not have been possible without the help of thousands of Negro Republican votes; furthermore, electoral reforms enacted by the Fusion legislature, such as direct election of County Commissioners, increased the number of blacks holding political offices, especially in heavily black sections of Eastern North Carolina—enough so that historian Joel Williamson suggests an "echo reconstruction."[15] Class and the agrarian agenda had briefly trumped race in the political struggle, and white landed farmers and the Negro had joined forces to overthrow "the party of the fathers." But the apparent triumph of class over race would ultimately prove hollow and sow the seeds of Populist downfall.

The Democratic Party in North Carolina received the Fusion coup with more than a little unease — not only were the Democrats out of power, but the social order of the South was under assault by the "disgrace" of Negro equality. A new generation was thus called upon to restore the Democracy to the seat of power — men such as Furnifold M. Simmons, Charles Brantley Aycock, Locke Craig and Josephus Daniels. These were younger men, whom Glenda Gilmore refers to as the "New White Men" for a commitment to industrialization, education and perhaps even the white race which exceeded that of their paternalistic, Redeemer-Bourbon fathers;[16] and they realized that the quickest way back to the seat of power was to break up the class interests of the Populists by appealing to what W.J. Cash calls the "Proto-Dorian Convention," the racial bond which stood above all other social and political considerations of the South.[17]

While at least one historian calls North Carolina's Fusion years an "historic experiment in interracial democracy,"[18] and the Populist program did originally call for "a united front between the Negro and white farmers,"[19] it seems clear that the coalition of the Populists and Republicans was an uneasy alliance from the beginning. Woodward suggests that the Populists' decision to fuse with the Republicans was simply an appropriation of the Democratic tactic of manipulating Negro votes in order to stay in power; "The binding force was plainly expediency...."[20] At best, the Populists and the Negroes of the Republican Party shared a "limited equalitarianism"—"'They are in the ditch just like we are.'"[21]

But the Populists' racial brethren in the Democratic Party would not allow this coalition of class interest to continue. In the white supremacy campaigns of both 1898, when they retook the legislature, and 1900, when they won approval of a constitutional amendment which effectively disfranchised the Negro in North Carolina and regained the governorship, Aycock, Simmons and other Democratic leaders employed the rhetoric of race. Part of the attack was directed at the Populists themselves. Thus the farmers "suffered [a] heavy loss in prestige under attack by the party of white supremacy for alleged racial disloyalty."[22] Some Democrats even went so far as to view Populists as "enemies of white civilization."[23]

However, for most of the Democrats the "real" enemy of white civilization was not the Populist "traitor," but the "infamy" of "Negro rule" or "domination." To understand how searing these words would be to the ears of a white man in the South of 1900, we must comprehend how deeply he felt this to be his country, how profoundly he felt himself the complete superior to the Negro—whom he considered merely "a vile and unclean thing," the lowest creature in a Southern hierarchy still so rooted in antebellum notions of *place* or "placeness," to use Joel Williamson's term.[24] Not only had many of the white men of that era known the Negro as slave, but they also had deep roots in their communities and their lives were imbued with legacies of forefathers who had made homes here from nothing, whipped Ferguson at King's Mountain and fought with Lee in Northern Virginia. Even the history lessons of a meager common school education would instill in them a belief in the absolute superiority of the Anglo-Saxon race. As Locke Craig put it in a speech in 1900, "this blood that thundered in the veins of Cromwell and the soldiers of the Covenant ... on Marston Moor and Naseby Field...."[25]

They were also men who were passionate about civic duty; court week and political participation, speeches and public life, were genuine and tangible for them in a way that they are not today — they believed that they counted, their world was smaller and did not extend much beyond Rutherford and Raleigh. It was from this sense of political efficacy that the agrarian revolt drew much of its power. But it was also a distinctly white, Southern edifice, in that it largely excluded the Negro — genuine power-sharing was unconscionable for most white men. Thus while many Populists and Republicans did dismiss "Negro rule" as propaganda, they were nonetheless susceptible to the insult to their race and forefathers which the prospect presented: "bottom rail" could never be on top.

Blacks actually held only a small proportion of the political offices in the State, mainly in the eastern counties. But Democratic papers such as Daniels' *News and Observer*, Joseph P. Caldwell's *Daily Charlotte Observer* and Rutherfordton's *Western Vindicator*, edited by Maj. L.P. Erwin,[26] were filled with propagandistic articles sporting headlines such as "Negro Control in Wilmington," "Greenville Negroized," and "Negroism in Lenoir County,"[27] and appeals were made to the Populists of Western North Carolina counties to "save" their brethren in the east from "Negro domination." Similarly Aycock and others toured the state — including stops in Forest City, Caroleen and Rutherfordton — "crying nigger, nigger, nigger," and raising the specter of social equality with the infernal "black beast" by equating the "goddess of North Carolina Democracy [with] the white womanhood of the State."[28] The Democrats even began "White Supremacy Clubs,"[29] and after South Carolina's arch racist Benjamin Tillman spoke in the state, gangs of Red Shirts[30] became an intimidating presence, especially in the southeastern border counties. Fear and propaganda proved an irresistible combination, and, under this assault, the pressure placed upon North Carolina Populists to return to "the party of the fathers" would be intense. "The Democracy" was eminently successful, and near the end of the campaign in 1898 white Populists and Republicans were seen marching together with Democrats at a Red Shirt parade.[31] Their victory would be punctuated with the so-called

"Wilmington Revolution," a carefully choreographed white riot which followed in the days immediately after the election — and cost perhaps a dozen or more black lives.

For the matter *did* finally come down to *power* and "redemption," and for these objectives Simmons and Aycock were willing to risk instability — so long as the risk remained with the Negro. When the Democrats of North Carolina had achieved black disfranchisement and regained both the Governor's mansion and the state legislature, they could thump their chests, declare the world righted, and the Negro "protected" and in his *place*. If it meant the sacrifice of a few black lives to Judge Lynch or a Wilmington race riot, then so be it.

* * *

The term "lynching" refers to an extralegal form of vigilante justice whereby alleged criminals are executed by mobs without due process of law. In the 19th century, these events were sometimes ironically called acts of "lynch law," perhaps conveying a sense of legitimacy as a form of *community* sanction. Just how the term "lynching" originated is unclear, though it has been traced to at least three different tales of Loyalist or Tory executions which occurred in North Carolina and Virginia between 1768 and 1780.[32] And perhaps every Rutherford schoolboy knows the tale of Tory hangings at Biggerstaff's Old Fields, near Sunshine, following the rout of Ferguson at King's Mountain in 1780.[33] But race had nothing to do with these early executions.

If there is an antebellum antecedent which links race to lynching, it is perhaps to be found in "the slave patrol," which Joel Williamson refers to as a "[court] on horseback ... with the power to try, judge, sentence, and punish offenders on the spot"[34] and Allen Trelease calls a sort of "institutionalized vigilantism."[35] The patrol was an organization peculiar to the slave-holding South which played an important part in the capture of runaways and securing the white population against insurrection, especially in the years following the Nat Turner uprising of 1831. But it lived on in the Southern imagination long after slavery had come to an end. In Negro folklore, the "patty roller" would continue to symbolize "terror" — even if it was only to admonish small children to behave; and, in *Intruder in the Dust*, set in 20th century Mississippi, when Faulkner uses the term "Beat Four"[36] he refers to the jurisdiction of a patrol, even though that body no longer had a "formal" existence. The patrol (though it had legal sanction) might thus be viewed as the "archetypal mob," a predecessor of the white lynch mobs that committed thousands of extralegal lynchings in the South during the late 19th and early 20th centuries — notwithstanding the caveat that it was more nearly analogous to smaller "terrorist" or "vigilante" mobs rather than the larger "mass mobs" so frequently associated with lynchings which rose to levels of community ritual.[37]

But regardless of pre–War antecedents, it was not until Reconstruction (ca. 1870) that the peculiar Southern correlation between lynching and race really began to manifest itself. Trelease, who documents numerous lynchings of blacks in his *White Terror*, a history of the Ku Klux Klan during Reconstruction, suggests that when blacks ceased to be property, "they became easier and safer targets for the pent-up fear, hatred, and derring-do of frustrated whites." Moreover, since there were no masters or slave codes to control the Negro, fear of "all-out race war" burdened the Southern conscience. Conservative political rhetoric against "Negro rule," perceptions of blacks "as only a degree removed from the wild beasts of the jungle," and the infamies of "social equality" and the "Southern rape complex" merged to create in whites a near "pathological fear" of their former slaves.[38] Randolph Shotwell described similar fears of "black brutes" following allegations of rapes in Cleveland and Rutherford counties during this period.[39] The patrol was thus revived in the form of the Ku Klux Klan and other vigilantism which through riots, murders and lynchings took hundreds of Negro lives throughout the South during the late 1860s and early 1870s.

However, in *The Crucible of Race*, Joel Williamson argues that it was still later, with the dawning of the South's era of "racial Radicalism" (1889–1915) — a period distinguished by dramatic moves toward black political disfranchisement and racial segregation, as well as increased violence against the Negro — that lynching became ensconced as the white South's *preferred* sanction for black criminality, especially for sexual assaults upon white women.[40] Williamson's theory is psychohistorical (an elucidation and expansion of the old "rape complex") and emphasizes that racial lynching really developed from the convergence of Victorian sexual repression and the decline of Southern agriculture. While his emphasis on unconscious sexual needs was anticipated by Jacquelyn Dowd Hall's observations on the New South's "folk pornography" and "the association between 'savagery' and sexual passion" in the 19th century mind,[41] Williamson goes further and links the rise of racial lynching during the Radical era to the fortunes of the agrarian movement.[42] Statistics do indeed indicate that racial lynchings in the South peaked ca. 1892, just as politicization of the farmers was cresting; and throughout the period between 1889 and 1901 (as the farmers' movement waxed and waned) lynchings were comparatively higher than they were in the decades immediately before and after.[43] During this period, the black man, according to Williamson, was more than just a victim of extralegal justice — he became a *scapegoat* for the ills of a society at the brink. Why did this happen?

As the agricultural crisis deepened, young, landless and alienated black males began flocking to the cities of the South in search of work. To white eyes unaccustomed to this in-migration, a young black man would seem threatening, a "nigger loose" or "strange nigra,"[44] and blacks were thus associated with crime and immoral sexual behavior. This image of the Negro was fed and buttressed by genuine increases in black criminality, especially murders, in urban environs,[45] and the perception that Negroes, as Hall puts it, lacked "family feeling, the cornerstone of social order." Above all, with respect to their sexuality, writes Hall, "black men were [seen as] acting upon the innate lasciviousness of the savage beast."[46] Finally, these so-called "New Negroes" were a generation of blacks who had been born after slavery and were less willing to submit to white domination, less willing to comply with the Southern "caste" system — that place reserved for them at the *bottom* of the Southern social hierarchy — than had been their slave forebears before them.[47] In short, whites perceived blacks as threatening in ways and to degrees they had not been before. All this combined to give rise to the myth of the "black beast rapist," legitimized by the pseudo-science of the day which portrayed African-Americans as a race "retrogressing" to savagery and primitivism.[48]

Both Williamson and Hall hold that the rise in racial lynching was at least in part due to the *unconscious needs* of sexually repressed white men. The "black beast" was thus a fantasy of white men who embraced a Victorian standard of restraint which led to sexual repression and guilt. As Williamson puts it, white men projected bestiality upon black men "because, they were, at varying levels, denying ordinary sexual behavior to themselves";[49] Hall writes that white men "project[ed] onto blacks the 'animal within.'"[50] This ultimately manifested itself in a fantasy whereby white men would protect the "purity" of their women from the savage "black beast." By lynching a Negro, Williamson argues, white men "symbolically killed" thoughts of sexual liberation for themselves;[51] or, as Hall says, "the buried parts of themselves could be objectified and controlled."[52] Black men were thus marked as scapegoats by a sort of psycho-sexual resentment.

Williamson *adds* that sexual repression was compounded by the self-doubts and failures associated with the transition from an agricultural to industrial economy during the Radical era. Since the economic decline had undermined the ability of white men in the South to provide for their families, it led to "feelings of inadequacy." "It seems fully possible," writes Williamson, "that the rage against the black beast rapist was a kind of psychic compensation. If white men could not provide for their women materially as they had done before, they could certainly protect them from a much more awful threat — the outrage of their purity, and hence their piety, by black men."[53] Thus he notes that, especially during the 1890s, white farmers alternated between periods of political action (through the vehicles of the Farmers' Alliance and the Populist Party) and victimage of the Negro. When there seemed to be hope for the farmers' cause, lynchings abated; but when there was failure, the black man was a convenient scapegoat.[54]

But though the "rape fantasy" thesis does indeed help to explain the rise in racial lynching during this period, it is weakened by the observation that the majority of racial lynchings had nothing to do with rape — as with the Forest City lynching of Avery Mills. Williamson himself observes that "[only] about a third of ... lynchings had anything to do with rape."[55] It was in fact the crime of murder which was most likely to lead to a lynching.[56] He asks us to accept this lacunae with a leap of faith: "Whites began the practice of lynching as a reaction against the presumed threat of the black beast to white womanhood," he wrote, "but it soon became an appalling habit, applicable to a wide range of offenses, real or imagined."[57] At no point does he explain how "the presumed threat of the black beast" could be transferred to other offenses, thus adding weight to the views of Fitzhugh Brundage[58] and Stewart E. Tolnay and E.M. Beck[59] that his explanation for lynching is *incomplete*. Though some historians choose to ignore the statistics — Donald Matthews has written that they make "no difference," that "[the] black rapist myth" fully deserves its "canonical status" as "one of the most pervasive expressions of white culture in the American South"[60] — there nonetheless remains the "smell" of reductionism.

Brundage addresses this problem most directly, and makes note of the "temptation to make it [the rape complex] the central theme and to explain both too much and too little by dwelling upon the prevailing sexual mores of the South."[61] Elsewhere he observes that psychological or psychohistorical interpretations of lynching have failed to account for variations by region and frequency; moreover, he argues that there is inadequate understanding of family life and sexuality in the postbellum South to provide a foundation for psychological interpretation.[62] Brundage's excellent analysis of the problem of lynching (especially his taxonomy of the mob) indeed reveals a very complex phenomenon which can admit no easy answers — the economic relationship between owner and tenant,[63] Southern honor,[64] religion,[65] Populism,[66] all these factors have heuristic value, as also does the rape fantasy thesis.

It is beyond the scope of this study to attempt a general explanation of racial lynching.[67] I have discussed Williamson's theory at length because his emphasis upon the role of the Populist movement and the rhetoric of the "black beast" have so strongly influenced my own thinking on the Forest City lynching — though I will add Southern honor to the mix. My thesis is basically two-fold. First, the Forest City lynching of 1900 took place on the heels of the North Carolina Democratic Party's successful white supremacy campaigns of 1898 and 1900. As we discussed above, both of these campaigns employed a highly-charged racial rhetoric which demonized the Negro in order to break up the Populist-Republican coalition, raising the specters of both black social and political equality and at least indirectly sanctioning violence. The successes of these campaigns in Rutherford suggest "the Democracy's" appeals were heard and persuasive. Secondly, this rhetorical destruction of the Negro took place against the broader context of a Southern code of honor which necessitated the defense of the white power structure. The "murder" of a prominent former Populist by a "lowly" Negro thus required the ritualized spectacle of prompt and lethal sanction by the white community.

* * *

It would be understatement to say that *words* themselves were a potent weapon used against the Negro. For the typical white Southerner of 1900, utterly convinced of Anglo-Saxon supremacy—and faced with a "New Negro," less willing to deny himself the political and social equality denied his slave forebears—the rhetorical dehumanization of blacks became virtually ubiquitous. Leon Litwack's recent *Trouble in Mind* is replete with examples of metaphors used by whites of the period to equate blacks to lower forms of life: "'noxious insects,'" dogs, disease, a "black poison in the body of the South," "'half-civilized gorillas,'" fleas, mules, and "'a lazy, lying, lustful animal' whose nature 'resembles the hog's.'" One white, cited by Litwack, likened the lynching of a Negro to "'killing a chicken or killing a snake.'" For many whites, the Negro was indeed barely more than vermin—to be white and think otherwise was to be "regarded as a traitor and an outcast."[68] The extent to which this "biophobic" degradation of "newfangled niggers" could have given rise to racial lynchings is unclear. But emotionally, it is simply easier to kill an animal than a human being.

Words provide a "pre-text" for action, and the anti–Negro rhetoric of the New South was also accompanied by a strong element of sadism, apparent in the gratuitous violence associated with many racial lynchings. Litwack describes in excruciating detail victims who were burned alive, shot, disemboweled, hung and mutilated. Their agonies as their blood boiled or eyes popped out of their sockets are almost indescribable. But people *wanted* to see these events—they were spectacles to be "cherished" in community memory. Crowds witnessing a lynching could sometimes number several thousand—and they often fought over macabre souvenirs, such as pieces of the victim's heart, liver, fingers and bones.[69] The elements of display and torture in these events begs explanation.[70]

It is true that not all lynchings were equally barbaric. Avery Mills' lynching had very little of the spectacle of cruelty—it came close to a "good lynching," at least in the sense that Mills was dispatched quickly. But it was unfortunately altogether typical in that the Forest City mass mob that ended his life was "not overly scrupulous about determining the guilt of the black victim."[71] One might say that lynching was ritual first and justice second.

The lynching of Negroes quite literally became a sort of white *birthright* in the New South, a right to destroy black lives with impunity — nearly 2,500 between 1882 and 1930[72] — egged on by the vituperative rhetoric of white supremacists. Rebecca Latimer Felton, a Georgian who would later be the first woman to serve in the U.S. Senate, would announce in a widely published speech in 1897, "'…if it takes lynching to protect woman's dearest possession from drunken, ravening beasts, then I say *lynch a thousand a week if it becomes necessary*.'"[73] But similar threats were often made with no reference to lynching or the protection of women. Another Georgian would remark, "Before we submit [compromise white supremacy] we will kill every Negro in the South."[74] During the white supremacy campaign in North Carolina in 1898, Democratic congressman — later governor — William W. Kitchen was quoted as saying, "Before we allow the Negroes to control this State as they do now, we will kill enough of them that there will not be enough left to bury them."[75] The most extreme of radicals came to believe that the Negro was so innately bad that he could have *no place* in American society.[76] Alfred Moore Waddell, who led the Wilmington Race Riot of 1898, "vowing to choke the Cape Fear River with carcasses,"[77] went so far as to assert that race war and the racial extinction of the Negro were inevitable.[78] The rhetoric of white supremacy had thus succeeded in projecting upon the Negro an absolute badness, in contrast to the white South's absolute purity, rightness and good.

The Negro was of course only one of many "devils" in the Southern mind — Catholics, Jews, Yankees, bankers and many others had their places in that firmament. But skillful and persuasive public men can move the incubi of men's nightmares like pawns on a chess board. Aycock, Simmons and Daniels were such men, and they realized that for the politicized "mid-road" white farmer of the 1890s, the devil had became the plutocracy: the wealthy, *non*-productive bankers, industrialists and railroad tycoons who controlled finance and by whom the farmer felt exploited. They also realized that the surest way to smash the farmers' movement was to substitute another devil: and the Negro afforded precisely this. If "the Democracy" could not deliver the heads of monopoly capitalists (i.e., figuratively speaking, by introducing reform) they could at least *deliver* the Negro. Put another way, money would continue in "short supply" and remain the "plaything" of the plutocrats — but there were plenty of "niggers" for the farmers.

The men of the land thus had wanted the destruction of the plutocrats and a new order, but had not realized this project. However, by participating in and witnessing a lynching — or perhaps by just being part of the same

Southern mind, the socio-historical fabric which sanctioned lynchings—they shared in a surrogate destruction which ritually reaffirmed white hegemony over the almost powerless Negro. Though Aycock and other Democratic leaders in North Carolina opposed lynching as mob rule, they would nonetheless orchestrate redemption—and ascend to power—using a rhetoric which exploited deep reservoirs of racial hatred which were indistinguishable from the same ones which gave rise to lynchings.

In this sense, the lynching of Avery Mills was about political power also—and it is for this dissimulation that it is most difficult to forgive men like Aycock and Simmons. The Forest City event occurred less than four weeks after the second of two white supremacy campaigns which these men led, and in a time in which the rhetoric of race and the assertion of white power had reached its zenith. When "the Democracy" cried "Negro rule" and "Negro domination" and appealed to white farmers to return to "the party of the fathers," they marshaled the fear of the "black beast" and the savagery of sadism in the name of political power and created a milieu which was conducive to racial victimage. It was a fear that infected Mills Flack and a mob in Forest City, and, in the person of Avery Mills, the Rutherford farmers made a ritual victim to re-forge the racial bond between themselves and "the Democracy."

* * *

Perhaps the South possessed no other "distinctive condition," as Brundage calls it, more ripe for the expression of the rituals of racism than the Southern code of *honor*; and, in the following, I will speak much of honor, a concept bound up with the import of *community*. For in the South of 1900, where bonds of community, church and political life were much stronger than now, honor vested one's self-worth in "the eyes of others," and lay at the heart of one's *public* reputation.[79] This meant that life in the small town or rural Southern community of one hundred years ago was more intrusive—as illustrated by Mills Flack's church, where members were investigated for fornication, dancing, drinking and cursing,[80] something which is unthinkable today. But also, strength in the bonds of men and community lent themselves to the defense of honor through acts of *repressive justice*; transgressions against the collective honor of Southern communities explain much of the propensity of "mass mobs" to lynch in retaliation for murder[81]—such as was the case in Forest City where the "murder" of a leader in politics and church was received as an insult to much of the community. Men and community took precedence over law. As Brundage writes, "Raw human emotion ... dictated the reactions to perceived transgressions ... [and] the culture of honor played a crucial role in directing the release of spontaneous emotions and passions in certain time-honored customs."[82] The code of honor was thus the justification for the murder of Avery Mills and hundreds of other blacks during the lynching era.

But though honor would suffuse the lives of white Southerners, the Negro just as surely could have no honor in the South. Brundage observes that the Negro was conspicuously dishonorable in a society which demanded honor and his "dishonor became intimately intertwined with black inequality and subordination."[83] Southern honor was indeed transformed by the presence of the Negro. Though certainly Bertram Wyatt-Brown is correct when he says that honor came before slavery, he also states that "over the course of a parallel and mutually sustaining existence, white man's honor and black man's slavery became in the public mind of the South practically indistinguishable."[84] As Ayers puts it, "...slavery by its very nature dishonored all members of one class and bestowed honor on another; in the American South, race codified and reified this class distinction."[85] With respect to lynchings, writes Brundage, these events were, "much more than just acts of vengeance. They also dramatized as few other rituals could the domination of whites and the degradation and dishonor of blacks."[86] It is as if white honor in the South was built upon the dishonor of the black man — that through a sort of perverse symbiosis, the former gained by the diminishment of the latter. Needless to say, the Negro was expected to acknowledge white privilege and respect the racial code which placed him at the bottom of the Southern status hierarchy.

Though the South of 1900 would begrudge little or no honor to the Negro, he was no longer a slave and wished to be treated like a man — especially if he was a young man, a "New Negro" born after slavery. This is evident in the case of Avery Mills; the Forest City lynching was triggered by the temerity of a young, black tenant farmer and his wife to disagree with a prominent white landholder *over the ownership of some peaches*— and a Southern code of honor which made this unthinkable to a man like Mills Flack. Virtually any Negro assertiveness— even violations of the racial code such as failure to tip a hat or obsequiously step aside when passing a white on the sidewalk — could ignite white rage against "the beast," and Avery Mills and his wife Raney evidently refused to be "good Negroes." Perhaps Mills Flack thought to teach them a lesson when he went armed to his farm that day. And though his friends and family would posthumously defend the code and his honor, Flack was finally "hoisted upon his own petard" by the very aggression and anger that the code condoned — and thus was himself a victim of what he sought to defend.

Furthermore, despite the complicity of community and honor in the destruction of Avery Mills' life, as the aftermath of the Forest City lynching unfolded it also reflected a decline in the import of community and a strain in the Southern code of honor — a strain which is mirrored in the ambivalences of Aycock and Simmons about lynching and white supremacy. For social processes of "atomization" or "individuation" were well under way in the South. As Palmer writes, "increasingly [the farmers were] threatened by collapse into economic servitude and social dependency while a world of cities, vast industrial developments, a complicated and stratified social organization, [and] a world of impersonality…, amoral in the traditional, personal sense of morality, destroyed the community and values they knew and understood and in which they believed."[87] The same feelings of chaos and disorder, of impending millennial doom, which had thus helped spur the farmers' movement,[88] would continue as the "old ways" inexorably eroded. Brundage keenly links these processes of social change to the decline of honor itself. He writes,

> Powerful solvents, in particular urbanization and industrialization, were at work on the code of honor during the late nineteenth century…. [It] fostered growing emphasis upon self-control and new conceptions of self-worth, all of which grated against the ideals of honor. In addition, … champions of the New South creed … extolled the virtues of discipline and personal dignity and implicitly denigrated the values of the Old South. The new values, of course, did not vanquish older southern values in one fell swoop. But with the construction of each new cotton mill and each new city block the survival of the code of honor was called into question.[89]

Undoubtedly, Rutherford farmers during the 1890s felt something of this gradual breakdown of community and honor as the old hegemony of independent agriculture gradually gave way to the mills. And certainly the Flacks experienced these changes. Mills Flack's boys were leaving the home of their ancestors to make their fortunes elsewhere — for example, Mills' son Thomas Millard would give up farming cotton and go to Mississippi[90] — and Mills would be the last of his line to make a living from the land. Lee Roswell, his eldest son, was a sewing machine salesman in Washington, DC, at the time of his death in 1904.[91] Many of his children, grandchildren and great-grandchildren would turn to the railroads and cotton mills for their livelihoods and lived — at least for brief periods — in places like Charlotte, NC, South Carolina, Georgia and Kentucky.[92] If you do not live *in* the community "of the fathers" you will necessarily feel less dependent upon it and less apt to defend it.

Of course, honor and community had not eroded enough to save Avery Mills, but perhaps their decline did play a role in sparing his wife Raney — who was later tried and convicted on charges of second degree murder in the death of Flack but subsequently *pardoned* by Aycock. The Forest City lynching thus reveals that men such as Aycock and Simmons straddled a fence, so to speak, with respect to the code of honor, racial hatred and lynching — with one foot in "our fathers' fields," the other in modernity. Gilmore notes that Aycock could describe the white supremacy victory of 1898 as a "glorious victory," and yet admit that "the extent of it frightens me," following the Wilmington riot in which at least eleven Negroes were killed and many more were forced to abandon their homes and property.[93] Cash observed in the "best men" of the South a "distinct moral uneasiness" with "Negro-lynching" and "Nigger hate."[94] Though a man such as Aycock (surely venerated as North Carolina's "best man," ca. 1900) could ruthlessly exploit the Negro for political purposes, he could also believe that the black man had a "place" in the South, even if it was only at the lowest rung of the social ladder. Aycock recognized that lynching threatened "rule by law," the foundation of stability upon which the New South would rest. Even Furnifold M. Simmons, generally described as the architect of the white supremacy campaigns of 1898 and 1900, "plead earnestly for respect for law" when a lynching was feared after a Negro allegedly murdered his father in 1903.[95] Mobocracy was as intolerable to Aycock and Simmons as it had been to the founders.

It is easy to demonize these men now, which revisionist historians such as Glenda Gilmore has indeed done, but they did — at least incrementally — try to marshal the forces of the state against lynching, culminating in the successful prosecution of lynchers in Salisbury in 1906.[96] Aycock's pardon of Raney Mills would symbolize his stand against mob rule in the Forest City case and also serve as a symbolic sanction against the community for what was slowly becoming a superannuated lawlessness. North Carolina's "progressive plutocracy," to use V.O. Key's oft quoted words, indeed did move slowly away from honor and toward the law.

But clearly the law was not the friend of Avery Mills in 1900. Though one could hardly point to a more deeply troubling manifestation of white supremacy than racial lynching, certainly the *legal double-standard* which sustained it was equally destructive, if not more so. As Leon Litwack writes, in addition to civil, common and statutory law, there was "Negro law," the untaught law of custom in the Jim Crow South which translated into "selective" justice.[97] Negroes rarely served on juries, their testimonies were hardly ever accepted, and they were given little chance against whites in court.[98] And while the "better class" of whites might occasionally denounce "nigger hate," white lynch mobs could destroy black lives with more or less impunity — and few lynchers were ever tried. Avery Mills' offense was the alleged murder of a white man, and for that the penalty was almost certain death.[99] Even if he had not been lynched, the law probably would have done little to save him.

* * *

What follows is really two stories that I believe are inseparable: that of 1) the Rutherford farmer Mills Flack and the agrarian/Fusion era of which he was a part, and 2) the racism which inflamed the passions of the Forest City mob that destroyed the life of Avery Mills. For while I will acknowledge that many factors played a role in racial lynching, the lynching of Avery Mills owed much to a desperate time of economic transition — not unlike the current textile decline facing Spindale and other mill towns in Rutherford — when proud men of the land were finally persuaded that their attempt to take a stand for man and against money, to paraphrase Walter Clark, had come to failure. But the realization of failure was indeed *forced*— or helped — by a rhetoric which transformed the *common enemy* of the farmer from monopoly capital into the Negro.

The lynching of Avery Mills in effect served a cathartic, ritual function, supplanting the rhetoric of revolt, a revolt against money, monopolies and concentrated wealth, which the farmers viewed as threats to their way of life, with the rhetoric of race. The Negro was thus the scapegoat, the sacrifice, which would symbolically right *another* disorder in society — implied by black political power and the threat of social equality — and affirm the necessity of white solidarity and hegemony implicit in the Southern code of honor. In other words, Avery Mills became the *object* of Populism's failure in Rutherford — a failure to a great extent engineered by the rhetoric of an out-of-power Democratic Party. While I will explore other themes here — such as the reluctance of family members who lived through this event to transmit it to the generations that followed —*The Forest City Lynching of 1900* is perhaps, finally, a tale of how the code of honor and rhetorical persuasion merged in the maintenance of power in Southern society — and how the "mortar" of the New South was mixed with Negro blood.

1

Mills Higgins Flack and the Agrarian Revolt in Rutherford

MILLS HIGGINS FLACK HAD DEEP ROOTS in Rutherford, descending from a line which can be traced to his great-grandfather, John Flack (?–1792), who settled in what was then Tryon County no later than 1778. Attached to the mid-18th century Scots-Irish migration to the Piedmont and Western North Carolina, John Flack was among the pioneers of the County and fairly prominent in the affairs of early Rutherford, being appointed a Justice of the Peace during the Revolution (1781), a capacity in which he served until his death. This appointment establishes that he was a Patriot, and it is even possible — though probably unprovable — that he was among the Rutherford militia who helped defeat Ferguson at King's Mountain (see Appendix VI).[1]

Mills Flack's father was a farmer, as was his father before him. His grandfather, George Flack (1778–1860), along with an older brother, Andrew Flack, Sr. (1775–ca.1865), inherited their father's Catheys Creek lands when they came of age in the 1790s, and would remain on the old farm the rest of their lives.[2] There they raised corn, oats, potatoes, a little rye and wheat, and livestock such as pigs, sheep and cattle.[3] Neither of these men were as active in public affairs as their father, but they were respectable farmers of modest means: each owned several hundred acres and a half dozen or so slaves.[4]

Andrew Flack, Jr. (1808–1890), the second son of George Flack, seems to have been a favorite of the latter. Andrew never left the family farm, but would remain even after marriage to Alvira Higgins (ca.1812–ca.1881) of Burke County in 1830.[5] There also he would sire twelve children, the fifth of which, born on November 13th, 1838, was named Mills Higgins after his maternal Grandfather.[6] When George Flack died in 1860, he left his eldest son "Major" John only $20, but the bequest of Andrew Flack, Jr. was nothing less than the entirety of his father's holdings on Catheys Creek.[7]

Growing up on the old Flack farm, it was surely the life of the land which Mills Flack would come to know best. But he received some "book learning" too, and as Andrew Flack, Jr. was appointed a superintendent of common schools in 1853,[8] it is probably safe to assume that education was valued in the Flack household. The 1850 census indicates that young Mills had attended school —certainly at one of the "common" or public schools of the day—in the previous year.[9] A later biography indeed confirms that Flack was educated in the common schools,[10] though his attendance was probably irregular and contingent upon the distance from his home to the school and the labor requirements of the farm. Flack also attended Golden Grove Seminary during 1858-59,[11] an academy which was located near present-day Spindale.[12] Any secondary or higher education was certainly atypical for the son of a rural farmer in antebellum North Carolina. As one of Mills Flack's last recorded public acts was a speech before the Rutherford County Teacher's Association,[13] it would seem that education was vital to him.

Mills was probably a life-long Baptist. His great-grandfather, John Flack, undoubtedly came to Old Tryon as a Presbyterian, for he was of Scots-Irish heritage and is associated with the early history of the Brittain Presbyterian Church, founded in 1768 near Camp Creek.[14] However, Brittain Church was some distance from John Flack's lands on Catheys Creek, and it seems the Flacks later joined nearby Mountain Creek Baptist (estab. 1787)—as evidenced by the fact that John's eldest sons, George and Andrew, are both buried there.[15] Mills Flack thus probably attended the Mountain Creek church as a youngster growing up on Catheys Creek. After his marriage and settlement near Cove Creek, it is possible he joined the congregation of Montford Cove Baptist Church, for this was the church of his in-laws, the Hemphills.[16] Following his removal to Burnt Chimney ca. 1883, Flack emerged as one of the leading brethren at the nearby Cool Springs Baptist Church (estab. 1848), which later became the First Baptist Church of Forest City.[17]

The Flack slaveholdings were modest. According to the 1850 slave schedule for Rutherford, Mills' father Andrew had seven slaves.[18] By 1860, his holdings had grown to ten.[19] Comparison of the ages of the slaves (the schedules did not identify slaves by name), which shows consistent +/- ten year increments as well as the presence of exact gender matches, strongly suggests that the same individuals counted in the 1850 census were also present for the 1860 census. From this observation we may infer that Andrew Flack, Jr. was not actively engaged as a breeder or trader and that his slaves (if they were indeed members of the same family) were not callously separated — perhaps indicating the presence of a benevolent master-slave paternalism in the Flack household.[20] Nonetheless, Mills Flack's upbringing in the antebellum South would have led him to expect deference and humility from the Negroes with whom he had relationships.

In November, 1859, Mills Flack married pretty, dark-haired Margaret Alvira Hemphill (1843–1875) of the Montford Cove community, located near the Rutherford-McDowell County line.[21] The young couple set up housekeeping on the Cove Creek lands of George Flack, not far from Margaret's father, John Hemphill.[22] With the death of his grandfather in 1860, Mills inherited several tracts of land, including the 250 acre Cove Creek farm,[23] and in October of that same year his young wife gave birth to their first child, a boy they named Leander Roswell (1860–1904).[24] But young Mills had barely begun the task of building a farm of his own and raising a family before the shots fired in Charleston harbor would announce the beginning of a bloody and protracted Civil War.

Margaret Hemphill Flack, first wife of Mills H. Flack (ca. 1870). (Helen Flack Cole)

* * *

Flack would indeed serve the Confederacy during the War Between the States, though his service was probably limited to militia and Home Guard duty and shaped by what we might call "the politics of conscription." In April, 1862, the Confederate Congress passed the Conscription Act to impress the manpower the fledgling government deemed necessary to supply the war effort. Many advocates of States' rights—such as Gov. Joseph E. Brown of Georgia and Gov. Zebulon B. Vance of North Carolina—held that the law was a "tyranny" of central government. But Vance nonetheless reluctantly agreed that conscription was necessary. When Chief Justice Richmond M. Pearson issued rulings against the use of militia to round up deserters and conscripts, Vance acquiesced in the legislature's decision to vest in the Governor himself that authority. To this purpose, the legislature bypassed Pearson with the creation of the "Guard for the Home Defense" or Home Guard.[25]

Yet Vance's acceptance of conscription was complex. Burton Hendrick insists that Vance "hated" the device "[with] all the energy of his vital nature ... because it took simple, hard working Southern folk from their humble homes ... and left North Carolina exposed to its enemies." Hendrick notes further that Vance used "exemptions" and "furloughs" as tools to withhold conscripts from the War Department.[26] However, at one point, Vance urged the legislature to draft militia officers.[27] Tarheel boys by the thousands never returned from the seemingly endless bloodlettings of Northern Virginia. Vance merely reflected the ambivalence that many other North Carolinians felt, especially those from the mountains where Whig-Unionist sentiment remained strong.

Flack first received a captain's commission in the Rutherford militia's 103rd Reg., 26th Brigade, on January 23rd, 1862, and was assigned command of Company No. 5. The 103rd was in the command of Lt. Col. Ceburn L. Harris of Chimney Rock.[28] When the legislature created the Home Guard in 1863, Flack's unit was reorganized as the NC Home Guard's 69th Battalion, also commanded by Harris.[29] No roster survives, but its five or more companies were probably led by many of the same men who held commands in the militia's 103rd Regiment, including Flack. Rutherford court minutes refer to "Capt. Flack's company" throughout the period between 1862 and 1865.[30]

Mills Flack also benefited from an exemption. Provided a commissioned officer of the State militia was elected prior to July 8th, 1862 (as was the case with Flack), he was exempt from service in the regular army.[31] Flack and other exempted militia officers probably encountered some prejudice,[32] and by the end of the War the number of exemptions was "embarrassingly large."[33] Nonetheless, as these men were elected by their companies, Flack's commission as an officer and company leader suggests that he was admired and respected in the community,[34] even as a very young man. On the other hand, as he could have disregarded his exemption and joined the regular army,[35] it is also possible that he had little use for a "rich man's war."

The "peace movement" was strong in Rutherford and seems to have infected the Guard and Flack's commander, Ceburn Harris. Mills Flack *may* have shared in this sentiment—though this is purely speculation. The Adjutant General's letter books indicate that Harris was often at odds with the authorities in Raleigh over medical exemptions,[36] orders[37] and military regulations[38]; he even granted furlough to a deserter.[39] The Rutherford Home Guard's complicity with the peace movement is further suggested by the failure of Harris's command "to respond to a Federal raid late in the war ... [motivating] several local women [to petition Governor Vance for] guns to defend themselves."[40] During Reconstruction, Harris would emerge along with Judge George W. Logan as a leader of the so-called "Harris-Logan group" of radical Republicans in western North Carolina — Logan was Harris's brother-in-law and during the War was one of the stalwarts of the peace movement in North Carolina.[41] But Flack seems to have been largely uninvolved in Rutherford's Reconstruction politics, and what little evidence that does survive indicates he was a Conservative/Democrat.[42]

What did the militia and Home Guard of Rutherford do during the War? The County court minutes shed some light, suggesting that one of their principal duties was to feed the families and livestock of volunteers; "feeders" were appointed in each captain's district and great pains were taken to assess the needs of families. The court minutes also include the appointment of patrollers from the various companies,[43] and a reference to prisoners in the charge of the Home Guard.[44] The routine duties of patrolling and "feeding" probably constituted much of the Home Guard/militia's responsibility.

But they did have other more dangerous duties. The Adjutant General's letter books indicate that the Rutherford Home Guard participated in a "secret" Cherokee County expedition to "recover ... State arms" in 1863,[45] and an action against deserters in Polk County in 1864-65 where "great depredations" were being committed.[46] In his historical romance, *Then and Now*, D.F. Morrow, whose father commanded a company, similarly describes the Rutherford Guard's confrontations with Union sympathizers and deserters, as well as worried rumors of a slave uprising, and even the hanging of a man for forging a slave pass.[47] Morrow's work (though of dubious reliability) and the AG letter books perhaps evoke the more gravid moments of Home Guard activity for Captain Mills H. Flack.

* * *

Following the War, Flack settled upon the task of making a living and raising a family. He seems to have made a fairly prosperous farmer — at least in these early years. In the 1870 population and agricultural schedules his real estate valuation was given as $3,000, and comparison with the valuations for his Cove Creek neighbors suggests that he was better off than most of them.[48] The agricultural schedules of 1870 and 1880 indicate that his principle crop was corn, though his farms also produced wheat, sorghum molasses, and, by 1880, even a little cotton.[49]

His family grew as well, and by 1875 Mills and Margaret had "tossed out" six more sons to help on the farm: Andrew Braxton (1862–1948), John Buford (1865–1924), Samuel Mills (1868–1942), James Ewell (1870–1910), Thomas Millard (1874–1907) and Posey Maggie (1875–1932).[50] But in August, 1875, just a few months after Posey's birth, Margaret, then only thirty-two years of age, died.[51] Her death is mentioned in a letter written to Mills' uncle, Major John Flack, by his aunt, Jane Lewis, then living in Yell County, Arkansas, who expressed concern for the welfare of Mills' "seven motherless children."[52] Margaret was laid to rest in the Hemphill Family Cemetery, located off Cove Road.

Margaret Hemphill Flack had an older sister named Sarah Elizabeth (1840–1894), who in 1860 married the son of a Baptist minister named Samuel J. Bruce. The Bruces also resided in the Montford Cove community.[53] Though the hows and whys are unclear, by 1870 Sam Bruce had either died or left Sarah.[54] In any event, perhaps not long after Margaret's death, Mills and Sarah began an affair which resulted in an illegitimate son given the name Alonzo (ca. 1876–?). This is evidenced by a $500 bastardy bond which survives in Rutherford records and charges Flack "with the maintenance of a bastard child, begotten by him upon the body of Sarah Bruce."[55] Many years later, Mills' grandson, Ralph Roswell Flack, wrote of playing with Alonzo at the Bruce home in Cove Creek,[56] but he never revealed that Alonzo was his uncle. The balance of public shame for the affair with Sarah perhaps fell upon Flack, for he would soon remove from Cove Creek.[57]

But though the liaison with Sarah Bruce may have been damaging, Mills Flack quickly found another wife. In April, 1876, he married Katie Harrill (1847–1934), the rather grim-faced, twenty-nine-year-old daughter of Alfred (1821–1903) and Ursula Harrill (1828–1895) of Cool Springs Township.[58] Though not pretty, Katie was a devoted member of the Cool Springs Baptist church who could restore an air of respectability to Flack. But more importantly, she was willing to be mother to his children. As her obituary later put it, she "mothered her step-children with the same tender devotion as she did her own...."[59] She would give Mills Flack seven more children, four of whom would survive to adulthood: Otho Gerod Remus (1877–1946), Lalla Chinara (1879–1970), Mary Lenora (1880–1944), and Effie (1885–1966).[60]

After his family, it was perhaps to the land and farming that Mills Flack was most devoted. The odium of the Bruce affair would thus be expunged, not only by a new wife, but by a new farm as well. Flack retained most of the Cove Creek lands until 1897,[61] apparently renting the farm to his sons during at least some of the intervening years.[62] But, according to Ralph R. Flack, about the time Mills remarried (1876), "he moved from Cove Creek to a plantation [at a place] called Hamilton Quarters, situated on the West side of Second Broad River, near Bostic Station and includ[ing] the mouth of Catheys Creek."[63] This property consisted of about eighty-seven acres.[64] Combined with the Cove Creek lands, Flack thus owned over 400 acres at the time of the 1880 agricultural census, though only about a quarter of these were under cultivation.[65] Mills seems to have remained at the Hamilton Quarters plantation until at least 1883.[66]

1. Mills Higgins Flack and the Agrarian Revolt

The 1880s and 90s were to be years of change and opportunity in Rutherford brought by the coming of the railroads and cotton mills, and Forest City — which did not even exist by name at the beginning of the decade — would be the locus of activity. Perhaps Mills Flack had the potential of the rails in mind when, in August, 1882, he purchased two tracts of land (together nearly seventy acres) just west of the then rapidly growing town of Burnt Chimney[67]— soon to be Forest City. On this small farm Mills Flack would eventually build a modest home for his family. When the Rutherford Railway Construction Company was chartered to construct a line from Rutherfordton to South Carolina "by way of Forest City" in 1883,[68] and Mills and Katie granted the company a right of way in 1885,[69] it must have seemed that a new age was just around the corner. But though Forest City would witness

Katie Harrill Flack, 2nd wife of Mills H. Flack, dressed in mourning for her deceased husband (ca. 1900). (Nelda Wilson Maxwell)

the completion of two rail lines by the end of the decade — the Seaboard Airline in 1887, followed by the Southern Railway in 1890[70]— there is no evidence that these developments brought prosperity to the farmer Mills Flack. Nor could the new cotton mills— Henrietta Mill No. 1 (1892), Henrietta Mill No. 2 (1896), and the Florence Mill (1897)[71]— offer hope to a landed, independent farmer such as Flack.

Perhaps during these years the Flacks found their hope in God and church rather than "in the world." The Cool Springs Baptist Church was adjacent to the Flack property in Burnt Chimney, and during the late 1880s and throughout the 1890s, Mills and his family were very active members.[72] They endured the storms of the Rev. Housen D. Harrill (1842–1926) crisis in 1887-88, when the Cool Springs' minister was charged with "unchristian conduct and language toward and about the brethren"[73]; and the move of the church and change of name to Forest City in 1889, when church records were withheld by an angry member of the Harrill family.[74] Though it is probable that the Flacks were unhappy with these events— the Rev. Harrill was a relative

The Mills Flack family standing before their home on the farm near Forest City where Flack was killed (ca. 1900). From left to right: Effie Flack, Katie Harrill Flack, Mills H. Flack, unidentified boy, Posey M. Flack, Chinara Flack, Ora Flack, Otho R. Flack and Lenora Flack. (Nelda Wilson Maxwell)

of Mills' wife Katie,[75] Flack apparently refused to trade the church a small parcel of land in early 1889,[76] and "letters of dismission" were issued to the entire family later in the year[77] — if the Flacks left the church, it was not for long.[78] Mills Flack was clearly a respected brethren, who throughout the 1890s served on committees and was frequently appointed to investigate wayward members of the church[79]; his wife, children, their spouses and his grandchildren were also very active.[80]

* * *

Yet, faithful or not, there must have been times when Mills Flack felt that God had deserted him. For as a farmer of that day, he likely found his finances pressed — by lower crop prices and higher interest rates— and began to lose his land. This is reflected in his sell-off of the Cove Creek farm between

1. Mills Higgins Flack and the Agrarian Revolt

Florence Mill (ca. 1900), Forest City, established in 1897. One of Rutherford's early cotton mills. (Helen Flack Cole)

1890 and 1897,[81] as well as the sale of his Forest City lands following his death in order to cover the debts against his estate.[82] Perhaps he had vaguely hoped for a windfall from the railroads which came to Forest City.

But problems for Flack and other farmers cut deeper than the mere loss of money or property. For there were also issues of prestige, honor, self-worth and the welfare of his family—which was very large. As Laura Edwards writes,

> With the land went a man's control over his own labor and that of his wife and children.... Gone was the basis on which he claimed political power. Gone was his independence and his very identity as a man.[83]

As we have noted above, the cotton mills—the panacea of the New South—were not a viable alternative to farmers with substantial landholdings. To a proud, independent farmer such as Mills Flack, it must have seemed his very way of life was being destroyed, and there perhaps grew a palpable sense of desperation—"many white farmers were teetering on the brink of collapse."[84]

Ralph R. Flack was raised in a very close knit, extended family and, as a child in the 1890s, observed at close range the struggles of his Father, Uncles and "Grandpa" Flack (with whom he lived several years) as the prospects for farmers worsened. An anecdote he preserves in his childhood memoirs is particularly illustrative of the struggles of the Flacks:

The Cleveland panic [of 1893] was now in earnest. In the fall, Father [Andrew Braxton Flack, Mills Flack's son] took three bales of cotton to [the market in] Caroleen-Henrietta.... [He] returned after dark, [and] when he had eaten supper he and Uncle Millard sat down at the dining table to figure out and divide the cash income for the year. The three bales [of] cotton brought seventy-two dollars and some few cents. First the guano bill had to be paid and other incidentals, then a percentage went to grandfather for rent of the land. [Papa] then gave Uncle Millard his share (don't recall how much) and he kept the rest. I remember very clearly the following: Uncle Millard said, "Braxton, you can continue to raise cotton if that is what you want to do, but I never expect to plant another cotton seed as long as I live."[85]

The First Baptist Church of Forest City, where the Flacks worshipped (ca. 1910). (Helen Flack Cole)

Woodward observes that cotton prices in 1894 were more than three times lower than they had been in "the panic year of 1873."[86] It is hardly an accident that Mills Flack was the last of his line to earn a livelihood exclusively from farming.

Of course, the Flacks were still better off than the hundreds of thousands of landless farmers caught in the nightmare of farm tenancy. Tenant farming (or sharecropping) developed as a post–Civil War, Southern response to the co-existence of cash-poor, landed farmers (who lacked money to pay laborers) with large numbers of poor, landless, blacks and whites. Many farms could remain productive in such circumstances only by allowing the latter to farm on a crop-sharing basis.[87]

But the system worked largely through "crop liens"

which in turn often caused "debt peonage"—an even greater evil than slavery, in the opinion of C. Vann Woodward. Poor, landless farmers needed credit for supplies, but in order to get it, they had to pledge part of an unplanted crop. This left the tenant at the mercy of his creditor, who could set exorbitant prices and interest rates for the goods sold to the tenant. Very often the tenant's crop was not large enough to cover the debt to his creditor and he would have to renew the lien season after season, trapped in a cycle of debt.[88]

* * *

Low crop prices, a tight money supply and the horrors of the crop lien led the farmers to believe that they were being exploited as a *class*, seeing in the *greed* and concentration of wealth in "Gilded Age" capitalists and industrialists—and the politicians who supported them—the ultimate causes of their problems. They believed that there was literally a *moral* difference between wealth generated by producers (farmers, laborers) and non-producers (bankers, railroad tycoons); that "productive" wealth was right and good and "non-productive" wealth was not; "'that wealth belongs to him who creates it, rather than to those who by chicanery, legislation and fortuitous circumstances manage to get possession of it.'"[89] As Theodore Mitchell puts it, at least some farmers saw themselves as "heirs to a Jefferson[ian] ... humanity," which devolved upon them the "right to stewardship in society" from their position as the *creators* of food.[90]

By the late 1880s, their frustrations had given rise to a mass agrarian movement, manifested in the spread of the National Farmers' Alliance and Industrial Union and eventually in the establishment of a powerful third party, the People's or Populist Party. Their aim was a sort of "revaluation of values," whereby producers would be elevated to the positions of influence and dominance they held in the agrarian-based antebellum economy, and the farmers believed that government could and should help in this endeavor. Bankers and rich speculators were literally evil. *Men* were more important than *money*.[91]

In North Carolina and much of the rest of the South, blame for the decline in agriculture eventually would be heaped upon the Democratic Party and their lopsided support for "New South" industrialization—though the farmers' movement attempted to work within "the Democracy" in its early days. Thus politics became mixed with class. Given the direct impact of the farm crisis upon himself and his family, it was perhaps only natural that Mills Flack's politics put him in opposition to the conservative "Bourbons," the old Redeemers of the Democratic Party, who favored the railroads and manufacturing interests and paid little heed to the plight of the farmer. Flack likely found his identity with the "wool-hat boys," the "land-poor" plantation owners and yeoman farmers (small holders), and perhaps felt like something of a "social misfit," uncomfortable with the "courthouse clique" of lawyers and businessmen who ran things in Rutherfordton.[92] The extent to which he and others of the landholding farmers may have identified with landless tenant farmers and sharecroppers is unclear — but Ayers holds that the agrarian movement was largely a revolt of the "landowning majority."[93]

Flack was certainly not alone in his dissatisfaction with the corporate plutocracy. Leonidas L. Polk emerged as the leader of North Carolina's farmers in 1886 with the establishment of the North Carolina Farmers' Association and the newspaper he edited, *The Progressive Farmer*. In 1887, this organization successfully lobbied for a state agricultural college — which would later become North Carolina State University.[94] However, by 1888, the Farmers' Association had been absorbed by an even stronger national organization, the Farmers' Alliance and Industrial Union, which had its origins in Texas, but was then sweeping the South and mid–West.[95] According to McMath, it eventually had an estimated 1.5 million members nationally.[96]

The Texas Alliance sent organizers all over the South to help set up state and county alliances,[97] preaching the virtues of cooperation and agrarian unity as means to solve the farm crisis. Soon, the newly-formed North Carolina Farmers' Alliance was also organizing in the field, by 1891 building a membership of about 90,000. Thus, about four in ten farmers in the State were at some point members.[98]

A State organizer named D.N. Caviness established the Rutherford Alliance in June and July, 1888, under "most encouraging" circumstances.[99] It initially consisted of sixteen sub-alliances and a county organization headed by Col. John L. McDowell,[100] who was installed as its first president at a July 16th meeting of the farmers at the academy in Forest City. On that Monday morning, residents of the town were "startled by a pouring in of hundreds of brawny fisted farmers...." When a man named B.B. McMahan spoke and "quoted the old adage, 'United we stand; divided we fall,' ... a round of cheers went up from as ... determined [a] set of men as ever met together in our county."[101]

By 1891 (the height of the movement) more than forty sub-alliances would exist in Rutherford with a total membership exceeding 300.[102] Mills Flack's name does not appear among the first officers of the Rutherford County Alliance or any of its sub-alliances. However, it is clear that he established himself as a leader of the farmer class and the Alliance in Rutherford. He would eventually serve two terms as president of the County organization, was also an Alliance lecturer,[103] and perhaps did as much as anyone in the County to fight for the rights of the farmers.

Contrary feelings of corporate exploitation coupled with an optimism that change was at hand helped to fuel the growing Alliance movement. These sentiments are well reflected in a letter to *The Progressive Farmer* from B.A. Barber, president of Rutherford's Sunshine sub-alliance. He wrote,

> The Alliance is a new thing in this County, but the farmers are very much interested, and are taking hold. Every farmer feels more sensibly every day the weight of oppression, and we believe that the Farmers' Alliance is a step in the right direction to remove this burden. So let every member ... put his shoulder to the wheel and come to the front....[104]

The key to relieving "the weight of oppression" was seen as cooperation, and cooperation was indeed the hallmark of the Alliance.[105] The national organization achieved a modest success in 1889 when it broke the "jute-bag trust," which had dramatically raised prices on the jute-bags used by cotton farmers, by organizing a switch from jute to cotton bagging.[106] In addition, Charles Macune's mixed success with the Alliance Exchange in Texas (which was able to sell supplies to farmers at near wholesale prices through bulk purchasing) led to similar experiments with exchanges in other states, including North Carolina.[107] However, the cooperative exchanges seemed only to work insofar as they operated on a cash-only basis,[108] and indebted farmers simply had little cash with which to participate.

The alternative was of course to extend credit to farmers, but when Macune's Texas Exchange attempted this through "joint notes" in 1888 it virtually collapsed.[109] Bankers and wholesalers simply would not give credit to the farmers,[110] adding fuel to the fire that corporate interests were aligned against agriculture. This failure would convince many Alliancemen that only radical changes in the economic system could save the farmer from his plight,[111] and ultimately led them to broaden their attack upon the concentration of capital and seek political redress through several egalitarian and even "socialistic" reforms: government ownership of communication and railroads; direct election of Senators (finally adopted in 1913); expansion of the currency through a bi-metallic monetary system; and, above all, the "sub-treasury plan," whereby the government would store crops for farmers and extend credit based on their value. These reforms were issued in the form of "demands" from annual National Alliance meetings, such as those held in St. Louis (1889) and Ocala (1890).[112]

Meanwhile, cooperation was also tried by Rutherford farmers. In early 1889, the County Alliance passed a resolution pledging "not to use a single sack [of guano] at ... advanced prices," and "not [to] buy any sewing machines from agents or other middlemen, but direct from the manufacturers through Alliance agents."[113] To this end, they made arrangements to do business with an agent called Blanton & Stough.[114] Later in the year, William O. Baber, of

Mills H. Flack, with the big, callused hands and confident look of a leader of Rutherford's "rebel farmers," about 1890. (Helen Flack Cole)

the Pea Ridge sub-alliance, wrote the *Progressive Farmer*, "The Alliance has done some good here. We have saved in guano and in other goods also."[115]

But times still remained tough in Rutherford. Though the County Alliance had adopted the *Progressive Farmer* as its organ,[116] L.C. Hardin of the Forest City sub-alliance was led to lament that "only four or five members of our Alliance ... subscribe.... [Several] say they will take it so soon as they sell some cotton and get some money."[117] Hardin described the Forest City contribution to the State Alliance Fund as "liberal,"[118] but Baber noted that Pea Ridge had as yet given little.[119] Crops were at least good in Rutherford that year though, and a Gray's Chapel sub-alliance member observed "a general good feeling among the farmers."[120]

The Alliance's "movement culture," as Lawrence Goodwyn called it,[121] was spread through a lecturing system which explained the farmer/producer's economic plight, the roots of the farm crisis in the selfishness of a non-producing corporate elite, and how agrarian reform could only be achieved through dramatic change. In other words, the farmers were politicized through a conscious educational effort — part of a plan agreed to at Ocala in December, 1890, and instigated by Polk, "for putting full-time lecturers in the field to conduct an all-out educational campaign in 1891."[122]

State and district lecturers came to Rutherford, as elsewhere, and W.L. Abernathy wrote of a large crowd which heard a speech by a State lecturer named Col. Long in Henrietta in 1891. He observed,

> Its effect was educational, but I chiefly remember its thrilling, inspiring force among [those] who heard it.... It was an economic discussion, so plain that everyone comprehended, and withal so eloquent and telling that not an enemy of the order would have averred his relation to it.... I give it

as my honest conviction that for its capturing eulogy, biting sarcasm and moving pathos in his descriptions of the destitution of labor, I have not heard that speech excelled in long years."[123]

Other lecturers who toured Rutherford included J.S. Davis[124] and L.N. Durham.[125]

But it was probably through social gatherings or rallies at the sub-alliance and county level that the lecture format had its greatest impact. As noted above, Mills Flack identified himself as a lecturer. Though he probably spoke only at sub-alliance and county meetings, these were critical events where the farmers bonded both politically and socially, and which "served to link the Alliance and its individual members more closely with their communities."[126] Sub-alliance meetings were typically bi-weekly, and were a critical part of the Alliance education program, functioning as "schools" in which members could exchange ideas and socialize.[127] As Robert McMath writes, "The men and women who gathered on Saturday afternoons in churches, schools, and homes sang hymns and Alliance songs, observed the rituals of the order, conducted business, listened to lectures on subjects ranging from 'Grasses and Clover' to 'monopolies ... and their relation to National affairs,' and generally enjoyed each others company.'"[128] Perhaps Mills Flack exhibited a special facility for public speaking at these meetings, one which led to his emergence as a leader in Rutherford's Alliance movement.

* * *

Little direct evidence of Flack's political ideology survives. Perhaps the most complete statement is a portion of a letter which was published in the *Progressive Farmer* in October, 1894. From Forest City he wrote,

> Suppose we farmers raise our own supplies of corn, bacon, flour and such things as it takes to support a family, having no surplus except in cotton, and just cotton enough to pay our taxes. What would become of the fellows who have been living full and fat off the hard earnings of the farmers? At a price below cost of production, do you not think there would be howling among the hungry wolves in less than twelve months? And would not prices increase by this plan and produce be in demand? Now, farmers, let's try this system next year and see how it will work, for we have been giving our surplus to Shylock until he has become the Pharaoh of these United States.[129]

Mills Flack's use of the agrarian rhetoric of revolt would suggest that he was a "mid-roader," fully in sympathy with the agrarian rhetoric against concentrated capital, plutocrats, monopolists, etc.— the "hungry wolves" or "Shylock" in his letter — who exploited the farmer. He also is clearly speaking the language of cooperation with his "subsistence plan" to strangle the non-producers who exploit the farmers; though, on the other hand, his reference to raising "just enough cotton to pay our taxes" perhaps suggests a cooperation of landowners, but not tenants or sharecroppers who would have no land on which to pay taxes and had long given *their* surpluses to the landed farmers. Later, when he addressed the House, Flack would also invoke the class issue when, using Leonidas Polk's words, he asked a colleague, "Are you for the masses or the classes?"[130] But did he see the landowners and the sharecroppers as a monolithic class with common cause? Probably not.

Use of biblical imagery to describe concentrated capital — "the Pharaoh of these United States" — was also not uncommon in the movement. Mitchell writes that "Alliance rhetoric resounded with Old Testament imagery," and suggested that the farmers had a "millennial" calling.[131] Bruce Palmer also notes the role of religious imagery and cites an Alabama farmer who "expressed his hopes and concerns for the reform movement with an elaborately mixed metaphor built around the flight of the Jews from Egypt."[132] As noted above, Mills Flack was an active member of the Forest City Baptist Church. When he entered the Legislature in 1895, he identified himself as a "Missionary Baptist,"[133] perhaps suggesting a zealous commitment to the spread of "the Word," but the true depth of his religious feeling is unclear.

Flack's use of the term "Shylock" — which he also used in debate on the floor of the State House — is suggestive of anti–Semitism, but it was not uncommon for the movement to associate the Jews with concentrated capital. Oliver Orr noted that Populist leader Marion Butler "charged that the major instruments of American commerce were dominated by J.P. Morgan, 'representing a foreign gold syndicate composed of London Jews, cold-blooded Shylocks, the descendants of the money changers whom Christ drove from the temple.'"[134] Mitchell would perhaps relate the anti–Semitism of Flack and other Alliancemen to the influence of "biblical injunctions against usury [which] reinforced Alliance condemnation of moneylending, liens, and mortgages."[135] And, of course, Richard Hofstadter made much of anti–Semitism in the movement in his *The Age of Reform*, linking it to what he felt was a paranoid Populist preoccupation with the "conspiracy of the international money power"— though Hofstadter did qualify the anti–Semitism of the farmers as "a mode of expression, a rhetorical style, not a tactic or a program."[136]

* * *

As the elections of 1892 approached, many Alliancemen in North Carolina were dissatisfied with progress made on the reform agenda. Most of these men were Democrats and, in 1890, when Alliance Democrats captured the North Carolina Legislature, the farmers were hopeful of dramatic change. But they found "the Democracy" largely unwilling to take up their radical agenda. For example, the venerable Senator Zeb Vance, certainly the most beloved politician in the Tarheel state during the second half of the 19th century, only reluctantly introduced the sub-treasury bill on the floor of the U.S. Senate in 1890; later, when his re-election to the Senate was in the hands of the Alliance legislature of 1891, Vance used his ample prestige to force the farmers to dilute a resolution requesting him to support the Ocala demands.[137]

By 1892, Alliancemen in Rutherford had also given up on "the Democracy." Early in the year the Rutherford organization endorsed the radical agenda set forth at Ocala "believing and feeling that the laboring masses of this country have not been represented, their interests have not been duly considered, and feeling necessarily compelled in the name of justice to make certain demands ... on account of grievous and unjust burdens upon the producers of this Republic...."[138] Later that summer, when the Pea Ridge sub-alliance entertained the County organization with "the finest dinner," the Rutherford Alliance "passed a resolution that we would not vote for any one for office who was opposed to our demands. We mean to stand square and flatfooted on our demands until trusts and combines die the death of the wicked." The Allianceman who made this report to *The Progressive Farmer* added, "Old Rutherford is coming, and that to stay...."[139] Another Rutherford Allianceman wrote, "Old Rutherford is in the middle of the road and up with the procession."[140] And Dr. Oliver Hicks, a prominent Rutherfordton physician who sympathized with the farmers, reported "that there exists now a profound sentiment in favor of combining the strength of all laboring classes in an effort to change the administration of affairs ... [by the] vast horde of corrupt, unscrupulous and mercenary demagogues, whom we all know are, most assuredly, dragging us to anarchy and ruin."[141] A third party movement of the farmer class was underway.

* * *

Many Alliance leaders in the South (most notably Macune) looked unfavorably upon a break with "the party of the fathers."[142] But Leonidas Polk was more warm to the idea, and in 1891 and 1892 he emerged as the leader of the radical "mid-road" wing of the Agrarian movement, having finally decided that he'd had enough of "'arrogant party dictation.'"[143] Polk's untimely death in June, 1892, robbed the nascent party of its most attractive candidate for President, but the mold was cast and in '92 the radical agrarians would break from the Democratic party and form their own which was known as the People's Party.

Leader of the Farmers' Alliance, Leonidas L. Polk (ca. 1890), whose words Flack echoed on the floor of the State legislature when he asked a colleague if he "favor[ed] the masses or the classes?" (North Carolina Office of Archives and History, Raleigh)

The People's Party competed in state and local elections throughout the South and mid–West in 1892, and fielded a presidential ticket as well, headed by a former Union general named James B. Weaver. By July, "[third] party talk was rampant" in Rutherford,[144] but allegiance to "the Democracy" was strong, and many of the farmers in the County were wavering in their support for the reform movement. At a Democratic rally "[several] erring brothers who have been beguiled into the Third party to-day openly confessed their sins and asked to come back to the fold."[145] A prominent farmer named Leonard Fowler "said that at the beginning of the Third party movement he was heartily in sympathy with it ..., but after careful consideration, and in view of the men whom he was called on to vote for against the Democratic nominees, he could no longer go with the Weaverites."[146] In early September, Wyatt P. Exum, the gubernatorial candidate of the People's Party, Marion Butler, North Carolina's heir to the mantle of Polk, and stalwart Rutherford Democrat and State Senator, M.H. Justice, spoke to a crowd of about four hundred in Rutherfordton — but only about seventy-five were estimated to be third party supporters.[147]

Nonetheless, the new People's Party nominated their ticket at Rutherfordton later that month, putting up Mills Flack for the State House. There was apparently some talk of Fusion with the Republican Party in the County, but this did not materialize.[148] A *Daily Charlotte Observer* correspondent covering a Rutherfordton debate between the district electors for the three respective parties said, "If there is any misunderstanding between the Republicans and the Third party they are certainly the friendliest enemies I ever saw."[149]

In October, rumors circulated at the County fair that the Populist ticket would withdraw.[150] But the mid-road farmers held fast, and in their quarterly meeting that month the Rutherford Alliance reaffirmed the radical program.

They resolved to make their own fertilizers, to raise their own food crops in a move toward self-sustaining agriculture, and, once again, to cooperate in the purchase of manufactured goods.[151] It was to no avail, however. The People's Party was soundly beaten, and the Democrats, who boasted carrying the Rutherfordton township for the first time since the War, enthusiastically proclaimed, "The coon is ours."[152] In his first bid for the House, Mills Flack had finished a distant third in a three-man field with only 289 votes.[153] But the story would be vastly different in the election of 1894.

2

The Fusion Era and White Supremacy in Rutherford

WITH THE DEATH OF LEONIDAS POLK in 1892, the mantle of the State Alliance's leadership fell to the opportunistic Marion Butler, the youthful, dapper editor of the Raleigh *Caucasian*. His immediate objective, as well as that of many other Populist leaders in North Carolina, was to attain office — if "the Democracy" would not enact the farmers' reforms, then they would do so themselves.[1] Furthermore, recognizing that the combined vote of the Republican and Populist parties could have swept a coalition party to victory in the state in 1892,[2] they concluded that elective offices could best be won by "fusing" with the Republican Party, at least on the state and local levels. A Fusion arrangement between the Republicans and the Populists would involve nominating "cooperative tickets"—i.e., the two parties would not compete with one another for elective offices and would unify against "the Democracy."[3]

The Democratic legislature of 1893 had furthered the alienation of the farmers through limitations enacted upon the Alliance charter. "By 1894," Helen Edmonds writes, "the gap between the Populists and the Democrats seemed irreparable."[4] And though the agrarian radicals were uncomfortable with the alignment of the Republican Party with corporate interests, they did find an important point of agreement on electoral reform at the county level. Both parties believed that county commissioners should be elected, not

2. The Fusion Era and White Supremacy in Rutherford

appointed by justices of the peace — who in turn had been appointed by a Democratic legislature. That such an arrangement might lead to a dramatic increase in Negro office holders in heavily black eastern North Carolina counties was something that the leadership of both parties was willing to risk. Regardless of ideological differences, expedience would carry the day. As Edmonds puts it, "to many white farmers, by 1894, the familiar cry of defending the state against Negro rule was becoming an outworn shibboleth"[5] — at least, for the time being.

Interestingly, Fusion was opposed by Rutherford's own Capt. John Baxter Eaves,[6] who was state chair of the Republican Party. Perhaps Eaves feared a backlash from the prospect of Negro rule in the East. In any event, the "dark and silent Eaves"[7] was defeated and lost his chairmanship following an overwhelming vote for Fusion at the Republican State convention in late August.[8] Not even the Rutherford delegation would side with him in opposing Fusion.[9] Much as with the Populists, the office-hungry carried the day and Republicans simply cast principle aside; as Steelman writes, "The singular appeal of fusion to Republican party strategists was that it afforded an opportunity to defeat the Democratic hegemony."[10] Following state party conventions which had taken place in August, the Republican and Populist state executive committees met in the early Fall and formally endorsed the Fusion arrangement — though cooperation seems to have actually been worked out by leaders of the respective parties at a "secret" pre-convention meeting on July 30th.[11]

Populist leader Marion Butler (ca. 1895). His visit to Rutherfordton during the campaign of 1898 helped engineer a Fusion ticket, albeit a weak one. (North Carolina Office of Archives and History, Raleigh)

On October 1st, 1894, county Republicans and Populists held their nominating conventions in Rutherfordton. Four of the county offices went to Republicans (clerk of court, register of deeds, sheriff, and surveyor); three offices were reserved for Populist nominees (treasurer, coroner, and State representative). Mills Flack was again the Populist nominee for the Legislature, but the Republicans were unhappy with Flack. "A prominent Republican," wrote the *Daily Observer* correspondent, "says that there is much objection to Flack among the Republicans, and that many of the delegates are disgusted with the action of the bosses in forcing upon them a Pop. candidate who was defeated in a race for the same position last election." Republican dissatisfaction with Flack was further evinced by the posting of broadsides which announced that a certain E. Lane[12] was a "straight-out Republican candidate for the Legislature." Precisely why the Flack candidacy had strained the Fusion coalition in Rutherford is unclear. However, the Populists were also uneasy as evidenced by their "dead silence" at the endorsement of "the Duke," Republican Richmond Pearson, for Congress—a silence which the venerable veteran of the Reconstruction era in Rutherford, Ceburn L. Harris, "punctuated by solemnly jabbing his Populist hat into the air on the end of his cane."[13]

There was also tension between the Populists and "the Democracy." The *Daily Observer* reported that the Secretary-Treasurer of the county Alliance, Alphonso DeKalb Wallace, "a Populist high priest," threatened the Democratic postmaster, M.O. Dickerson, with a knife when the two had a confrontation at Dixon's Store. Wallace had charged that the Democrats paid for the announcement of the Republican bolter Lane.[14] In the North Carolina politics of that day, threats and even physical violence were not particularly uncommon, even among prominent politicians.[15]

At any rate, neither political tricks nor threats would salvage "the party of the fathers" in 1894. The Fusion ticket swept all the elective offices in Rutherford—including the coveted house seat where Mills Flack defeated his Democratic challenger, S.F. Harrill, receiving 2,035 votes to Harrill's 1,836.[16] Thus, Flack was to be a member of the first of two Fusion assemblies of Populists and Republicans which briefly swept the Democratic Party from power for the terms 1895-96 and 1897-98.[17]

The only session of the 1895-96 legislature met from January 9th through March 13th, 1895. It was extraordinary for its combativeness. As it was through the aid of Negro Republicans that the Fusion triumph had been possible, the predominant issue of the session was race. A Republican legislator boldly proclaimed (just as Democrats in Rutherford had boasted in 1892), "We have got the Coon" and we will reverse twenty years of "Redeemer" legislation.[18] Democrats, on the other hand, berated the Fusionists over such trivialities as the alleged replacement of a "one-legged Confederate" doorkeeper with a Negro appointee.[19] Ultimately, the Fusionist Assembly of 1895 was able to push through a number of democratic reforms, such as the popular election of local officials.[20] But, the victory of 1894 would also sew the seeds of a Democratic Party backlash which would lead to the Wilmington race riot of 1898 and Negro disfranchisement in 1900.

* * *

2. The Fusion Era and White Supremacy in Rutherford

It was probably shortly after Christmas, 1894, that Flack made his way to Raleigh to serve in one of the most controversial assemblies of the post–Civil War period. His performance in the floor debates, as recorded in the staunchly Democratic Raleigh *News and Observer*, was not conspicuous, though his comments at times evinced both common sense and wit.

In a January 14th debate on the public printing contract, for instance, he avoided partisanship and stated he "was in favor of letting the contract as low as possible whether to Democrat, Populist or Republican. [']If the lowest bidder be a Democrat and he wants to work for us, all right.'"[21] Flack also interjected himself into a February 12th debate on fixing interest rates at 6%. Obviously in favor of a bill which he believed would ease the credit crisis for the farmer, and in response to the argument that it would draw capital from the State, Flack said on the contrary that he "thought this would cause Shylocks [sic] to invest his capital here" and the enactment of the bill was long overdue.[22] Still later, on February 20th, a discussion of election law reform led the Democratic representative from Mecklenburg County, J.D. McCall, to defend "the Democratic Party as the restorer to their rights of the men who followed the cause of the Confederacy under the cross of their convictions." To this Flack retorted, "[If] the Democratic law was so pure why did the contestees here lose their seats?"[23]

But the most interesting floor exchange involving Flack occurred very late in the session, on March 8th, when he was sharply rebuked by several colleagues for his insistence upon an amendment to a special appropriation for the Normal and Industrial School in Greensboro.[24] Flack argued that "these are days of economy," and the appropriation should be reduced by $1,000. When a Populist colleague, Rep. R.S. White of Bladen, again argued in support of the bill without amendment, Flack asked, "did he favor the masses or classes?," thus echoing the words

Mills H. Flack sat for this photograph when he was in Raleigh for the Fusion legislature of 1895. (Nelda Wilson Maxwell)

of the Populist hero Leonidas Polk. To this the Bladen man responded "both," and continued to pontificate on the "good work of the school."[25]

Flack's emphasis upon the class issue evidently stirred the ire of a Republican colleague, the formidable H.G. Ewart, a skillful Hendersonville lawyer who had previously served a term in the U.S. House of Representatives.[26] When Flack continued to insist on the rights of the "plain people" and asked, "what were they going to do with the poor ones at home?," Ewart declared, "If Mr. Flack refused this appropriation, he would never be returned to this house in which he is now a member only by the grace of God and the blunders of the Republicans." At this jab, the State House shook with laughter. Then Ewart asked Flack if "he would join him in his proposed amendment to the Revenue Act to tax whiskey five cents a gallon for education or was he in the hands of [the] whiskey ring?" Now the more polished Ewart was himself playing the class issue. He was trying to humiliate the Rutherford man by insinuating that the masses with whom Flack identified included illicit distillers—perhaps conjuring images of Cherry Mountain's notorious Amos Owens.[27] Flack could only respond that "he was misunderstood, and, avoiding Ewart's question, said his position was simply that of economy in appropriations."[28]

But Rep. Edward V. Cox of Pitt County took issue with Flack's explanation. No, said Cox, Flack had made it plain that his interest was in more than matters of economy, for he had "asked White was he in favor of *the classes or the masses.*" Cox then skillfully argued "that these normal school students were directly from the masses; he knew from personal experience that those from his county went there directly from the free schools; that these masses were the hope of the people…, and that members would be cowardly to refuse to vote for this bill."[29]

Flack had been careless in his use of the rhetoric of class, and his arguments had been exploded. While his support for the masses was entirely consistent with radical Populist ideology, his hesitance to fully back the Normal and Industrial School also betrayed a lack of support for one of the land grant colleges that his own Farmers' Alliance had helped to establish.[30] Of course, even South Carolina's Ben Tillman, the "Edgefield farmer," who was instrumental in the founding of Clemson University, was at great odds with the "aristocracy" of the University of South Carolina.[31] Perhaps the strength of Mills Flack's ties to the land and the narrow interests of the farmer did little to cultivate a respect for the "ivy halls" of *higher* learning—though I think he would have acknowledged the importance of education in general.[32]

Rep. Ewart's reference to "the blunders of the Republicans" also suggests that Flack was not always a cooperative Fusionist. The farmers had continued to work within the Democratic Party until the election of 1892, and there can be little doubt that it was difficult for Flack and other Alliancemen to warm to cooperation with the Republicans, especially insofar as the latter either directly or indirectly promoted Negro influence and office-holding.[33] Above, we noted that the Republicans in Rutherford were less than comfortable with the nomination of Flack for the Legislature in 1894. On the other hand, the Democrats may not have found Flack inordinately objectionable. A propagandistic Democratic Party pamphlet of the period referred to "the stench left in the air by the Legislature of 1895," but, as Mills Flack was mentioned only once,[34] perhaps the Democrats thought his contribution to "the stench" very modest. In any event, a few days after his exchange with Representatives White, Ewart and Cox, the business of the Fusion Legislature of 1895 was done.

* * *

As the elections of 1896 drew near, Populist leaders in North Carolina had largely abandoned much of the radical "mid-road" agenda and chosen rather to stake their hopes in currency reform: the establishment of a bi-metallic currency, the "free silver" crusade. Rutherford Populists seem to have been ambivalent about this prospect. As A.D'K. Wallace wrote to his "Dear Brother," Marion Butler, in May, 1896:

> Believing as I do, that all the principles of Populism are right and necessary[,] I regard the free coinage of silver as but restoring the straw with which we would be able to make our full tale of bricks. We would still be left on the Egypt side of the Red Sea when that victory was won. If we succeed in getting the Silver men together we will find opposition to the Government ownership of all monopolies, national banks, telegraphs, etc., must continue to satisfy the greed of those who want to fatten on the industries of the Country....[35]

Of political conditions in Rutherford, Wallace observed that the "sound money and Silver Dems" were very friendly, but he regarded them as still bound to the "shackles of partyism." Writing before the Democratic National Convention that July and the nomination of "free-silverite" William Jennings Bryan, he foresaw that the Democrats "would not abandon their friends — the Golden calf worshipers — and their blood [would] be on their own [hands]." "I would expect a snowstorm on the 4th of July," Wallace wrote to Butler, "as readily as I would expect you to help reinstate the old Democratic Party in this State." He concluded his epistle by prophetically "point[ing] to the necessity of co-operation [with the Republicans] in State and County matters next fall, however repugnant such a course is to a true reformer." Wallace's first priority in 1896 was to remain in power. He staked his hopes for principle upon the election of 1900.[36]

State executive committees of the Populist and Republican parties would indeed agree to cooperate upon state and local offices again in 1896 — though on the national ticket, Populists would support the Democrat Bryan.[37] Fusion between Rutherford Populists and Republicans was effected for the 1896 election in a conference of party leaders on September 7th. The terms were similar to those of 1894 — the offices of sheriff, register of deeds, and surveyor went to the Republicans, while the offices of treasurer, coroner and State Legislature went to the Populists. In addition, each party was allowed two nominations for the now elective three-member board of county commissioners.[38]

However, the agreement was conditional upon the willingness of the Populist candidate for Legislature to support Republican Jeter Pritchard for Senate. Many Rutherford Populists were unhappy with Pritchard because he was unwilling to support free silver.[39] The county Populist convention, which was to have been held on the same day as the Republican, was delayed nearly two weeks, and many Populists in the county were threatening a straight ticket over the Pritchard issue.[40] Though it is not clear, this may be why Flack did not run for re-election to the State House in 1896 — perhaps he just could not in good conscience support a man (Pritchard) who was against the expansion of the currency.

The Pritchard issue, as well as the ideological tightrope that North Carolina Populists were walking that year, may also explain the silence of Wallace, Rutherford's Fusion candidate for State Senate, on free silver during the campaign which followed. In a debate with Wallace in Ellenboro in late October, his Democratic opponent, Michael Hoke Justice, "made an appeal for free silver, and said he had tried to get Wallace to help him, but to date Mr. Wallace ... spoke not a word." Wallace rather argued "[that] a 'free ballot and a fair count' was more precious than silver or gold."[41] But he was beaten by Justice in the election that year.[42]

Though Flack's replacement on the ticket for State Legislature, Lindsay Purgason, managed a very narrow victory over his Democratic opponent for Rutherford's House seat,[43] and at the State level the Fusion coalition tightened its grip, capturing the governorship and large majorities in both the Senate and House, Democrats in Rutherford made considerable inroads in 1896. In addition to Justice's victory over Wallace, "the Democracy" recaptured the offices of treasurer and surveyor, and also won a seat on the county commission.[44] The *Daily Charlotte Observer* reported that enthusiasm for the election in Rutherford was not as great in '96 as it had been in 1894,[45] and noted a large "stay-at-home" vote.[46] Perhaps mid-roaders, unhappy with the disintegration of the radical agenda into a Fusion arrangement for office-seekers, were coming back to "the party of the fathers." But Edmonds also notes a state-wide decline in Populist support in 1896, due in part at least to "fear created by Democratic propaganda of Negro rule."[47] It was almost exclusively this fear which the Democrats would seize upon to "redeem" themselves in 1898.

* * *

The rhetoric of "white supremacy" and the campaign of 1898 loomed ahead, and the principal role of the Populists in that tumultuous year would be their return to the fold of "the Democracy," the re-forging of the Proto-Dorian bond with their Democratic brethren. Populism and the agrarian revolt in Rutherford were not dead, but they were perilously close to their death agony, and it was the appeal to Anglo-Saxon brotherhood which would seal their fate.

This was evident in Rutherford as early as May of 1898, when the Populists organized a meeting in Forest City to select delegates to the party's state convention.[48] A few days before they were to convene, the *Rutherfordton Vindicator*, a Democratic weekly, in a brief article entitled "Are They?," made an appeal to the Rutherford Populists which foreshadowed the coming campaign's emphasis upon Negro domination and officeholding in eastern North Carolina. "We do not believe," wrote the *Vindicator*, "[the Populists of Rutherford] are made of the same material that some of their eastern brethren have shown themselves to be."[49] The Populists in their state convention in May in fact voted to fuse with "the Democracy," but confident Democrats "'respectfully declined'" this offer. Unperturbed by this show of disloyalty, later that summer Republicans again voted to cooperate with the Populists,[50] and the state executive committees of the two parties finally came to agreement in late August.[51]

Thus another Republican-Populist "caucus" was held, this time in Republican Sheriff J.V. McFarland's office at the County Courthouse in Rutherfordton on September 5th — behind closed doors. The principal question on the table: would Populists in Rutherford once again fuse with the Republicans.[52] The *Vindicator* was able to elicit little about this meeting, though a Republican offered that there would be no "division of the pie"— suggesting that inter-party cooperation was finished.[53] The *Daily Charlotte Observer* also reported that the Republicans and Populists had failed to fuse because "it was impossible for the Republicans to agree to the fusion arrangement had two years ago."[54]

The bone of contention between the parties in 1898 centered on the much coveted House seat. Rutherford Populists had been allowed to control the nomination for the Legislature all four years of the Fusion arrangement. In 1896, Fusion in Rutherford had nearly broken down due to Republican insistence that the Populist nominee support the "gold-bug" Pritchard for

U.S. Senate. They had finally come to terms, perhaps because Mills Flack, the committed agrarian radical, had relinquished the seat to Lindsay Purgason. However, Purgason, himself "a Populist of some determination," had in fact voted against Pritchard. According to the Charlotte daily, "that action of Purgasson's [sic] is probably the cause of failure to fuse this year."[55] As Edmonds observes, "Pritchard's election had shaken Fusion to its foundation."[56] Republicans in Rutherford now demanded the right to nominate the Fusion candidate for the House seat and in exchange offered the Populists the register of deeds.

However, four hours of discussion in Sheriff McFarland's office could not bridge the gap between the two sides. The meeting adjourned and the Populists announced that they would field a straight ticket. A full slate of candidates was named: Purgason would once again be the Populist nominee for the Legislature, and Mills Flack was named as candidate for clerk of court. The *Daily Observer* correspondent opined that Purgason's nomination "tends to put an end to fusion in this county." But he also noted, "If any fusion arrangement is made in the future during this campaign his name will be taken down. The belief is general here that the ticket nominated yesterday will be taken down before election day, but I do not think so."[57] There was thus still a gleam of hope for Fusion, but the radical Populists of Rutherford seemed bent to another course.

Republicans in the county had other problems besides recalcitrant Populists. Rutherford's Negro Republicans, who in the past had always been counted upon to vote a straight party ticket, were threatening to bolt from the party of Lincoln, chiefly because under Fusion they had lost control of their schools. As the *Daily Observer* explained it,

> Under Democratic administrations they were allowed to control their own schools, being elected committeemen in their own districts, employing their own teachers and building their own school houses. But upon the advent of the Populist-Republican administration those offices were taken away from the negro in this county, and that action enraged the negro toward the Republican party, the board of education in this county being composed of three Republicans. The negroes therefore determined that they would show the white Republicans that without negro votes their ticket would be overwhelmingly defeated in this county.[58]

"The Democracy" in Rutherford no doubt reveled in the dilemmas of the Republicans, and the staunchly Democratic *Vindicator* generously obliged Negro leaders of the revolt by publishing their letters, which were extremely critical of the Republicans. For example, in calling a political meeting of the colored people in the county at New Hope School House on August 6th, Jacob Whiteside had written, "Formerly our schools were located by our best citizens of the county, to our best interest and where our children could all get to attend them. Now a few men have been allowed to tear our schools to pieces."[59] A week later, Lafayette W. Hamilton complained, "The board of education met and declared the Negro too big a fool to attend to his schools and say who should teach our schools." He added, "We are going to nominate a full county ticket of the dusky sons of Ham.... [We] know that we cannot elect them, but our defeat will be the defeat of our so-called Republican friends."[60] John V. Carrier warned that "[unless] the Republican party agrees to change the white man's government ... Republican office holders will be harder to find than the wadding from one of Admiral Sampson's heaviest guns."[61] The New Hope meeting resulted in the appointment of a delegation to bring the grievances of the Negroes to the Republican county convention of September 12th.[62]

In late August, the embers of race and discrimination in education were once again stirred by the refusal of whites attending the county teacher's institute in Rutherfordton to enter the courthouse "until the negro teachers had been excluded from the building."[63] The board of education was forced to schedule a separate institute for the Negro teachers the following week.

All this acrimony meant that as the Republican convention date approached there was neither a Fusion agreement with the Populists nor even the assurance that the Negroes would support the party. Republicans determined that a "big show" was needed to rally the Negroes back and rekindle hopes for Fusion; thus they planned a day of speech-making by a large delegation of prominent Republican officials—including Senator Jeter Pritchard—on Republican convention day (September 12th).

Before the speeches began at the courthouse in Rutherfordton, the visiting delegation was housed at the old Central Hotel. Through the morning hours "the faithful" called upon them. "Very often a negro leader was taken in tow and introduced to Senator Pritchard and others," reported the *Daily Observer*, "and every effort was used to show the colored man the error of his way."[64]

The speeches began at 11:30 with L.B. Wetmore, Republican candidate for Solicitor in the eleventh district, whose speech was characterized as "one long wail and beg for the negroes to vote the Republican ticket." He was followed by Burke's Charles McKesson, a former Democrat, whose effort was characterized by the Charlotte paper as "a great speech on 'nigger, nigger, nigger.'" "He talked to the negroes and told them stories ... in dialect, and had the negroes laughing and once or twice the negroes shouted a little, but the old time negro Republican enthusiasm was lacking." But when Senator Pritchard finally rose to the podium, his words gave little indication that he sought to appease the Negro dissidents in Rutherford. "He ... did not deny any of the statements which have been made of negro rule in the eastern

Jeter Pritchard (ca. 1890), Republican U.S. Senator and later federal judge, spoke in Rutherfordton during the difficult campaign of 1898. (North Carolina Office of Archives and History, Raleigh)

section of the State, but tried to show how Democrats appointed negroes or did favors for negroes while they were in power."[65] Perhaps his words were meant for Populists then under siege with the rhetoric of racial bonding.

Such an appeal was necessitated by stories of the "black beast" and Negro misrule, which had begun to fill the state's papers, engineered by the Democratic triumvirate of Aycock, Daniels and Simmons. The *Vindicator* was hardly aloof from the racist propaganda machine, with news from down east featuring bold front page headers on the "REIGN OF RUIN!" of New Bern's "incompetent" Negro magistrates[66]; "WILMINGTON'S FUSION-RULE" of eighty-six Negro office-holders[67]; "SAD PLIGHT OF THE EAST," "Worthlessness and Corruption" among Negro office holders in Bertie County[68]; and "NEGRO DOMINATION IN THE EAST," again on Wilmington and New Hanover County.[69] Likewise, articles designed to attract Populists back to "the party of the fathers" were also run with headlines such as "DOOR WIDE OPEN," addressed to "our Populist friends,"[70] and "FOOLING THE POPULIST FARMER: He Has Gotten None of the Things That Were Promised Him, but the Opposite."[71] One of the *Vindicator*'s final articles before the election asked "SHALL WE MARCH BACKWARD NOW?," and implored its readers to "SAVE THE STATE IN NOVEMBER."[72] The Populist "soul" was under assault. L.E. Green of Ellenboro received attention in both the *Vindicator* and the *Daily Observer* for a letter he wrote the Clerk of Superior Court in New Bern in which he inquired as to the veracity of the reports which followed these headlines.[73]

The papers also made a prominent Rutherford Populist an instrument of scandal in efforts to discredit the Fusion administration in Raleigh. Following his loss in the district Senate race in 1896, A. D'K. Wallace had been appointed the chief clerk to the Secretary of State, Cyrus Thompson. Thompson, in a debate with Aycock in Concord,[74] "held up the sobriety of the present administration in contrast with the drunkenness of Democratic administrations." But upon his return to Raleigh, Thompson was confronted with the alleged discovery of his chief clerk, "helplessly drunk behind the water cooler in his office." Thompson promptly fired Wallace. In a letter to the editor of the *News and Observer*, Wallace admitted to the indiscretion and explained that he was distraught "after committing his wife to the insane asylum at Raleigh."[75]

Soon after the Wallace story broke, Negro Republicans in Rutherford held their threatened renegade convention. Following considerable debate, the convention decided to close nominations for county offices after putting up only two men: Martin Miller for register of deeds, and William Logan for county commissioner.[76] Later, Negro independent candidates announced for sheriff and clerk of court.[77] Ultimately, these candidates seem to have withdrawn.[78]

Newspapers were not the only weapon in the arsenal of the Democrats in their drive to re-establish Anglo-Saxon hegemony. Charles B. Aycock's tour of the State, giving firebrand speeches, put intense pressure upon white men — and especially straying Populists — to return to "the party of the fathers." On the 10th of October, Aycock came to Forest City, where he spoke before a crowd of about 300.[79] The *Vindicator* called it "such a speech as has never before been heard,"[80] and the *Daily Charlotte Observer* said it was "the strongest speech ever [given] at Forest City."[81]

At Caroleen that night he spoke again, this time to more than 600. The Forest City talk must have made an impression, for when a blind man named Wiley Spurlin "heard of Mr. Aycock's great speech at Forest City [he] insisted upon being led 5 miles through the dark to Caroleen in order to hear the truth so ably expounded."[82] While the *Vindicator* said nothing of the substance of either talk, it did remark that "the ill concealed chagrin of the opposition who were present is the best evidence that the effort was anything but pleasant to the hopes of the fusion negro party."[83] The Charlotte paper opined that "the [two] speeches ... are worth a good many votes to the Democratic ticket."[84] At Shelby the following day, H.E.C. "Red Buck" Bryant reported Aycock was

> much pleased with the outlook in ... Rutherford county. The white people seem to be aroused to the true condition of affairs in the State. Everywhere he has spoken the people have heard what he had to say and in many cases Populists have come to him and told him that the east must be redeemed.[85]

A week before Aycock's appearance in Forest City, a prominent Rutherford Republican also made a speech against the continuation of the Fusion arrangement. Capt. J.B. Eaves, who in 1894 had lost the battle with the Fusionists, as well as the State Republican chairmanship, addressed a large crowd at the courthouse in Rutherfordton on October 3rd. Eaves unequivocally defended the gold standard and asserted that leaders in the Republican Party who had advocated silver had "sold out" and "were traitors to their own party." Then he turned to the matter of race. "To the colored people," Eaves said, "...you may think that you are Republicans to-day, but if you do you are mistaken." He told the Negroes that they were "simply joint stock-holders in a joint stock company formed for the purposes of controlling the offices in the State," and advised them "to stay at home." To the white men, the old Captain of the 50th NC said that Fusion was "a disgrace to a heathen nation." "I am not in favor of putting negroes in office over white men."[86] The "dark and silent" Eaves, who had been humiliated by his own party four years before, had broken a perhaps embittered silence to attack Fusion. Predictably, the staunchly Democratic *Daily Observer* appreciated Eaves' salvos and lauded him as "the farthest-sighted Republican in North Carolina."[87]

But the Fusionists had not yet given up. Marion Butler came to Rutherfordton on October 15th to help fill the ever widening breech in the Fusion lines. Events did not seem to favor him. He was late arriving at the courthouse, and embarrassed when he paused during his speech to argue with the editor of the *Western Vindicator*, Major L.P. Erwin. He apparently made few converts. However, Butler may have succeeded in helping engineer a Fusion agreement in the County, for such was announced by the embattled Republicans and Populists of Rutherford soon after his courthouse appearance. On the day of Butler's speech prospects had looked dim for agreement — a candidate on the straight Populist ticket had indicated that there would be "dissatisfaction" among the faithful, with or without Fusion. But two days later, agreement was announced following a conference of the Republican and Populist committees — with a Populist on the ticket for the coveted House seat.[88] The "straight Pop" ticket was withdrawn.

Nonetheless, for many Populists all was still not well. They had only been allowed nominations for three offices, while the Republicans had gotten seven, and the Populist nominee for the Legislature, Francis Freeman, was reported to have previously been both a Democrat and a Republican. "The above ticket is an exceptionally weak one," reported the *Daily Observer*, "and no ticket which could have been put up could have been more acceptable to Democrats than the one finally settled upon." Moreover, the rhetoric of white supremacy was clearly eroding Populist support for Fusion — and apparently even Populist support for Populism. "Very few of the leading Populists of the county were present at the conference."[89]

It seems probable that most of these "leading Populists," including Mills Flack, had finally given up the cause of the "plain people," the crusade against monopoly capitalism, and come back to "the Democracy." This appears to be the meaning of the following obscure reference to Flack in the *Vindicator* of October 20th:

> Does Mr. Mills Flack, the head and front of the People's party in Rutherford, realize how pleasant and delightful it is for brethren to dwell together in unity, when he is asked to step down and out ... for the honor of who shall be hindmost in the race for Clerk. Mr. Flack is thankful and we offer congratulations.[90]

The biggest political rally of the year was held in the yard of Dr. Oliver Hicks' home in Rutherfordton on the last day of October. Approximately 1,500 people heard W.T. Crawford, Richmond Pearson, and George Boggs, the Democratic, Republican, and Populist candidates for U.S. Congress. It "was a cool day, but the air was fine and the sky clear" as the candidates spoke — perhaps an auspicious sign for the Democrats as election day neared and Republican and Populist defections continued. After the speeches, an old man came up to Crawford and said, "'I have never voted anything but a Republican ticket during my life, but this time I expect to vote for you and the whole Democratic ticket.'"[91]

Indeed, hundreds of Rutherford Republicans and Populists did vote for "the party of the fathers" in 1898. The *Daily Observer* reported that there had "never [been] such a Democratic victory in the County before." It was a complete sweep — the Democrats won every Rutherford office — and the majorities were huge — "ranging from 639 to 410."[92] Results were similar throughout most of North Carolina. The rhetoric of Negro domination and misrule had worked, and "the Democracy" had been "redeemed."

But the election of 1898 in North Carolina is probably best remembered today not for the redemption of the Democrats but for the violence against African-Americans which followed in its wake, the infamous Wilmington race riot. In Rutherford, the only report of violence occurred at a polling place in Camp Creek township. There it was reported that "a Negro had used insulting language to a party of Democrats and several shots were fired, but none of them took effect, and a dangerous and tragical fight was narrowly averted."[93] However, in Wilmington denunciation of the Negro as a "black beast" had been challenged by a courageous mulatto newspaper editor named Alexander Manly. In an editorial, Manly had the temerity to suggest that white women occasionally entertained the thought of sexual relations with black men. This was an intolerable indiscretion to whites in Wilmington who found the notion of social equality with the Negro even less acceptable than political equality.[94]

Two days after the election, on November 10th, led by Col. Alfred Moore Waddell and George Rountree, Wilmington erupted. A mob of several hundred white men marched to the offices of Manly's paper, broke in, destroyed the presses, and set the building on fire. A shot, perhaps from a Negro, was fired into the crowd. The riot then began in earnest, and a slaughter of the "nigra savage" which perhaps knows no parallel in North Carolina's history followed. Probably at least fourteen blacks were killed and large numbers were forced to flee the City, abandoning property and livelihood.[95] In his memoirs, Waddell estimated that about twenty Negroes were killed in his "Wilmington Revolution." But he defended the Wilmington riot as "the spontaneous and unanimous act of all the white people ... prompted solely by an overwhelming sense of its absolute necessity in behalf of civilization and decency."[96] For him and many others, the white men of Wilmington had merely been the defenders of the Anglo-Saxon heritage that was the bequest of their *fathers*.

* * *

In June, 1900, as the summer and the political season approached once again, residents of old Rutherford were grieved by the death of the venerable Capt. J.B. Eaves. He might yet have served in other capacities, but the gods would not allow it. After being near death for about a week, he succumbed finally on June 16th. The crowd at his graveside at Rutherfordton City Cemetery was said to have been "the largest gathering that has ever assembled at that cemetery."[97] The brave Captain of Co. I, 50th NC, had "passed to the undiscovered country."

There would be more grief to follow in Rutherford that summer, but not before another white supremacy campaign could be waged and won by Simmons, Aycock and company. The principle objective in 1900 was the disfranchisement of the Negro. A joint committee of the Democratic Legislature of 1899 proposed an amendment to the State constitution which would require "the electorate to pass a literacy test before registering and to pay a poll tax before voting."[98] Aycock (who was the Democrats' choice for the governorship) insisted that the disfranchisement amendment "be submitted to the people for ratification rather than to a constitutional convention"[99] — as had been the case in other states, such as neighboring South Carolina. In order to ease fears among illiterate white men that they too would lose the vote, the amendment included the infamous "grandfather clause," which stipulated "that no one who could vote on or before 1 January 1867, or his lineal descendant, should be denied the right to vote, whether he could read or not, provided that he registered before 1 December 1908."[100] The Democrats also cleverly moved the vote on the amendment and state and local elections up to August, so as to separate state issues from national ones.[101]

2. The Fusion Era and White Supremacy in Rutherford

The old County Courthouse in Rutherfordton (ca. 1905), the center of political activity in Rutherford. It burned in 1907.

Many white Republicans, of course, were adamantly opposed to the amendment, seeing with its passage their own demise.[102] At least initially, many Populists also opposed it on the grounds that poor, illiterate whites of the farmer class would be disfranchised along with blacks.[103] Nor did the exemption from the literacy requirement until 1908 help to ease the anxieties of many white men; they feared this provision "would work a hardship on future illiterate white children."[104] The solution Aycock proposed was to educate them, and he promised that no white child would be disfranchised because of a lack of education.[105] The grandfather clause's six-year time limit, as Gilmore writes, "lent immediacy to Charles Aycock's proposed educational crusade for whites,"[106] and he toured the western part of the state promising illiterate white mountaineers that North Carolina would educate their children.[107] In late June it was announced that he would speak in Rutherfordton.

The day that Aycock spoke, July 2nd, 1900, was an oppressively hot one, wrote "Red Buck" Bryant, the *Daily Observer* reporter. But the old courthouse in Rutherfordton was "filled like a sardine box with fish," and most of the fish seem to have been farmers, "every face dripping with perspiration." They were enthusiastic too. When Rutherford's state Senator, M.H. Justice, rose to introduce the beloved man from Wayne County, "the audience as one man yelled and cheered." "The issues are great issues," Justice said, setting the tone. "It is a fight between the races, the black and the white, and it is a battle with the peaceful ballot." Aycock dwelled at length upon the disfranchisement amendment and the grandfather clause, and when he "declared that no white boy should lose his vote after 1908 for lack of educational advantages the audience roared with applause." Bryant concluded that the Democrats had "broken the backbone of the opposition."[108] A week later, M.L. White (writing under the pseudonym "Corn Cracker") concurred with Bryant that "sentiment for the amendment is gaining ground in ... Rutherford."[109] There could be no doubt in 1900. The farmers were once again in the embrace of "the Democracy."

The agrarian revolt in Rutherford was now all but over. On July the 4th, two days after Aycock spoke in Rutherfordton, the Populist county convention was to meet to nominate its ticket. It must have been a pathetic sight for the proud men who had led the farmers' revolt in Rutherford. Only *eight* men were in attendance at the convention, and it was therefore determined that nominations would be delayed until the 11th, when the Populist Secretary of State, Cyrus Thompson, was scheduled to speak at the courthouse. In fact, there would be no Populist nominations. Republicans in Rutherford rejected Fusion, and there seems to have been no consideration of a straight Populist ticket. "It is understood," reported the *Daily Observer*, "[that] the Populists will vote the Republican ticket and there will not be fusion." But there were likely few old Populists in the county who kept this understanding. The Proto-Dorian bond and the rhetoric of white supremacy had captured the hearts and minds of the farmers of old Rutherford. Even the county's Populist "high priest," A.D'K. Wallace, made it clear that "he would vote for the amendment and would not vote for any man who was not in favor of it."[110] Reports of Republican defections were also numerous.[111]

Clearly the momentum was on the side of the Democrats—both in support of the amendment and the recapturing of the governorship. But they left nothing to chance. On July 26th, in Forest City, they staged "[the] largest and most enthusiastic political rally ever held in this county"[112] when an estimated 4,000 people came to hear M.H. Justice and Wilmington's Col. Alfred Moore Waddell. The speakers were preceded by a parade

> led by 50 boys and girls on wheels handsomely decorated in pure white and followed by 100 ladies attired in white on horseback. Then came Col. Waddell and the speakers ... and the general procession, led by the King's

2. The Fusion Era and White Supremacy in Rutherford

Left: Governor Charles B. Aycock (ca. 1900), who pardoned Raney Mills following her conviction for second degree murder. The old courthouse in Rutherfordton was "filled like a sardine box with fish" to hear his speech during the campaign of 1900. *Right:* The leader of the Wilmington race riot, the Hon. Alfred Moore Waddell (ca. 1900). When he addressed a huge crowd in Forest City during the White Supremacy campaign of 1900, he reduced the question to one simple formula: "Are you white or black?" (Both: North Carolina Office of Archives and History, Raleigh)

> Mountain and Cleveland bands.... Two banners were carried before the 100 ladies on horseback bearing the words: "Save Your Vote for Us."[113]

Once again, the rhetoric of race: symbols of white "purity" (white clothing and women) coupled with an appeal to white men to protect their women from "the black beast."

Race and the amendment were indeed the chief themes that day as the politicians mounted the rostrum. Justice said, "a negro ... was never the equal of a white man, and was not as good as any white man, and was not capable of holding any office of any kind at any time.... North Carolina's whites were the people to rule and they would rule." After he was introduced, Col. Waddell defended the "Wilmington Revolution," and reduced the essence of the campaign of 1900 to this simple formula: "Are you white or black?"[114] The "race feeling" in Rutherford and the determination to once and for all end "Negro rule" had perhaps reached their zenith.

As August 2nd and the referendum approached, there were also indica-

Leading Rutherford Democrat, state senator and later judge Michael Hoke Justice (ca. 1910), who declared in 1900 that the disfranchisement of the Negro would put the government back in the hands of the white man, "and thank God for it." (From *The Sun*, Rutherfordton, 13 February, 1919, p. 5)

tions that racial tensions in the region had gone beyond mere words. On July 16th, in the Union Mills area of northern Rutherford, a Negro named Joe Lewis was shot to death by Levi Thomason, allegedly for making "impudent remarks" to his wife. The *Daily Observer* reported, "Thomason has not surrendered or been arrested. The negro is one of the meanest in the county."[115] On the day of the election, another Negro named John Ponder was apparently lynched in neighboring Polk County. He was said to have "fired on the white men first, whereupon they shot him several times and then cut his body up with knives."[116]

Many men of Rutherford must also have been aware of the extraordinary and widely reported events which took place in New Orleans in late July. There, a single, remarkable black man named Robert Charles, who would be admired by a later generation as a sort of *proto-militant*, took on nearly the whole of the city himself, picking off several cocksure white policemen with almost superhuman marksmanship. Smoked out of a house on Saratoga St., Charles was finally killed. Bullet after bullet was pumped into his lifeless body, and the son of a slain policeman took a macabre pleasure in stomping upon the face of the corpse.[117] "Finally," writes Joel Williamson,

> officers brought up a police wagon. They flung Charles' body onto the floor between the seats, leaving his head hanging over the end. As the wagon rattled down the street toward the morgue, the battered head, flattened, almost unrecognizable now, jerked crazily about.[118]

New Orleans then disintegrated into a full-scale white riot.[119]

Back in North Carolina and Rutherford County, the victory of "the Democracy" on August 2nd was total. The amendment ultimately passed by a vote of 182,217 to 128,285.[120] Most blacks in the state were now effectively disfranchised, Aycock was Governor-elect, and the Democratic sweep in Rutherford was even more convincing than it had been in 1898. The day after their "great victory," the Rutherford Democracy convened at the courthouse to celebrate. Senator M.H. Justice took the podium, fresh from a decisive victory over his Republican opponent. "'The amendment adopted will put North Carolina in the hands of white men,'" he said, "'and thank God for it.'"[121] In fact, so complete was the victory that total white hegemony in North Carolina politics would not again be threatened until the 1960s.

* * *

Thus, in the midst of the white supremacy campaigns of 1898 and 1900, Mills Flack and the agrarian radicals of Rutherford seem to have finally abandoned any illusions they had that the farmer's revolt would somehow succeed. They turned away from class interests and the conviction that the Democrats had done little or nothing to help agricultural interests, and back to race as the bedrock of power. Primordial racism was simply bred too deeply for them to resist its call. This was the mind of Mills Flack and the mob that would avenge the honor of their "ole Cap'n" on a fateful day in August, 1900.

3

The Forest City Lynching and Its Aftermath

O F AVERY MILLS AND HIS FAMILY we know very little. The U.S. Census of 1900 indicates that he was a Negro born in North Carolina in December, 1879, and that he could read, but not write. His wife's name was Raney (b. November, 1882), and he had an infant daughter named Massey (b. July, 1899).[1] At the time of the lynching, Raney was pregnant with her second child.[2] The *Charlotte Daily Observer* reported that Avery Mills had a "bad record," meaning a criminal record.[3]

But this was perhaps just a typical white stereotype of the "new Negro," i.e., African Americans born outside slavery — and both Raney and Avery were of these new Negroes. Woodward wrote, "As the old type of Negro bred in slavery died off and the new type bred to caste increased, it seemed from within the white world that the Negro was losing his manners and his morals."[4] The proportion of crime committed by blacks increased dramatically, and though lynchings, the convict lease system, etc., took their toll on black lives, "[the] great truth is," as Williamson remarked, "that most blacks died by black hands."[5] But the new Negro was defined by more than crime or a lack of morals and manners. According to Williamson, the failure of Reconstruction "brought a rising disengagement and alienation of black people from the white world."[6] The new Negro consequently grew up without the "paternalism" and sense of "place" of slave society that his father and grandfather had known. It is thus hardly surprising that there was a dissonance in the relationship between Avery and Raney Mills of the new generation of post–Civil War blacks, and Mills Flack, of an older white generation that had known slavery.

3. The Forest City Lynching and Its Aftermath

We otherwise know only that Avery Mills was a tenant farmer on lands owned by Mills Flack near Forest City. Most tenants worked on a crop-share basis; however, some of the landless farmers were renters, and it is possible that Avery Mills rented from Flack. The *Charlotte Daily Observer* was unclear on this point, referring to Flack's farm "which is rented to Mills, or who is, by some agreement, making a crop this year."[7] Following Flack's death, his wife, Katie Flack, was awarded a widow's allowance which was based upon property which included "Rents from Avery Mills" of $3.40.[8] But this seems far too little for back rent due on an entire farm, and probably refers to rent for a mule or equipment.

In any event, crop-share arrangements were typically one-year, verbal agreements (Though there were written agreements in use in Rutherford County. See the instrument on page 64). Most importantly, landowners had full authority to dictate whatever settlement terms they wished to their tenants. Thus, as landlords naturally sought to maximize profits, tenant farmers were often exploited in settlements.[9] The potential for resentment in an exploitative landlord-tenant relationship, exacerbated by a hot August, a weak farm economy and the explosive racial climate of 1900, may have simply proven too deadly a mix.

* * *

A few days before his death, Flack had stopped to pick some peaches on a parcel of his Forest City farm, then worked by the Negro tenant farmer Avery Mills. According to various reports, Mills' wife, Raney, confronted and argued with Flack, apparently questioning Flack's rights to the fruit. One report has it that she threatened Flack with a pistol and ordered him off the property, though Flack's son, Otho,[10] indicated that they had only argued. In any event, the Flacks left before the confrontation escalated to violence.[11]

Confrontations such as these, between blacks and whites, were common during this period, and, according to Laura Edwards, usually grew out of the refusal of African Americans "to defer to whites in authority"[12] — in this case, the refusal of a tenant to defer to the property rights of her landlord. Gilmore cites a number of examples of "black insolence" which occurred during the white supremacy campaign of 1898 — and provided fuel for the Democrats' propaganda machine. These incidents ranged from blacks forcing whites off sidewalks, to attacks with umbrellas.[13] In one well-publicized confrontation, a group of black children compared some prominent, white Wilmingtonians to the "nether regions of a horse."[14]

We may chuckle at some of these so-called "offenses" today. But by defying a white man in the South of 1900, Raney had committed a serious offense. For she had violated the "unwritten code of racial etiquette which

A Rutherford County crop lien instrument for $50 (at 6% interest), executed in 1901. Mills Flack and Avery Mills may have had a similar agreement. This loan was docketed by the Clerk of Court and registered in Rutherford County mortgage books by the Register of Deeds. These books have since been destroyed.

had to be obeyed; [that] all whites, regardless of individual merit, [had to] be accorded the deference due to members of the superior, ruling race."[15] Moreover, Mills Flack wasn't just any white man. He was a prominent figure in the community, a former state legislator and a leader in Forest City. Now *his* honor was at stake. As Ayers explains:

> When black gestures signaled flagrant contempt, many white Southern men literally knew no way to react other than with violence. If a black man insulted a white man and the white did not strike back immediately, he had, in his own eyes and the eyes of his peers, no honor left to lose.[16]

Glenda Gilmore wrote that for "whites a hundred years ago character did not exist apart from reputation...."[17] And as a South Carolinian put it in 1877, "'To swallow an insult from a Negro would be perpetual infamy.'"[18]

3. The Forest City Lynching and Its Aftermath 65

It was undoubtedly with honor and the incident with the peaches on his mind that Flack made his next trip to his tenant's farm armed with a shotgun. At about 9 o'clock on Tuesday morning, August 28th, Mills Flack, Otho, and an unidentified boy, made their way to the plantation, this time with a wagon to collect fodder. According to Otho, whose eyewitness account seems to be the most reliable,

> the negro [Avery Mills] stopped them and was abusing them about a few words which had passed between them and the negro's wife some days before, and threw a rock at Mr. Flack [i.e., Mills Flack]. Mr. Flack then shot the negro [in the hip, though he was not badly hurt] and he [Mills] started to the house, Mr. Flack following, breaking his gun over the negro's head. In the meanwhile the negro called to his wife to bring his pistol, which she did and the negro shot Mr. Flack then, when Mr. Flack was trying to get the pistol away.[19]

Thus, *it was Flack who shot first*, not Avery Mills. While the Negro had escalated events by throwing a rock, Mills Flack had shot an *unarmed* man — "black beast" or no. Was this the act of a dignified community leader, a man who not only would have been expected to defer to rule by law, but who had himself been a lawmaker? On the other hand, can we say this was the rash act of a man consumed by the problem of a white man's "racial honor"? Perhaps, for Otho's description of events gives the impression that his father was so assured in his "superiority" that he believed he could simply *take* a loaded weapon from the "lowly nigra" Mills. Could Avery Mills — in the moment of their confrontation — have somehow come to represent for Flack all the pain and frustration that the farm crisis had wrought upon his family and class? Or, could the "martial spirit" of the South with its comfort in violence have destroyed the "ole militia Cap'n," Mills Higgins Flack? Whatever the explanation for his rashness, Flack may not have collected any fodder that August morning, but he made plenty for the "courthouse clique" in Rutherfordton who thought the farmers better suited as followers than as leaders.

Yet must we necessarily conclude that Flack did indeed shoot first? The *Charlotte Daily Observer* reporter who conducted Otho's interview stated that the account "was believed to be a true statement by most all the people at Forest City.... Had the mob known the facts were as they were, probably the negro would have been in jail to-day."[20] Certainly the townspeople of Forest City and Rutherfordton must have been shocked by the August 31st article — two days following the lynching — with the headline, "Flack Shot First."[21] But it is difficult to conclude otherwise since it was Mills Flack's own son who was the source of this account (see Appendix IV). The *Daily Observer* reporter also noted that Otho's story largely concurred with that

Otho Remus Flack (ca. 1900), who was likely in the party that lynched Avery Mills and later confessed that Mills Flack had shot the Negro first. (Nelda Wilson Maxwell)

of Avery Mills' wife, Raney — except that she denied giving Mills the pistol with which Flack was shot.[22] Furthermore, the actions of the Judge who presided over Raney Mills' subsequent trial in Cleveland County suggest that he too accepted this account.[23]

But on that morning in August, 1900, confused and unreliable reports of the incident (and Avery Mills' culpability or lack thereof), would be heard by Flack's friends and other townsfolk — a confusion which is illustrated by the differing accounts of Mills Flack's demise which appeared in the press. The Raleigh *News and Observer* of August 29th actually published three different accounts, based on wires from Charlotte and Shelby. The first from Charlotte stated:

> Flack had gone to Mills' house to get some fruit, Mills being his tenant. Mills refused to allow the fruit to be taken. Flack, who had a shot gun in his hand, fired it off in order, it is thought, to frighten the negro. Mills then had his wife bring him a pistol, and opened on Flack, shooting him dead.[24]

The Shelby report made no mention of Flack shooting first and portrayed a rather more cold-blooded Avery Mills who "told his wife to hand him his pistol, whereupon he stood in the door and began shooting Mr. Flack...."[25] A third wire, also from Charlotte, differed from the other accounts in that the taking of the peaches was assigned to the Negro Mills.[26]

Even the *Charlotte Daily Observer* reporter, who was a witness to the later lynching, got the story wrong the first day. His initial report, which was reprinted or summarized in many newspapers throughout the State, gave the following account:

> This morning at 9 o'clock Mr. Flack, his son, Otho, and another boy went to the plantation in a wagon to pull fodder. Mills' house is about 100 yards from the road. He appeared and halted Mr. Flack and began to renew the

talk about the fruit, when Mills' wife brought him his pistol. He took it and deliberately shot Mr. Flack just under the heart. Mr. Flack, having a shot-gun, drew it and fired, the shot taking effect in the negro's shoulder, and then took the gun and pounded the negro over the head with it until it was broken.[27]

In the confusion, anger and heat of the moment, perhaps the reporter and the townsfolk of Forest City accepted without question an account of a mortally wounded man still possessing the stamina to shoot another and then break a gun over his head. Sure, Mills Flack could take a mere "savage" even with his dying breath — reminiscent of the old regime's notion that any Southerner was worth ten Yankees. But regardless of what they *may* have thought, a mob bent on vengeance is moved by emotion, not reason. Moreover, their minds were saturated with the "rhetoric of race," and the honor of an important white man and the community itself was *apparently* at stake.

The scene on the Flack farm immediately after the shooting must have been chaotic. Perhaps Otho remained with his father and attempted to staunch the flow of blood with a rag or shirt while the unidentified young boy[28] ran to a nearby neighbor for help — a doctor would have probably been just minutes away in Forest City. It was mid-morning on a weekday and the dusty, hot, August streets of the little town would have been full and bustling. Word of the shooting would have spread quickly, and it could not have been long before dozens, if not hundreds, had gathered at the scene, by foot, horseback and wagon.

Officers immediately arrested Avery Mills and his wife Raney. But this would have been little consolation to the growing crowd. The Flacks were a family of considerable influence; Mills Flack was a friend and respected leader[29]; and he had been shot by a trifling "nigger" tenant farmer. The anger at the scene would have been extreme and palpable. The discourse of racial bonding undoubtedly seized the moment, and the herd mind was suffused with images of "retrogressing black beasts" and "loose niggers."

Mills Flack would die in less than an hour, and it was obvious to Flack himself that the wound was mortal. His friends gathered round to offer what little solace they could and to hear his last words. The *Daily Observer* described his last moments,

> Mr. Flack said to his friends before he died that he could not live long; that the negro had killed him and that he wanted him hanged and wanted his friends to see it done. He was then taken home [to die].[30]

Thus, with his dying breath, Mills Higgins Flack had called his friends to lawless revenge. How could they refuse the honor of their "ole Cap'n" and the man who had fought for the rights of the Rutherford farmers in Raleigh? The seeds of a lynching were thus sown.

* * *

Perhaps one reason for the obscurity of Mills Flack's demise[31] and the subsequent lynching is the loss of contemporary files of Rutherford County newspapers—not a single County paper survives for the year 1900. But, by a great stroke of luck, the Rutherford County correspondent for the *Charlotte Daily Observer*[32]—whom I have unfortunately been unable to identify—not only reported on the incident in great detail, but actually witnessed the lynching of Avery Mills (see Appendix III). And while it is possible that there were other eyewitness accounts in the papers of Forest City and Rutherfordton,[33] his report is to the best of my knowledge the only one which survives.

After their arrest, according to the *Daily Observer* correspondent, Avery and Raney Mills were brought before Justice J. Cicero Greene[34] in Forest City. No doubt a large and angry crowd was present outside Greene's mortuary as he charged the couple with murder and ordered the town's law enforcement officers to move them to the County Jail in Rutherfordton.[35] These officers were Town Marshall Sam Hamrick[36] and Constable William C. Hardin.[37] They proceeded in a wagon west-northwest toward Rutherfordton (six miles away) with their cargo, Avery and Raney.

The reporter, who was probably in Rutherfordton when word of the shooting reached him, hurried to the scene and met the officers and their prisoners in route to the jail at the Seaboard Air Line depot on the outskirts of Forest City. "Not stopping, but going on toward the city," he wrote, "I saw crowds on horseback and in vehicles armed and coming at full speed."[38] The crowd overtook the officers about "two and one-half miles from Forest City at the old Eaves place, on the right of the Seaboard Air Line road," and held up the wagon, driven by Hamrick.[39] Another crowd, which had probably followed Sheriff Elijah Martin[40] and Town Marshall J.D. Justice[41] from Rutherfordton, was also on the way, and Martin "stopped down the road a few hundred yards to keep them back."[42]

The crowd was apparently quite large. According to the affidavit later submitted by Raney Mills' lawyer to the Rutherford County Superior Court, "the mob was composed of about two hundred and fifty men."[43] If true, this would be equivalent to just under one-quarter of the population of the Town of Forest City at that time.[44]

Now obstructed by an angry mob, the officers pleaded with the crowd "to let the negro alone, and let him go to jail and take the full course of the law."[45] Officers Justice and Hardin both tried to dissuade the mob from violence, as also did O.C. Erwin,[46] a respected veteran of the Spanish-American War. The reporter sensed that "it did seem that they would submit, but someone would then make a remark about the killing and stir the crowd again."[47]

"But that nigga killed Mills Flack!," someone would yell. Or perhaps one of Flack's sons cried, "*He* murdered my Daddy!" Surrounded by Mills Flack's friends and relatives, the pressure upon the officers would have been extreme. The smell of the land and the horses, the hot August sun close in the sky, the air tense and heavy. Moreover, it was broad daylight. These were men they knew and who knew them, and they were all white and they all shared the bond of whiteness, a bond that demanded *honor*. Pleas to allow the law to take its course meant nothing, because power did not reside in intangible abstractions but in flesh and blood. And flesh and blood demanded honor, and honor demanded ritual, and ritual demanded blood. "Thar ain't no justus but ta kil 'im!"[48]

Though the mob remained unpersuaded, Town Marshall Justice of Rutherfordton would not yield his prisoners. The *Daily Observer* correspondent wrote,

> [He] told Mr. Hamrick to drive on. He got in [the] wagon, took out his revolver and told the crowd that he was a marshal and had the prisoner in charge and was going to take him to jail. He started to drive a second time, but was stopped and one of the crowd pulled the negro out of the back end of the wagon. He was left sitting there a few minutes and then, when more men arrived, one man called: "Grab him up!" and so they did in the midst of all the pleading that could be done, and took him down the road.[49]

The mob led Avery Mills off the main road to Rutherfordton and a short distance down a narrow dirt road, then known as the Ledbetter Road.[50] Raney was left behind — escaping a fate similar to her husband's only because she was "big with child."[51] Sheriff Martin and the other officers followed in pursuit of their charge. At this point, according to the reporter,

> some one yelled, "There comes the sheriff!" Immediately the negro was thrown against the bank of the road and the small mob ahead began firing, and he was dead in less than a minute. He groaned once and kicked once.[52]

Avery was shot about twenty times, and the mob then quickly dispersed through the pine woods.[53] Though the reporter did not identify any of the men who did the shooting, he stated that they "did not number over a dozen."[54] One can only imagine Raney's terror as her husband was murdered before her eyes. But she mustered enough composure to try to save herself and her unborn child, for, while the crowd and officers were occupied with Avery, she attempted to escape. She "was later caught and brought to jail."[55] The death of Mills Flack was thus avenged.

* * *

The corpse of Avery Mills, August 28, 1900, probably taken near the scene of the lynching just off Ledbetter Road. The original photograph was allegedly found among some old Ku Klux ephemera many years ago. Its current whereabouts are unknown. (From a photocopy in the possession of Helen Flack Cole)

How to explain the Forest City lynching? Certainly the season in which it occurred and the exploitation inherent in the landlord-tenant relationship may have set the stage. In their study of lynching in the South, Tolnay and Beck found that lynchings "were especially concentrated during the hot summer months of June, July, and August."[56] Jacquelyn Dowd Hall argued further that the higher incidence of summer lynchings was at least partly explained by sharecropping and the crop lien system of the South; after "the hard work of planting was done and only the lucrative harvest remained" the "tenant with the best crop [would be] run off."[57] It is indeed possible that, in addition to a white man's honor, Flack had Avery's crop in mind when he packed his shotgun that day, and that greed was in part the trigger that ultimately led to the Forest City lynching. But while this may explain a trigger to the lynching or the conditions which preceded it (i.e., the death of Flack), it does not really illuminate the event itself. Moreover, Brundage argues that "[b]ecause a defense of white authority, and conversely a challenge to that authority, were never far beneath the surface of any labor dispute involving whites and blacks, more than just economic motives could be at work in both the murder of a white planter by a tenant and the subsequent lynching of the tenant."[58]

Rather, the size of the mob, the rapidity with which it formed and reacted, and the boldness of a daylight lynching, all point to the reaffirmation of white racial hegemony through *community ritual* which Brundage, in his taxonomy, associates most strongly with "mass mob" lynchings.[59] On the one hand, the large numbers of the mass mob afforded participants anonymity, ensuring "that no single individual would be held responsible for the execution," and thus giving the act a "communal" rather than personal character.[60] Similarly, the sheer momentum of communal feeling often meant that mass mob actions took place within twenty-four hours or less of an alleged crime.[61] Moreover, the occurrence of the Forest City event in broad daylight (a rarity in this state) especially suggests a unanimity of public outrage over the death of Flack. Of thirty-three North Carolina lynchings between 1888 and 1906 identified by Walter Samuel Lockhardt (he actually missed the Forest City event), he stated, "Every lynching during the period happened after dark — almost invariably between midnight and daybreak."[62]

Furthermore, in light of the efforts of the constable and sheriff to resist the mob, perhaps much of the explanation for the mob's boldness rests not only in its size but also in the "quality" of its membership. Hall writes that "a lynching typically involved large segments of the population, and it was the presence of 'men of property' that tipped the balance against sheriffs who sought to uphold the law."[63] Brundage also notes the roles of "the best citizens" and "locally prominent" men as typical of mass mob lynchings.[64] Though we do not definitely know the identities of any of the men who comprised the mob which murdered Avery Mills, it is fair to assume that such a large crowd — as noted above, nearly equivalent to one-quarter the population of Forest City — would have included "men of property" and that their presence tended to offset the pleas of law enforcement.

But Hall also argues that large size and the presence of prominent figures in the community were "typical" of lynch mobs,[65] so these characteristics alone perhaps can not explain the audacity of a daylight lynching. What may have tipped the balance was Flack's high status in the community. One recent study, by Roberta Senechal de la Roche, is particularly suggestive as an explanation for how Flack's status as "victim" may have played a role in the Forest City event.[66]

Senechal de la Roche analyzes lynching from an ahistorical, sociological perspective, as a form of "social control," i.e., a response to deviant behavior. Generally, she argues that where "social distance" is great between alleged wrongdoers and their alleged victims (differences in class, socio-economic status, ethnicity and so on), lynchings are more likely to occur.[67] The differences between Avery Mills and Mills Flack in social status and political influence were perhaps at least as antithetical as their race — Mills, a simple, black tenant farmer with little or no power or influence, and Flack, a prominent white landowner and a former state legislator. Thus, Flack's high status fostered a social distance which was especially ripe for a lynching and likely contributed to the boldness of the mob.

But, notwithstanding these observations, an historical context especially conducive to racial hatred remains a compelling vehicle for understanding the lynching of Avery Mills. We need look no further than the "racial zeitgeist": a dehumanizing anti–Negro rhetoric which filled white minds with images that made blacks vulnerable to white violence; the propaganda of two white supremacy campaigns which saturated the media with its discourse of the "black beast" and "Negro domination"; a "caste system" rooted in inflexible antebellum notions of "place" and "honor" which relegated the Negro to the bottom of Southern society; the slaughter of the "Wilmington Revolution" of '98; murders of blacks in Rutherford and Polk counties, the much-publicized riot in New Orleans, and the hundreds of Negroes lynched during the 1890s; a legal system which denied blacks even a pretense of justice; and the disorder left in the wake of the transition from independent agriculture to industrialization, unabated by a failed agrarian movement and requiring scapegoats. The temper of the times, the newspapers and the politics, could not have failed to fuel the racial passions of the white men of Rutherford County.

When we weave this history with *symbolism* we then find the ritual meaning of the Forest City lynching. Mills Flack, on the one hand, as a former President of the Farmers' Alliance and a Populist politician, was a symbol of the agrarian movement in Rutherford. Put another way, he was the embodiment of the *honor* of those who had struggled for "man over money," a struggle which had only just been lost. When Avery Mills "murdered" him, it was as if all the propaganda the farmers had been fed by "the party of the fathers" was true — the death of Mills Flack made explicit their basest fears of the "black beast." Avery Mills' misfortune was to step into *that* "whirlwind"[68] at just the right moment in time. And then he too became a symbol, a ritual sacrifice to the white hegemony to which the Rutherford farmers had only just "sacrificed" their movement. Money had indeed triumphed over men but it was not white men but black who would be crucified upon William Jennings Bryan's "cross of gold."[69]

This analysis is wholly consistent with Brundage's observations upon "mass mob" lynchings as communal ritual, where he believes "the racist component of mob violence became more explicit." "Mass mobs," he writes, "more than any other type of mob violence, gave vent to the most fulsome and virulent expressions of the racist pathology at the heart of southern mob violence." Such events had a particularly important role in ritually "unit[ing] whites and reaffirm[ing] commonly held values ... preserv[ing] the social and racial foundations of southern society."[70] The "collective honor" of the community had been threatened[71] by Mills Flack's death—it *had* to be reaffirmed.

On the other hand, the Forest City event lacked much of the ritual symbolism that Brundage observes as typical of "mass mob" lynchings.[72] The site of execution was not traditional but was rather chosen arbitrarily; there seems to have been no attempt to exact the usual confession from the accused; Mills was not hung, as is typical, but only shot; there is no evidence that the victim was tortured or his body mutilated, nor of the taking of gruesome souvenirs; nor is there any evidence that the body was placed on public display (save the taking of a photograph).[73] The event was in fact characterized by great haste—no doubt attributable to the resistance of the sheriff and the other officers. The mob would have their victim, but the presence of an uncomplicit authority was too close to allow them to "play" with the corpse. Rationality and rule by law were not dead that day in Forest City, nor were they asleep; but they were too weak to overcome the most deadly consequences of the bond of honor.

Certainly, the lynching of Avery Mills represented the high watermark of racial tension in Rutherford during the Fusion era—indeed, the Forest City event was probably the only racially motivated lynching in the history of the County, as the *Daily Observer* correspondent reported that citizens lamented "a lynching has occurred in this county, something that never occurred before."[74] Though Rutherford was infamous for Ku Klux Klan activity, including violence, during Reconstruction, Trelease observes "that, in Rutherford at least, the Klan committed no murders."[75]

The community, both black and white, had suffered a great trauma. But there would be no riot. Blacks in Rutherford, whether out of fear or disinterest, made no outward protest to the lynching.[76] Likewise, though there were still some grumblings about Raney Mills and threats would build to lynch her as well, the Proto-Dorian bond had been reaffirmed by ritual sacrifice. The next day, as families and friends gathered to pay their last respects to Flack and Mills, it was reported, "Everything is quiet at Forest City. The negroes are very quiet everywhere. They have said nothing one way or the other about the matter."[77]

* * *

Mills Higgins Flack was buried in the Cool Springs Cemetery in Forest City the day after the lynching at 2 P.M.—very close to his farm and the scene of his death. A "large concourse of friends and relatives" was in attendance.[78] Avery Mills' body was turned over to his mother on the day of the lynching; he was also buried on the 29th.[79] His burial place is unknown.

The *Daily Observer* correspondent's reports of the 28th and 29th seemed to indicate that arrests of the lynchers was imminent. He stated on the former date, "I learn to-night from officers that arrests of the lynchers will be made tommorrow."[80] But no arrests were made on the 29th and he wired that day, "I am reliably informed that arrests will certainly be made; that such a bold affair could not be let go by, and that the crowd who did the shooting will be prosecuted to the full extent of the law."[81]

However, the reporter's optimism was unfounded. Authorities were typically reluctant to punish parties guilty of involvement in lynchings. According to Lockhardt, only three of the thirty-three North Carolina lynchings he identified during the period 1888–1906 even led to investigations,[82] and Williamson observed that "probably the first lynchers ever to be sent to jail for murdering blacks were two of the leaders in the Salisbury case [of 1906]."[83] Still, as late as November, the reporter looked for justice to be done. After Judge Thomas J. Shaw[84] wrapped up Fall Court in Rutherford, the *Daily Observer's* Rutherford County coverage headlined the lament that "[none] of the lynching crowd has yet been arrested."[85]

The truth is perhaps as Charles Z. Flack, Sr. ascertained in his research in the 1980s: "Warrants were issued ... but those for whom warrants were issued skipped the County for several months and the matter was then somewhat forgotten."[86] The identities of those who shot Avery Mills to death can probably never be known with certainty—the coroner stated simply that Avery Mills had been killed "by pistol balls from the hands of unknown persons," a typical verdict in a lynching.[87] One of the wires to the Raleigh *News and Observer* reported that Raney Mills was asked of the identities of her husband's murderers to which she replied, "she does not know a single man who was in the mob, although no disguises were used."[88] Of course, she may have feared reprisals.

* * *

Brundage observes that "the family ... often took part and assumed a prominent role in mass mob lynchings."[89] The Forest City event was probably no different in this respect, as family tradition has it that some of Mills Flack's sons either participated in the lynching or were under suspicion for having done so, and were forced to leave Rutherford County for a while. Evidence seems strongest for the involvement of Otho and Posey Flack, as court proceedings for Mills Flack's estate indeed indicate that both were out-of-state in January, 1901—though the U.S. Census indicates they both resided in Forest City in June, 1900.[90]

Perhaps in support of their prolonged absence, Nelda Maxwell recalled that her Mother, Mills Flack's daughter Chinara, spoke of great hardships following the death of Mills Flack.[91] His death alone would have been a blow to the farm, but, if the sons had left the County in order to evade the authorities, the work of the farm would have been idled — with the Fall harvest looming. To this can be added the death of Avery Mills and imprisonment of his wife, which probably resulted in the loss of the tenant's crop — especially if Flack's sons were unavailable to harvest it. Ms. Maxwell also wrote of a tradition that the Sheriff frequently checked on the home, perhaps indicating that officers were watchful in order to serve warrants or arrest the boys should they return — or that local authorities helped the family.[92]

Moreover, Flack was in debt at the time of his death, owing creditors $500–$600.[93] In order "to create assets for the payment of debts against the estate ... of Flack,"[94] in January, 1901, the Rutherford Superior Court ordered that Flack's 87 acre farm on the Second Broad River (the Hamilton Quarters farm) be sold at public auction; there were no bidders at the first auction in March, but at a second auction on September 21st, 1901, the farm was finally sold to Flack's son, Samuel Mills, for $7 per acre.[95] This was barely enough to cover Mills Flack's debts. Final settlement of the estate was approved by the Court in January, 1903.[96]

Posey Maggie Flack, who, along with Otho, was probably part of the lynching party (ca. 1910). (Helen Flack Cole)

* * *

But the hardships of the Flack family paled in comparison to those of Raney Mills. Not only was her husband killed before her eyes, but she found herself jailed, charged with murder for providing her husband with the gun which killed Flack. Moreover, she had a baby not yet two years old and was pregnant with a second child. The *Daily Observer* reporter interviewed her after she had been removed to the County jail:

> The woman was seen at the jail this evening by *The Observer* correspondent and asked for a statement. She did not seem to be worried either at the jail or when her husband was taken from the wagon. She told me the whole story ... [but] says she did not take the pistol to Mills, but that he had the pistol in his pocket to kill crows. "When he stopped Mr. Flack," she said, "I tried my best to stop the fuss. I begged Avery and Mr. Flack not to fight. I was not scared at all...." When told by the correspondent that she would be tried and was guilty of murder if she carried the pistol, she became very much scared and nervous and said repeatedly that she would be tried then for something she did not do.[97]

Raney Mills had reason to fear the mob would return as well, for there remained considerable anger in the community over the allegation that she had supplied the weapon with which Mills Flack had been killed. By the 29th, the day after Avery's demise, there was a vague report "that a mob talked of lynching the negro woman," though it was discounted.[98] Then, on September 1st, the *Daily Observer* reporter wired,

> A report reached here yesterday afternoon [August 30th] that a mob was organizing at Forest City to come here [Rutherfordton] and lynch Avery Mills' wife.... Hearing this, the sheriff and deputies moved the woman from the jail and carried her a few miles above town and flagged down and put her on the South Carolina & Georgia train going toward Marion. Last night Sheriff Martin was 'phoned that a mob had organized and was coming, when he promptly informed them that the woman had been taken away. I learn that she was taken to Statesville. Every night since the killing she has been removed from the jail and heavily guarded.[99]

But in response to this article, the Statesville *Landmark* reported, "This is not correct. She was not brought here."[100] In fact, from Rutherford County Court records and the minutes of the Board of County Commissioners, it can be established that she was confined in Marion, where she probably gave birth to her second child.[101] Thus the dramatic report of the flagging down of a train "going toward Marion" had more than a hint of truth in it. About one month later, on or around October 1st, Raney Mills was returned to Rutherford County.[102] It is unclear where she was held during the interval between her return from Marion and the beginning of Fall Court in Rutherfordton during the second week of November — perhaps she was hidden by relatives or a compassionate family.

One can imagine court day that Fall of 1900 at the old Courthouse in Rutherfordton. Word of Raney's impending trial would have spread like wildfire among the "wool-hats" of Forest City — and they would be there to ensure that honor was done to the memory of Mills Flack. As Raney entered the Courthouse, the icy stares of the white men gathered about the front portico would alone have been terrifying. More likely, there were cat calls also: "Well boys, I believ'in we're gonna have us some fun tonight!" (Laughter).[103]

The Court proceedings began with a grand jury inquiry which indicted her.[104] However, on November 16th, her counsel filed a detailed affidavit with the Court which proclaimed Mills' innocence, argued that she could not receive a fair trial in Rutherford County, and expressed concerns for her safety (see the complete affidavit in Appendix V).[105] Judge Thomas J. Shaw thus ordered her case moved to Cleveland County's Spring Court.[106] Her affidavit also indicated that fears of further mob violence had necessitated the posting of a guard at the Rutherford jail while Fall Court was in session.[107] It was therefore determined that she should be jailed in Cleveland County until she could stand trial there.[108] A note appended to the Court record in a different hand suggests urgency, as it requested her "immediate removal ... on account of the unsafe condition of the jail for Rutherford County."[109]

We should not assume that Raney's gender guaranteed her safety. Patrick Huber has recently studied the case of Harriet Finch who was lynched in Chatham County in 1885. Though he noted that hers was apparently the last lynching of a woman in North Carolina, he cites Walter White's research, which identified ninety-two female victims of lynch mobs nationally between 1882 and 1927.[110]

Mills was finally tried in Shelby

Judge Thomas J. Shaw (ca. 1910), who heard Raney Mills' case in Rutherford and moved her trial to Cleveland. (From *North Carolina: Rebuilding an Ancient Commonwealth*, vol. III, published by The American Historical Society, Inc., Chicago, 1928)

in April, 1901. She pleaded not guilty, but was found guilty of second degree murder and sentenced to two years in the State Penitentiary in a trial that took about two days.[111] *The Rutherfordton Tribune* reported that she was "convicted because she gave her husband a pistol and told him to shoot."[112]

But the judge who presided over her trial, William S. O'Brien Robinson,[113] disagreed with the jury's verdict. He therefore wrote to Governor Charles B. Aycock to urge her pardon, a pardon which was granted on May 6, 1901.[114] Unfortunately this letter is now lost, but the Governor's pardon of Raney Mills and, more importantly, his reason for the pardon do survive. He wrote,

> This woman was convicted of murder in the second degree in aiding her husband to kill another man. The husband was himself shot before prisoner handed the pistol to him with which he did the killing. Her husband was then taken by a mob out of the hands of the officers and hung almost in her presence. She is about twenty years of age and has a young baby. The pardon is recommended by the Judge and the Solicitor.[115]

Judge William S.O'B. Robinson (ca. 1910), judge in Raney Mills' Shelby trial and who urged her pardon. (From *Editor in Politics* by Josephus Daniels. Copyright ©1941 by the University of North Carolina Press; used by permission of the publisher)

While the Governor was erroneous in stating that Avery Mills was hung, the pardon does emphasize that it was Mills Flack who fired first. Other than Aycock's strong aversion to lynching, this would appear to be the main justification for the pardon.

* * *

To an extent, party politics and class may have inspired Raney Mills' pardon. Flack was a Populist and Aycock, a Democrat, could have and perhaps did know this; moreover, the farmers also were out-of-step socially and culturally with the New South, and especially its leadership class of lawyers and businessmen. The association of mob violence with the death of a former People's Party politician would be consistent with what was undoubtedly the view that

STATE OF NORTH CAROLINA.

..........................., Governor and Commander in Chief,

To all who shall see these Presents—GREETING:

WHEREAS, *Raney Mills* .... at the *Spring* Term, one thousand *nine hundred and one* of the Superior Court of *Cleveland* County, *was* convicted of *Murder in the Second degree* and by judgment of said Court sentenced to *two years in States Prison*

And Whereas, It has been made to appear to me that the case is one fit for the exercise of Executive clemency:

Now, Therefore, I, *Charles B. Aycock*, Governor of the State of North Carolina, in consideration of the premises, and by virtue of the power and authority in me vested by the Constitution of the State, do by these presents PARDON the said *Raney Mills* .... upon the condition that this pardon shall not extend to any other offence whereof the said part *y* may have been guilty. In Witness Whereof, I have hereunto set my hand and caused the Great Seal of the State to be affixed.

Done at our City of Raleigh, this *6* day of *May* in the year of our Lord one thousand *nine hundred and one* and in the one hundred and *twenty fifth* year of our Independence.

Charles B. Aycock

BY THE GOVERNOR: *M. Council*
Private Secretary.

Governor Charles B. Aycock's pardon of Raney Mills (1901). (North Carolina Office of Archives and History, Raleigh)

lynchings were the coarse "nigger hate" of the uneducated, lower class, agrarian masses, a perspective which the quasi-patrician Aycock, bred to the leadership class of lawyers who have seemingly run this state since time immemorial, would have likely held — though with some irony, as it was from this same class of "wool-hats" that the Democrats drew much of the support which helped them engineer the defeat of Fusion in 1898 and disfranchise the Negro in 1900. Judge Robinson, though a staunch eastern North Carolina Republican,[116] was a "devoted" friend and supporter of Aycock. Though he had little love for the Negro,[117] he was of the same professional-class ilk as his friend, and no doubt had a similar view of lynching.

But to reduce the pardon to mere politics or class would be an injustice to Aycock, who indeed strongly opposed "lynch law" throughout his administration and was a great champion of rule by law. The very stability of society and republican government demanded obeisance to reason and law and that a stand be made against "mobocracy"—code of honor or no. He stated,

> The best way to safeguard society is for good people themselves to obey the law. We cannot stop crime by committing it; we cannot teach obedience to the law by disobeying it; we cannot preserve order by the means of a mob....[118]

Eleven lynchings occurred in North Carolina during Aycock's administration[119] (this does not include the lynching of Avery Mills because Aycock did not assume office until January 15, 1901). Oliver Orr, in his biography of Aycock, noted that the Governor "[on] numerous occasions ... ordered out the militia ... to prevent mobs from lynching men...."[120] Aycock even took the step of personally offering a $400 reward for persons involved in lynchings, and, in 1903, appealed to the legislature to design a law which specified punishment for those who participated in lynch mobs—though the legislature failed to act on this proposal.[121] But though his administration did not succeed in putting an end to lynching, certainly more than any North Carolina governor before him, Aycock made a stand against Judge Lynch.

On the other hand, the necessity for rule by law also provided much of Aycock's justification for eliminating the Negro from politics through the grandfather clause. Once the Negro was stripped of political power, there would be no need to resort to "lynch law," or so went the argument.[122] Moreover, as we have argued above, Aycock bore his own responsibility for violence against the Negro through his adoption of the rhetoric of white supremacy. His biographer, Orr, attributed Aycock's rhetorical extremes to his capacity to "excell [sic] in extravagance." He wrote,

> In Aycock's lifetime, as to some extent today, the unwritten code of ethics of political oratory permitted a type of behavior that was disapproved in personal relationships. In political arguments, orators ... made charges of incompetence, misconduct, and malicious intent that in any other area of relationships would have led to legal suits, serious social schisms, and violence. Aycock followed a code similar to that of the lawyer in the courtroom ... he would minimize his party's faults, and he would exaggerate the faults of the opposition.... To lack extravagance was to lack an audience.[123]

But I think Orr's argument is disingenuous. Ultimately, the objective of Aycock's rhetoric was *power*, pure and simple—and in 1898 and 1900, his design was the restoration of power to a "party of the fathers," revitalized by a renewed commitment to white supremacy. He seems to have been willing to sacrifice black lives to that "higher" purpose.

The "racial Conservative" Aycock thus shared the podium with the fire-eating Radical, Ben "Pitchfork" Tillman of South Carolina, made incendiary speeches against "Negro domination" across North Carolina, encouraged "Red Shirt" intimidation of Negroes (at least indirectly), and appealed to whites to cast votes to protect the purity of their women from the "black incubus" in their midst. Whether outwardly opposed to lynching or not, Aycock and other Democratic leaders exploited the dark needs that the troubled white man of the 1890s — often a poor farmer — had for ritualized racial victimage. The political climate which led to the Wilmington coup as well as the many lynchings of North Carolina's Fusion era consequently owed much to Aycock. He may have pardoned Raney Mills, but he was hardly a saint. Yet if we accept the premise that lynchings were owed to the broader socio-historical context, then we must qualify the guilt of men like Aycock with this caveat: that they were the leaders of "willing executioners."

4

Epilog:
The Silence of Dishonor

ONE QUESTION STILL REMAINS: why the Flack family's silence? With all his passion for family history, Ralph R. Flack, who was fifteen at the time of the Forest City lynching, never once discussed the incident with his daughter, Helen Flack Cole.[1] Charles Z. Flack, Sr. once wrote to Ms. Cole, "My father [Andrew B. Flack] and your father [Ralph Flack] never discussed the matter with me."[2] And Nelda Maxwell was also struck by the silence of her Mother, Chinara Flack Wilson (1879–1970), daughter of Mills Flack. She states, "It is so strange to me that my mother chose to *not* talk to us about the death of her father and its problems." But she "never, and why I don't know, talked about this tragedy."[3] The loss of Mills Higgins Flack was so devastating to the family that even decades later the survivors were compelled to repress the event. It appears that it was not until the investigations of Charles Z. Flack, Sr. in the 1980s that anyone in the family took up the question of what really happened.

Of course, the economic hardships endured by Katie Flack and her children could explain at least part of the silence — it was indeed a difficult time for the family. But there seems to have been something more, a crisis of the soul as well, perhaps suggested by Otho Flack's religious fervor and his "calling" to the lay ministry in later life — he served as pastor for several Baptist churches in Rutherford County.[4] Helen Flack Cole recalled her Mother, Emma Harrill Flack, derisively referring to Otho's habit of asking nearly every man he met, "Brother, have you been saved?"[5] Perhaps the trauma of his father's death played a part in leading Flack to the ministry — though it is true, of course, that Otho Flack came of age during those years when the Southern "Bible Belt" was in ascendence.[6]

However, Ms. Maxwell suggests something more: that Flack's death and the subsequent lynching may have placed a *stigma* on the family's name, a name that had been very respected in Rutherford County.[7] I think Ms. Maxwell is correct, but explanation of just what this stigma was is still left begging. I do not think that it was simply the lynching itself that brought shame — not in an era in which "white supremacy" all but condoned "lynch law," notwithstanding the ambivalence of those such as Aycock.

In my opinion, the stigma was that *Flack was largely responsible for his own death*— this is the great family secret of the Forest City lynching. According to Otho's account, Mills Flack had impulsively shot an unarmed man with no more provocation than some heated words and a rock — we do not even know if the rock hit Flack. Only *after* being shot in the shoulder and struck by the butt of a gun did Avery Mills then ask his wife for a pistol so that he could defend himself. Moreover, Flack was himself shot when he foolishly tried to take the gun from Mills. Even the cause of the dispute tended to diminish Flack — for two men to ultimately lose their lives in an argument over the ownership of some peaches bordered on absurdity.[8] As the *Charlotte Daily Observer* correspondent concluded with respect to Flack's culpability for the events, "Had the mob known the facts were as they were, probably the negro would have been in jail to-day."[9]

But the Rutherford farmers, who had venerated Mills Flack as a leader, had acted promptly to defend his honor against the "black beast," thereby preserving the "social distance" that his position in the community demanded, and re-forging the "Proto-Dorian" bond in an act of ritual victimage. When, in the days following the lynching, these same men learned of Otho's account of events on the Flack farm that day, some surely must have concluded that in defending the honor of Flack, they had, in a sense, dishonored themselves by rashly taking the life of a man who deserved his day in court. As Brundage argues, the bonds of honor and community which supported lynching were gradually being weakened by the onslaught of industrialization and modernity.[10]

Disapproval of the lynching also likely had a *class dimension* which rested upon the acceptance — or lack thereof — of violence, especially the violence of the mob. Flack's responsibility for his own death and the subsequent lynching must have been offensive to at least some of Rutherford's upper class, the better-educated, well-to-do professional class and the "courthouse clique," with whom Flack would have crossed swords in local politics. Those of "higher station" would have seen the rashness of his act and the subsequent lynching as consistent with the violent propensities of "vulgar," uneducated farmers and indicative of the class's ill-preparedness for leadership. Though violence pervaded all the classes of the old South (e.g., the *code duello* of the upper class), Dickson Bruce observed, "The violent planter was a deviant.... The violent yeoman was not."[11] Flack's landholdings and status made him much more than a yeoman, but his political allegiance was with "forgotten" men of the land, rich or poor, many of whom knew a life of violence only too well.

Of course, perhaps most of those who participated in the execution of Avery Mills that August day continued to maintain the lynching was justified — even after Otho's account became common knowledge. We know that there were threats against the *Rutherford Press* following editorials condemning the lynching[12]; and this is also evidenced by the threats to lynch Raney and the on-going concerns for her safety in Rutherford County as her November court date approached.[13] The racial bond was a powerful thing. But surely many also would have shared Aycock's ambivalence: a contempt for the Negro combined with a strong commitment to rule by law. Moreover, when the Governor pardoned Raney Mills, he in effect sanctioned the community for the lynching. The shame of the community could have in turn manifested itself as a subtle resentment directed against the surviving members of the Flack family. And the family would have experienced this resentment as "dishonor" to the memory of an otherwise respected husband and father.

The historian Bertram Wyatt-Brown has made the definitive study of the role of honor in the Old South. Perhaps at the bedrock of Southern honor lay familial honor, the "veneration of forefathers and their traditions," the honor of blood. As he states,

> The weight of tradition within a family was the first yoke upon the rising generation. "Blood" was not an abstract concept but a determination that could so type a child that a sense of unworthiness could develop. Like a horse, human beings were supposed to exhibit traits of lineage. "I know him very well," wrote James Simmons to Governor Manning in reference to a young aspirant for political appointment. "He comes of first rate Carolina stock and his breed is good. You can rely on him."[14]

But how could the senselessness of Flack's end, his responsibility for his own death, ever be reconciled with the "yoke" of a family tradition? He had been the sire and patriarch of a large and extended family — a family with deep roots in Rutherford County. For Ralph Flack, he would be remembered as the beloved Grandpa who gave him his first pocket knife,[15] not as a man slain in a dispute with a Negro tenant farmer, and certainly not as one who could have somehow sown the seeds of his own destruction. Mills Flack *had* been hoisted on his own petard, but the events of his death had to be *repressed*, for remembrance might have caused the Flacks to question whether they were in fact "good stock."

Even more pointedly, Wyatt-Brown relates an example of how "manner of death" actually could be integral to the way Southerners honored their ancestors. He writes,

> In a letter to "Cousin Eloise" a North Carolina clergyman recalled how ... a Mrs. Jacobs of Wilmington had written to say that "she was a grand-daughter of Col. Axalla Hoole who was killed at Chickamauga. I never had heard of her before," the minister said, but she declared that "I was her only relative in North Carolina" and should baptize her little daughter. Thus, last Sunday "I baptized the great grand-daughter of Col. Axalla Hoole who died at Chickamauga...."[16]

But the Forest City lynching of 1900 was no Chickamauga. The Flack family could never be comfortable with a "remembrance" of Mills Flack as a man who died because of an argument with a trifling, half-literate, "nigger" tenant farmer over the right to pick some peaches. Their very denial, their very silence, *affirmed* how enduringly painful the awful hours of that hot August morning were and would remain to those Flacks who lived through them. So, in their dreams, and perhaps their nightmares, they made a bargain with their unconscious minds which I call the *silence of dishonor*.

Yet the Flacks *would* go on. The mantle of leadership passed to Mills Flack's son, Andrew Braxton Flack, who would be elected to Forest City's Board of Aldermen in 1901, run unsuccessfully for Sheriff in 1904, and serve on the School Boards of Forest City and Rutherford County.[17] Mills' grandsons, Ralph Roswell Flack and Charles Z. Flack, Sr., would also be active in local politics and serve terms as mayors of Rutherfordton and Forest City respectively.[18] Perhaps the silence protected them.

* * *

But we have said enough about honor and violence and class. We should rather ask: where was the *law* when Avery Mills was murdered by a mob? Or, for that matter, where was *justice* when Raney Mills was sentenced to the State Penitentiary by a "neutral" Cleveland County court? Well, it was right there of course, the law *was* there. It was simply transcended by the racial bond between white men — for they were "flesh of one flesh and blood of one blood," these men of the South.

I am reminded of the film adaptation of James Dickey's brilliant novel *Deliverance*. You will know the famous scene. A four-man party of Atlanta businessmen decides to take a weekend canoe trip down a wild river in the Georgia mountains — which in a matter of weeks will be dammed and lie on the bottom of a lake. Part-way through the trip, two of these men are "set upon," assaulted at gunpoint by a pair of mountain "crackers." But the other half of the party rescues them, killing one of the mountain men.

Then ensues a debate over what to do with the body. The leader, Lewis, played by Burt Reynolds, argues that they can dispose of it themselves and avoid a trial, that it will never be found after the river is dammed. But another member of the party, Drew, insists the killing is "a matter of the law." To this, Lewis responds, "The law! The law! What law? Where's the law Drew?" As if to legitimize Lewis' argument, the silence of the remote forest scene is punctuated only by the sounds of bird calls and the steady motion of the nearby river.[19]

The law, for Avery Mills, and thousands of other African Americans during the lynching era, was silent like that forest. So, while for the Flacks there was the silence of shame, for Avery Mills there was the *silence of justice*. This was the *sin of the fathers* — a sin of privilege which allowed them to destroy a man with impunity because he was a Negro. His ritual death at the hands of a white lynch mob, for a "murder" which was arguably self-defense, was contrary to reason and justice. The fact is that judging by the group is anathema to the very notion of justice. Men must be judged one at a time.

There is an irony in this story also, for the Populism which Mills Flack symbolized to those men of Rutherford was very much about justice, about treating men as men rather than as instruments of profit — about man over money, about *economic* justice. As Lawrence Goodwyn has brilliantly argued, the agrarian revolt, at its very root, was "a people's movement of mass democratic aspiration"[20] — an affirmation of the *humanity* of the tillers of the soil, an *authentic* rebellion against what Foucault would later call "the political technology of power," embodied in the marriage of the state and capitalism. But the agrarian crusaders failed, the defenders of New South industrialization won, and the defeat of that egalitarian promise has *now* evolved into "mass resignation" to the corporate state, political inauthenticity, and escapism through comsumption.[21] Moreover, the panacea which industrialization offered to Rutherford in place of Goodwyn's "moment of democratic promise" — the textile industry — is now seemingly in its death throes.

Sadly, neither government, nor academia, nor the mass media have acted in a way that suggests they have foreseen this crisis or understood its significance. The State of North Carolina should have been studying the problem of "rural prosperity" and the decline of manufacturing decades ago; now it plays a desperate and perhaps largely futile game of catch-up as the gulf between urban haves and rural have-nots steadily widens. Academia has long since resigned itself to *laissez faire* capitalism, as evidenced by the diminution of attention to systemic socio-economic problems and alienation in the humanities; the universities have invested their "capital" in the promulgation of a "cookbook" post-modernism (diversity, multiculturalism, etc.) with its emphasis on the empowerment of the disempowered: gays, women, minorities. As for the media, the contrast between the attention given the *purely symbolic* Confederate flag issue in South Carolina and the human cost of the closing of Stonecutter Mills in Spindale says quite enough. The corporations will march on and over us in the name of profit before we realize that the *culture game* is the one they *want* us to play.

But then perhaps this is the price of our fathers' sins: that we be doomed to the limbo or hell of the Ur-principle of *power* and the paradise of reason and justice be forever beyond our grasp. There seems no satisfactory alternative to a faith in reason, yet power seems ultimately to dictate; and every time justice is compromised by the relativistic post-modern notion that "everything is political," enlightenment rationality—which gave birth to our laws and this nation our fathers made from nothing—is consigned to the dung-heap of history. Race war may not be inevitable, as Colonel Alfred Moore Waddell asserted over one hundred years ago, but the endless cycle of wars of words and cultures rooted in the injuries of the past and an incurable racism which no one seems able to face *is* seemingly *beyond redemption*. Good or bad, "the fathers" abide with us still.

Appendix I

A Partial List of Members (Chiefly Officers) of the Farmers' Alliance in Rutherford

Note: The following is largely based upon newspaper articles and a register of sub-alliances in the Farmers' State Alliance Secretary's Records at the State Archives (ca. 1894). A quarterly report in the Marion Butler Papers identified 350 members in Rutherford in Fall, 1891. The eighty or so members identified here (drawn from sources dating between 1888 and 1894) are equivalent to less than 24 percent of that total.

Most of those identified were officers in the Rutherford County Alliance and the various sub-alliances in the County. The County Alliance had a large array of officers and each sub-alliance had a President and a Secretary. Few rank-and-file members are known.

Name	*Title* (if any)	*Sub-alliance*
Alexander, W.C.	Serg't at Arms	Rutherford*
Andrews, D.W.L.	Secretary	Camp Creek
Andrews, J.S.M.	Secretary; Asst. Door Keeper	Cane Creek; Rutherford
Baber, W.O.	State Delegate** ('92); President	Rutherford; Rutherford

*Rutherford = Rutherford County Alliance.
**State delegates were delegates to the annual State Alliance Convention.

Appendix I. Members of Farmers' Alliance in Rutherford

Name	Title (if any)	Sub-alliance
Barbee, T.L.	Business Agent	Rutherford
Barber, B.A.	President; Chaplain	Sunshine; Rutherford
Beason, J.	Secretary	Liberty
Blanton, G.W.	Secretary	Oak Grove
Brooks, A.D.	Secretary; President	Shiloh; Union
Byers, W.F.	Secretary; Secretary	Rutherford; Oak Grove
Callahan, J.T.	Secretary	Tanner's Grove
Calton, J.M.	Secretary	Sunshine
Camp, J.J.	Secretary	State Line
Cathey, R.A.	Secretary	Frog
Cooper, J.A.	President	Oak Grove
Early, J.L.	President	Golden
Erwin, L.P.	Secretary	Rutherfordton
Fowler, L.	————	Rutherford
Flack, J.F.	State Delegate ('90)	Rutherford
Flack, M.H.	President; Lecturer	Rutherford; Rutherford
Freeman, Francis***	————	————
Freeman, G.T.	Secretary	Pea Ridge
Freeman, W.B.	President; Asst. Lecturer	Mt. Vernon; Rutherford
Gettys, William C.	Secretary	Duncan Creek
Green, A.J.	Secretary	Bostic
Green, F.M.	Secretary	Walls
Green, M.J.	Secretary	Rutherford
Gray, D.J.	President	Gray's Chapel
Griffin, J.W.	Secretary	Piney Grove
Guffey, J.P.	Secretary	Brittain
Hamrick, Elias***		
Hamrick, J.L.	Secretary	Walls
Hardin, J.E.	Secretary	Mt. Vernon
Hardin, J.N.	Secretary	Cedar Springs
Hardin, L.C.	Secretary	Forest City
Hardin, M.C.	Secretary	Cedar Springs
Harrill, A.W.	Secretary	Hamrick
Harrill, H.A.	President	Cedar Springs
Harrill, S.F.	State Delegate ('88/'89); Secretary; Secretary	Rutherford; Factory; Rutherford
Harris, S.B.	Secretary	Golden

***Alliance membership assumed based upon Populist Party affiliation.

Appendix I. Members of Farmers' Alliance in Rutherford

Name	Title (if any)	Sub-alliance
Harris, W.G.	Secretary	Sulpher Springs
Higgins, M.A.	President	Otter Creek
Hill, W.T.	Secretary	Henrietta
Hoge, John***	————	————
Holland, O.W.	Secretary	Factory
Jones, The Rev. A.T.	President; Lecturer	Shiloh; Rutherford
Jolly, G.W.	Secretary	Grass Creek
Kizer, Jonas***	————	————
Ledbetter, A.J.	Secretary	Otter Creek
Logan, J.F.	Secretary	Bill's Creek
Logan, M.W.	Door Keeper	Rutherford
Long, A.B.	President; Treasurer	Pea Ridge; Rutherford
Lynch, H.P.	Secretary	Holly Springs
McClure, J.A., Jr.	Secretary	Union
McDaniel, D.F.	Secretary	Sandy River
McDaniel, J.W.	Secretary	Providence
McDowell, Col. J.L.	President; President	Sulpher Springs; Rutherford
McFarland, D.B.	Secretary	Pea Ridge
McLure, J.A.	Secretary	Union
McMahan, B.	President	Factory
Miller, Mrs. Wm. G.	Secretary	Gray's Chapel
Moore, F.	President	Piney Grove
Morgan, A.F.	County Organizer	Rutherford
Morgan, J.W.	Secretary	Otter Creek
Philbeck, J.A.	President; Vice-President	Bostic; Rutherford
Philbeck, J.M.	Secretary	Rutherford
Powell, R.B.	Secretary	Floyd's Creek
Purgason, Lindsay***	————	————
Simmons, M.W.	Secretary	Liberty
Thompson, Dr. W.A.	President	Cane Creek
Turner, Richard***	————	————
Walker, J.P.	Secretary	Robbins
Wall, S.F.***		
Wallace, A.D'K.	Secretary; Sec.-Treas.****	Rutherford; Rutherford
Watson, W.P.	Secretary; Secretary	Cane Creek; Sunshine
Webb, R.A.***	————	————

***Alliance membership assumed based upon Populist Party affiliation.
****The County Offices of Secretary and Treasurer seem to have been combined by 1894.

Appendix I. Members of Farmers' Alliance in Rutherford

Name	Title (if any)	Sub-alliance
Webb, W.J.	President	Walls
Wilkins, D.S.	Secretary	Shiloh
Wilkins, L.T.	Secretary	Gray's Chapel
Wilson, W.B.	Secretary	Mt. Vernon
Withrow, J.P.D.	Secretary	Withrow
Womack, Willis	————	Walls
York, A.A.	————	————

Appendix II

Populist Candidates in Rutherford (1892–1898)

Note: Griffin's *History* is inaccurate and incomplete with respect to Rutherford's Populist or People's Party candidates. The following is offered as a corrective.

1892   Populists ran a separate slate (though there was some talk of Fusion with Republicans). All Rutherford Populists were defeated.

Mills H. Flack, State House
Elias Hamrick, Register of Deeds
John Hoge, Sheriff

Frank Moore, State Senate
R.A. Webb, Coroner

1894   First Fusion election. The balance of county offices (Sheriff, Clerk of Court, etc.) went to the Republicans because the Populists were allowed the nomination for the coveted House seat. All offices were won by Republicans and Populists.

W.O. Baber, Treasurer
Mills H. Flack, State House

Frank Moore, Coroner

1896   Second Fusion election. Baber and Wallace were defeated, but Purgason, Wall and Webb won.

W.O. Baber, Treasurer
Lindsay Purgason, State House
S.F. Wall, County Comm.

A.D'K. Wallace, State Senate
R.A. Webb, Coroner

1898   Last Fusion election in Rutherford. In early September, when Rutherford Populists and Republicans were unable to come to a Fusion agreement, County Populists met and nominated a separate slate of candidates. But the Populist ticket was withdrawn when Fusion was worked out in mid–October. All Fusion candidates were defeated.

Populists (separate slate)*
Mills H. Flack, Clerk of Crt.
Elias Hamrick, Reg. of Deeds
Jonas Kizer, Treasurer
Lindsay Purgason, State House
Richard Turner, Sheriff
R.A. Webb, Coroner

Populists (after Fusion)
Francis Freeman, State House
S.A. Wall, County Comm.
R.A. Webb, Coroner

---

*It is unclear if separate candidates were named for seats on the County Board of Commissioners.

Appendix III

The Charlotte Daily Observer *Article of 29 August 1900*

A Negro Lynched at Noon

Flack's Slayer Shot by a Mob

In a Dispute Over the Ownership of Some Fruit, Avery Mills Killed a Well-Known Rutherford County Farmer, and Was Soon After Shot to Death, Near Forest City — The Officers Tried in Vain to Get the Crowd to Allow the Law to Take Its Course — The Negro Dragged From a Wagon and Shot to Death 100 Yards From the Road — Particulars of the Crime.

Special to The Observer.

Rutherfordton, Aug. 28.—Mr. Mills H. Flack was shot and killed on his plantation, near Forest City, this morning at 9 o'clock by Avery Mills, a negro, and later Mills and the officers in charge of him were overtaken by a crowd on the way to Rutherfordton jail and the negro carried to the woods and riddled with bullets.

It seems that three days ago Mr. Flack went to his plantation, which is rented to Mills, or who is, by some agreement, making a crop this year, to get some fruit,

Appendix III. *Charlotte Daily Observer* 29 August 1900

whereupon Mills' wife ordered him off. He refused to go and she went to the house and secured a pistol and went back the second time and ordered him to leave. He left rather than have a difficulty. This morning at 9 o'clock Mr. Flack, his son, Otho, and another boy went to the plantation in a wagon to pull fodder. Mills' house is about 100 yards from the road. He appeared and halted Mr. Flack and began to renew the talk about the fruit, when Mills' wife brought him his pistol. He took it and deliberately shot Mr. Flack just under the heart. Mr. Flack, having a shot-gun, drew it and fired, the shot taking effect in the negro's shoulder, and then took the gun and pounded the negro over the head with it until it was broken. The negro attempted to shoot Mr. Flack's son, but he hit the negro in the head with a rock and took his pistol away from him and shot him in the hip. The negro was not hurt badly.

Mr. Flack died in less than an hour. The news soon spread and the Forest City people were gathered at the scene. The negro and his wife were arrested. Mr. Flack said to his friends before he died that he could not live long; that the negro had killed him and that he wanted him hanged and wanted his friends to see it done. He was then taken home and the negro and wife brought before Justice J.C. Green, who at once committed them to jail. They were placed in the custody of Town Marshal Hamrick and Constable Hardin.

After learning of the affair The Observer's correspondent started to Forest City to learn the particulars, and reaching the Sea Board Air Line depot in Forest City met the officers and prisoner [sic] coming to jail. Not stopping, but going on toward the city, I saw crowds on horseback and in vehicles armed and coming at full speed. I returned and overtook the officers and prisoners and informed them that an eager-looking crowd of men were pursuing them. They moved on as rapidly as possible, but the crowd overtook them just two and one-half miles from Forest City at the old Eaves place, on the right of the Seaboard Air Line road. Sherrif [sic] Martin, leading another crowd was on [his] way, and stopped down the road a few hundred yards to keep them back. In the meantime the first crowd had held up the wagon, and were waiting for a second squad. The town marshall, who was driving, attempted to push on, but the small crowd held the horse and told him not to move.

The crowd was appealed to to let the negro alone, and let him go to jail and take the full course of law, and at the time it did seem that they would submit, but someone would then make a remark about the killing and stir the crowd again.

Town Marshal, J.D. Justice, of Rutherfordton, made the crowd a most sensible talk; as also did Mr. O.C. Erwin and Constable Hardin. They tried to persuade them one at a time. Mr. Justice told Mr. Hamrick to drive on. He got in his wagon, took out his revolver and told the crowd that he was a marshal and had the prisoner in charge and was going to take him to jail. He started to drive a second time, but was stopped and one of the crowd pulled the negro out of the back end of the wagon. He was left sitting there a few minutes and then, when more men arrived, one man called: "Grab him up!" and so they did in the midst of all the pleading that could be done, and took him down the road.

When the mob had gotten the negro out of the wagon Sherrif Martin was coming close behind with the officers and some one yelled, "There comes the sherrif!" Immediately the negro was thrown against the bank of the road and the small mob ahead began firing, and he was dead in less than a minute. He groaned once and kicked once.

Appendix III. Charlotte Daily Observer *29 August 1900*

The firing had hardly ceased before the crowd was quickly making its way through the woods. The Sherrif was very much surprised and worried over the affair. The crowd that did the shooting did not number over a dozen. About 20 shots took effect.

The coroner's verdict was to the effect that the negro came to his death by pistol balls from the hands of unknown persons.

While the crowd had taken the negro to the woods the woman was left in the wagon alone and escaped, but was later caught and brought to jail.

Mills H. Flack was 60 years of age and a Christian and a worthy citizen. A wife, seven boys and three girls survive him. He will be buried Thursday. Several of his sons in other States have been wired for. Mr. Flack represented this county in the legislature in 1896.

The negro Mills had a bad record. The woman was seen at the jail this evening by The Observer correspondent and asked for a statement. She did not seem to be worried either at the jail or when her husband was taken from the wagon. She told me the whole story, which tallies with the above, except she says she did not take the pistol to Mills, but that he had the pistol in his pocket to kill crows. "When he stopped Mr. Flack," she said, "I tried my best to stop the fuss. I begged Avery and Mr. Flack not to fight. I was not scared at all. I am 19 and Avery is 21." When told by the correspondent that she would be tried and was guilty of murder if she carried the pistol, she became very much scared and nervous and said repeatedly that she would be tried then for something she did not do.

I learn to-night from officers that arrests of the lynchers will be made tomorrow. There is no talk of lynching the woman.

Appendix IV

The Charlotte Daily Observer *Article of 31 August 1900*

Flack Shot First.

And Broke His Gun Over Mills' Head Before the Negro Shot — Had the Mob Known This, the Lynching Might Not Have Occurred

Special to the Observer.

Rutherfordton, Aug. 29.—The lynching of Avery Mills for the killing of Mr. Mills H. Flack, yesterday morning at 9 o'clock, about a mile from Forest City, as told in yesterday's Observer, has been the chief talk since that time. Nothing has ever happened that has been regretted so much by the people of the county. Mr. Flack was not only an excellent citizen, but one of the county's most successful farmers, and the worse of it is that a lynching has occurred in this county, something that never occurred before.

The negro's body was turned over to his mother yesterday and buried today.

Mr. Flack was buried this afternoon at 2 o'clock in the presence of a large concourse of friends and relatives.

Everything is quiet at Forest City. The negroes are very quiet everywhere. They have said nothing one way or the other about the matter. Dr. W.A. Thompson, county physician, went down and examined the negro's body yesterday and found 18 shot in his body, one in his leg, one in his hand, one in his head, and that he had been

Appendix IV. Charlotte Daily Observer *31 August 1900*

shot with a shot-gun in the hip. There was a rumor afloat last night that a mob talked of lynching the negro woman but it was all fake.

I am reliably informed that arrests will certainly be made; that such a bold affair could not be let go by, and that the crowd who did the shooting will be prosecuted to the full extent of the law.

It was difficult yesterday to obtain a true statement of the affair, there being so many rumors afloat. The truth about who did the shooting first was not known until to-day, when Mr. Flack's son, Otho, who was along, and took part in the difficulty, talked. He said the negro stopped them and was abusing them about a few words that had passed between them and the negro's wife some days before, and threw a rock at Mr. Flack. Mr. Flack then shot the negro and he stated [*sic*] to the house, Mr. Flack following, breaking his gun over the negro's head. In the meantime the negro called to his wife to bring his pistol, which she did and the negro shot Mr. Flack then, when Mr. Flack was trying to get the pistol away. This is also about the negro woman's statement, except that Mills had his pistol with him, she stating that she did not take it to him.

The above is believed to be a true statement by most all the people of Forest City. It was thought at the time of the lynching that the report in yesterday's Observer was correct. Had the mob known that the facts were as they were, probably the negro would have been in jail to-day.

Appendix V

Affidavit Submitted by Raney Mills to Rutherford County Superior Court, Fall 1900, and the Order of Judge Shaw, Etc.

North Carolina Superior Court
Rutherford County Fall Term 1900

State
vs. Affidavit
Avery Mills &
Raney Mills

The defendant Raney Mills being duly sworn deposes and says,

1 That she is the wife of her co-defendant Avery Mills and that her co-defendant and husband is dead.

2 That she is not guilty of the crime alleged to have been committed by herself and her husband, on the 28th day of August 1900, as charged in the bill of indictment, has so pleaded and that she has a good defense to make to said charge.

3 That she has probable grounds to believe and does believe that she cannot obtain justice in the County of Rutherford, and that she cannot have a fair and impartial trial in said County of Rutherford owing to the great prejudice against her.

That the man Flack, whom it is alleged was murdered by affiant and her husband as shown in said bill in this criminal action, was a man of great influence in Rutherford County, and was a member of a very large family, the members of which family live in different sections or parts of Rutherford County and are people of great influence, and that she believes said influence has been used and is being used to her prejudice.

That while affiant and her co-defendant Avery Mills were in the custody of the officer of the law, on the 28th day of August 1900, between Forest City and Rutherfordton, a maddenned and angry mob, composed of about two hundred and fifty men, took from said officer, her husband and co-defendant and shot him to death, and that affiant was informed by the officers in whose custody she and her husband were at that time and place, Mr. J.D. Justice, and others, that she would have suffered the fate of her husband, had it not been for her pregnant condition at that time, she being pregnant and big with child, to which she has since given birth. That she was about to by [sic] lynched anyhow, after she had been taken to Rutherford jail, and that the authorities of sail Rutherford County, sent her to McDowell County, where she remained a month. That since the birth of her child she is informed and believes that efforts have been made to lynch her and threats have been made to that effect, and that while the Superior Court of said County of Rutherford has been sitting or in sitting or in session, a guard has been placed around the Rutherford jail, in which affiant has been confined, to protect her from mob violence. That affiant believes that those who murdered her husband, and the friends and relatives of Mr. Flack, will make every effort to convict her of a crime of which she is innocent. That affiant is informed and believes that the ends of justice demand that her cause be removed from said County of Rutherford to another county for trial.

signed Raney Mills affiant

Sworn to and subscribed before me this 16th day of November 1900.

M.O. Dickerson C.S.C.

North Carolina	In Superior Court
Rutherford County	Fall Term 1900

State
vs   Order
Avery Mills and
Raney Mills

This criminal action coming on for trial and the prisoner Raney Mills, having been arraigned and it appearing to the Court by affidavit of defendant Raney Mills, that her co-defendant is now dead and that she probably cannot obtain justice from a Rutherford County jury owing to the great prejudice which the court finds is against, and that she cannot have a fair and impartial trial in said County of Rutherford, it is therefore on motion of defendant Raney Mills, through her counsel, ordered that this case be removed to the Superior Court of Cleveland County for trial. That the Clerk of Superior Court for Rutherford County, transmit to the Clerk of the Superior Court for Cleveland County, a transcript of the records of the case, with all depositions and written evidence, if any, properly certified, to the end that

Appendix V. Affidavit by Raney Mills to Judge Shaw

it may be there docketed and placed by the Clerk of that Court on the criminal calender for trial at the Spring Term 1901 of said Superior Court of Cleveland County.

                         Signed   Thos. J. Shaw
                                             Judge Presiding*

State
vs
Avery Mills
and Raney Mills

        The defendant Raney Mills being present in Court and arraigned upon a charge of murder for herself pleads not guilty. And it appearing to the Court by the affidavit of defendant setting forth that she could not come safely to trial in the County of Rutherford and other matters relative to the same, that said cause should be removed. It is therefore ordered by the Court that this cause be removed for trial to the County of Cleveland, and that the Clerk of this Court certify all the papers and records in this case to the Clerk of the Superior Court of Cleveland County.

        The said Raney Mills is remanded to the custody of the Sheriff and it is ordered by the Court that she the said Raney Mills be taken to the County jail of the said County of Cleveland and there safely kept until the next regular term of the Superior Court for said County, then and there to be dealt with according to law. *The order for the immediate removal being made on account of the unsafe condition of the jail for Rutherford County as reported by grand jury.***

---

*From: Rutherford County, NC, Minutes of the Superior Court, 1894–1902, pp. 268–271 (microform).
**From: Rutherford County, NC, Minutes of the Superior Court, 1894–1902, pp. 244 (microform). Emphasis in last statement added. This statement appeared in the Clerk's minutes in a different hand.

Appendix VI

Research on the Origins and Revolutionary Services of the Flacks of Guilford and Rutherford Counties

The Flacks of Rutherford County trace their ancestry to William and John Flack, believed to be brothers, for whom the first evidence of establishment there is William Flack's application for a Colonial land grant in what was then Mecklenburg in 1768.[1] Previous researchers have been able to glean a fair amount about these men, chiefly using surviving court and land records of old Tryon and Rutherford counties. However, no one to date has been able to ascertain exactly where the Flacks of Rutherford came from; their relationship to Flacks elsewhere, such as those in Guilford County, NC, and Lancaster County, PA; nor their origins in the Old World.

What follows is an attempt to assemble and assess the various evidence relevant to these questions, building upon the work of others such as Dudley W. Crawford, Dr. Horace E. Flack, Ralph R. Flack, Charles Z. Flack and Ivarea Flack. Particular emphasis will be laid upon the value of Crawford's early article; previously untapped primary sources in Rowan/Guilford and Pennsylvania; collateral or associated family research linking the origins of the Rutherford Flacks to Lancaster County, PA; and some general suppositions suggesting Flack ties to Ulster and England. In addition, readers familiar with previous work will find herein new details pertaining to the Revolutionary services of the Flacks of both Guilford and Rutherford. While the problem of John and William Flack's ancestry remains unresolved, it is my hope that the following will serve as a useful corrective to previous errors and as a groundwork for further research.

Appendix VI. Origins of the Flacks

* * *

The line from which Mills Higgins Flack descended was that of John Flack (?–1792), whom we know bought 300 acres of land along Catheys Creek in what was then Tryon County in 1778,[2] and served as a justice of the peace in Rutherford during and after the Revolution.[3] John Flack was preceded in Tryon by William Flack, almost certainly a brother,[4] who, as noted above, applied for a land patent on Camp Creek (in what was then Mecklenburg County) in 1768. Based upon the family tradition first penned by Dudley W. Crawford, in conjunction with the Flack reunion held at the Bottomless Pools, near Chimney Rock, NC, in 1927, "brothers" John and William Flack were associated with two other "brothers," one named Thomas, the other Jefferson, both of whom settled in what is now Guilford County, North Carolina. In support of Crawford, we do find a Thomas Flack, who was more or less a contemporary of John and William, in Guilford, ca. 1760. However, if there was another "brother" who settled in Guilford, he was probably named James.[5] In addition to these four "brothers," Crawford also held that there were two Flack "cousins" who settled in Pennsylvania and New York.[6]

But before we can take up what I will call the "Crawford tradition," and the various problems associated with the origins of these men, we must first address the widely circulated theory (and, I believe, an erroneous one) that the Flacks of Rutherford came from Bucks County, Pennsylvania. Between 1908 and 1910, the Bucks County Flacks apparently held one or more reunions and a newspaper article followed at least one of these events, accompanied by a photograph of some of the venerable old men of the Bucks County clan. In his valuable essay on the family, Dr. Horace E. Flack, who apparently saw this photograph, added fuel to a Bucks County connection by noting the resemblance between the Flacks of Bucks and the Flack elders of Rutherford.[7] A James Flack (1708?–1802?), who migrated from Ulster to Pennsylvania about 1730, was progenitor of this line, and he apparently *did* have sons named William (b. 1748) and John (1752–1802).[8]

In her *Flack Heritage*, Ivarea Flack "adopted" this James Flack as the missing link between the Rutherford Flacks and those of Pennsylvania and Northern Ireland.[9] However, comparison of the *known* facts of the two lines would seem sufficient to disprove an association between them. For example, when the "anchiant" James Flack made his will in 1793, he named his son John Flack as his co-executor[10] — yet John Flack of Rutherford had died the year before in North Carolina. Other inconsistencies: William Flack of Bucks was said to have moved to Kentucky, not Rutherford; John Flack of Bucks was said to have married an Ann Wilson, of whom we have no mention in Rutherford; and tax records indicate that men named John and William Flack still resided in Bucks County in 1775 (long after William of Mecklenburg/Tryon/Rutherford first bought land).[11] The only way to reconcile the two lines is by arguing that James Flack of Bucks had two *other* sons named John and William. While it is indeed true that the Doylestown reunion article refers to two other sons named John and William, the article also states that they were presumed to have died in infancy,[12] and there is certainly no evidence that they rather survived and were the same as John and William Flack of Rutherford.

The "Bucks County theory" thus discounted, we now return to the aforemen-

Appendix VI. Origins of the Flacks

tioned Crawford tradition. It is, I think, particularly important to note that Dudley W. Crawford's work on the Flacks (which consists of an article published in several Rutherford papers in conjunction with the Flack reunion of 1927) is the first version in writing of what must have been up to that time an *oral* tradition. This tradition likely would have been conveyed to Crawford through the old men of the Flack clan in Rutherford — men like Christopher Jason Flack (1844–1929), George Andrew Flack (1849–1937), Millard B. Flack (1851–1929), J. Mills Flack (1854–1943) and Joseph F. Flack (1856–1937). All of these men were born before the deaths of John Flack's eldest sons, Andrew Flack (1775–ca. 1865) and George Flack (1778–1860); and Christopher Jason, Andrew's grandson, was already an adult at the time of the latter's death in late 1864 or early 1865.[13] It seems perfectly reasonable to assume that these old men of 1927 could have been recipients (as well as transmitters) of an oral tradition on the origins of the Rutherford Flacks which had some basis in fact.

It is curious that in the later work of both Horace E. Flack and Ralph R. Flack, Thomas Flack of Guilford was never identified — that they both assumed Andrew Flack (1769–1845), who was actually a son of Thomas Flack,[14] was one of the Guilford "brothers" of John and William Flack. It was Crawford who apparently first wrote of the Guilford connection with the Flacks of Rutherford, and it was also Crawford who first recorded that one of these Flacks was named Thomas. A careful perusal of early Guilford County records (and Rowan, as she was the parent county of Guilford) clearly establishes the existence of a Thomas Flack. But I think it is extremely unlikely that Crawford made any investigations of early Guilford records. The Thomas Flack and Guilford connections recorded by Crawford must have been part of an oral tradition which was handed down over several generations. Let us give Crawford his due for preserving this very valuable clue to the origins of the Rutherford Flacks.

* * *

Though the first definite evidence of Thomas Flack (?–ca. 1776) in Rowan/Guilford is a 1761 Granville grant, it is possible that he was living in North Carolina as early as 1754. For among a list of sixty names in Capt. Andrew Hampton's company of Granville County militia (dated December 6, 1754) can be found the names Samuel and Thomas "Flaick."[15] Some researchers believe that this is the same Andrew Hampton who would later settle in Tryon/Rutherford and in 1780 distinguish himself as the commander of the Rutherford men at the Battle of King's Mountain.[16]

There is no further mention of a Thomas Flaick in Granville records, but a Samuel "Flake" was recorded in a 1755 Granville tax list,[17] and quite possibly the same Samuel Flake applied for a land patent (never issued) in Johnston County in 1753.[18] By late 1762, a Samuel Flake (?–ca. 1802) had purchased a 150 acre tract in Anson County;[19] in 1763, he was recorded in an Anson tax list with a slave named Mingo.[20] Samuel Flake of Anson was a Regulator (as was Thomas Flack of Rowan/Guilford), but the State records indicate that during the Revolution he was among Anson's "disaffected" and was jailed for refusing to take the loyalty oath then required by law.[21]

It is tempting to entertain the possibility of some relationship between Samuel

Flake of Anson and the Flacks of Guilford and Rutherford. The name Flake is arguably a variant spelling of the more common Flack or Fleck.[22] Furthermore, descendants Osmer D. Flake and Julia Flake Burns preserved a vague tradition of three older "sons" of Samuel Flake coincidentally named Thomas, William and John.[23]

Of these supposed sons, only John Flake can be found in Anson records. He was a chainbearer for a survey for Samuel Flake's neighbor, John Smith, in 1768,[24] and served in Capt. Thomas Wade's "Lt. Horse & Independent Company of Foot" during the Cross Creek expedition in early 1776.[25] He last appears in Anson records in June, 1778, as a petitioner of Gov. Richard Caswell in a controversy over a disputed election of officers in that county in the company of Capt. George Wilson.[26] It is interesting that he vanishes from Anson records in 1778, just as John Flack appears in Tryon/Rutherford, though a Flake family researcher named Osmer Flake observed that a John Flake who served in the South Carolina militia "as Private previous to the reduction of Charleston," and settled accounts there as late as 1785, might be the same as John Flake of Anson.[27]

Withal, there is no conclusive evidence that Samuel Flake of Anson is related to the Flacks of Guilford and Rutherford, or that John Flake of Anson is the same as John Flack of Rutherford. Perhaps most damning to efforts to connect the Flakes and Flacks is that they do not seem to share any associated or collateral families — which in the case of the Flacks of Guilford and Rutherford points to a Lancaster County, PA, connection. A Flake researcher named William F. Joiner has in fact used a collateral family named Harris to argue that the Flakes came to North Carolina from Virginia.[28]

* * *

Thomas Flack of Guilford obtained a grant from Lord Granville for 181 acres along the Walnut Branch in Rowan County (now Guilford) in 1761,[29] and operated a grist and saw mill on or near these lands.[30] The entry "1758=1762" in the Rowan deed index perhaps suggests that he applied for this land in 1758.[31] He was an early member of Buffalo Presbyterian Church, and Rankin's *History* refers to him as "a young man" at the time of his arrival.[32] Buffalo Presbyterian was established by Scots-Irish who were part of the Nottingham Colony that purchased a large tract of land (over 20,000 acres) on Buffalo and Reedy Fork Creeks and were among the first settlers of present-day Guilford in the early 1750s. It is famous as the pastorate of the venerable the Rev. David Caldwell (1725–1824), born in Lancaster County, Pennsylvania.[33] Many of the other Nottingham colonists also came from Lancaster — townships such as Bart, Coleraine, Drumore, Little Britain and Sadsbury, and parts of that Pennsylvania county which were disputed by Maryland.[34]

Could Thomas Flack of Guilford also have come from Lancaster County, PA? There are indeed a number of Flacks in the 18th century tax records of Lancaster. These lists (1750–1780) include variant spellings such as Fleck and Flick (which could well be German rather than Scots-Irish) and correlates with the North Carolina first names of Thomas, James, John and William.[35]

Of particular interest is a John Flack or Fleck who obtained a patent for 318 acres of land in the northwestern extremity of Drumore Township in 1751.[36] His

Appendix VI. Origins of the Flacks

name consistently appears in surviving Drumore tax lists from 1757 through 1780.[37] In the Drumore list of 1757, his name is in close proximity to a James Porter (a surname with whom the Rutherford Flacks are closely associated),[38] who obtained a patent for a 248 acre tract adjacent to Flack's in 1754.[39] The 1759 list indicates that Flack worked as a "joiner" or carpenter.[40] Flack and his wife Jean sold their Drumore lands in 1781.[41] This township, Drumore, was located in the southern-most portion of Lancaster County, near the Maryland border, an area settled predominantly by the Scots-Irish.[42]

Probably soon after his arrival in Rowan/Guilford, Thomas Flack married Jane or Jean McQuiston (1735?–1802), the daughter of one of the original Nottingham colonists, James McQuiston (1700–1766), who was born in county Derry, Ireland, and received a Granville grant along the Reedy Fork in 1753.[43] Thomas Flack witnessed James McQuiston's will which was proven in Rowan court in 1766.[44]

But before his removal to Rowan, James McQuiston lived in Drumore Township, Lancaster County, PA. In 1735, he was among a group of petitioners from Drumore to the county court of Lancaster who sought "a road from 'James Alexanders to Octoraro Creek at a place Called Miles' ford to Joyn a Road in Chester County Leading to Christian Creek.'"[45] This part of Drumore became Little Britain Township in 1738,[46] and in 1740 McQuiston and others in Little Britain again petitioned the court for a road "'by James Porters Store … betwixt the plantations of the Said Porter & James McQueston Thence Down the Said Lane.'"[47] Thus, just as John Flack or Fleck of Drumore, McQuiston lived next to a James Porter when he resided in Lancaster.

James McQuiston was joined in America about 1735 by a possible brother named Robert McQuiston (?–1765), who appears in the records of Cumberland and Lancaster Counties, PA, by the early 1750s, and died only about a year after a move to Rowan County, NC, ca. 1764.[48] He married Ann Denny, the daughter of Walter Denny of Little Britain Township in Lancaster, and obtained a land patent in West Pennsboro Township, Cumberland County, PA, in 1752.[49] When he purchased a 353 acre tract on the Reedy Fork in Rowan/Guilford from James McQuiston in 1764, Thomas Flack was a witness.[50] Robert McQuiston's will, proven in Rowan court in 1766, was also witnessed by Flack.[51]

Surviving records indicate that Thomas Flack was a patriot of some note. Active as a leader in the Regulation Movement of 1770–71, he was apparently implicated with the Hillsborough mob that attacked the infamous Tory Edmund Fanning, demolishing his house and brutally whipping him.[52] *The Colonial Records of North Carolina* contain a very interesting document signed by Flack, as well as, among others, a Captain James Porter (again, the Porter surname which is closely associated with the Rutherford Flacks), and dated November 20th, 1770, indicating the support of Haw River Regulators in bringing to justice those responsible for the outrages against Fanning.[53] It also appears that he participated in a Regulator grievance committee which met in Rowan in March, 1771,[54] just two months before the Battle of Alamance, and it is not unreasonable to suggest that he was present at that important event.[55]

Later, during the Revolution, Thomas Flack served as a Captain and commanded a company in a Guilford militia regiment led by Col. James Martin.[56] Sur-

Appendix VI. Origins of the Flacks

viving Revolutionary War account books indicate that he participated in expeditions to Cross Creek (now Fayetteville) and Wilmington in early 1776; while it is unclear, it seems possible that he was at the Battle of Moore's Creek.[57]

In the Wilson Papers in the Southern Historical Collection at the University of North Carolina at Chapel Hill, there survives an old store ledger kept by one John Tate in Guilford during the 1770s. Thomas Flack was among Tate's customers between 1774 and 1776, and in the ledgers we can find Flack's purchases for items such as nails, brimstone, alum, buttons, rum, a quire of paper and other sundries. Next to an entry made by Tate concerning a "note payable Jany 1st 1776" is the curious notation, "taken by Violence."[58] Flack's account, which was in arrears L 151, was settled on March 5th, 1776, "By 1 Tract of Land returned."[59]

Could "taken by Violence" mean that Flack was killed in early 1776 about the time of the Cross Creek expedition? This is speculation, but it is certain that Flack was dead by 1778. A 300 acre Guilford land warrant applied for in August of that year by "Jane Flack widow" was issued for lands upon which Thomas Flack had "formerly lived ... including an improvement whereon the said Thomas Flack had a grist and saw mill."[60] This grant was issued to Jane Flack in 1783.[61]

Thomas Flack and his wife Jane sold their Walnut Branch tract (the original Granville tract) in 1773 to a John Chambers.[62] Rankin suggests that Flack then left the Buffalo Presbyterian congregation and "located near Haw River Presbyterian Church and joined there,"[63] perhaps because in 1770 we find him named in a deed for land purchased for the establishment of the Haw River church,[64] located just a few miles across the Guilford line in what is now Rockingham County. However, it seems more likely that Flack and his family remained on unclaimed land in present-day Guilford, on or near Reedy Fork Creek. A Guilford land entry for one Adam Lowman in 1779 refers to lands bordering the property of the "Widow" Flack "on [the] waters of Redy fork."[65]

* * *

The second of the Flack "brothers" to acquire land in North Carolina was William Flack (ca. 1740–ca. 1805?), who in August, 1768, purchased a 100 acre tract along Camp Creek from one Samuel Givens, though this deed was not proved in court until 1773.[66] In 1775, he received an adjoining land patent of 224 acres.[67] We know that there was a relationship between William Flack and John Flack because a petition brought before the Rutherford County Court, following the latter Flack's death in 1792, named William Flack as the guardian of John's children.[68] William Flack did not play the prominent role in public affairs that we find in the cases of John and Thomas Flack. There is even a family tradition that he was a Tory,[69] supported by the testimony of a neighbor in a letter of 1881 in the Draper manuscripts,[70] though this is perhaps refuted by records of his contributions of beef and corn to the militia of NC, Virginia and SC, probably during the King's Mountain campaign.[71] At any rate, his name appears rather infrequently in public documents. Nor do we find any documentary evidence which links him to Thomas Flack of Guilford. He probably died between 1800 and 1810, but I have located no record of the settlement of his estate.[72]

Appendix VI. Origins of the Flacks

* * *

Thus we come to John Flack, the third of the "brothers" in the Crawford tradition. The first documentation of John Flack in Tryon/Rutherford is his purchase of 300 acres on Catheys Creek from Henry Hays of the Ninety-Six District, SC, in June, 1778 (proved in October, 1778, court).[73] There is no convincing evidence that he was in old Tryon before that date.[74]

Above, we discussed the question of whether or not John Flack of Rutherford might be the same as John Flake of Anson. A similar (albeit weak) case can be made for a John "Fleck" who resided in Rowan/Guilford in 1768. In Rowan records there survives a tax list for that year which identifies a John Fleck in the household of a notable Whig named Samuel Clark or Clarke, who at that time owned a large tract of land on the Deep River,[75] just inside present-day Guilford and about 10 air miles from the Thomas Flack lands on Walnut Branch.[76] Fleck was perhaps in the employ of Clark, and his appearance in the list as a taxable poll indicates that he was at least 16 years of age at the time. It is entirely plausible that John Flack of Rutherford could have first resided in Rowan/Guilford before migrating to Tryon.

But while it may be well nigh impossible to prove that John Fleck of Rowan/Guilford was the same as John Flack of Rutherford, there is considerable evidence (especially collateral family evidence) to suggest that John Flack had a Guilford connection. For example, Dr. Horace E. Flack (and Ivarea Flack following him) pointed to Rutherford land conveyances from John Flack to a "John Anderson of Guilford" in 1784.[77] Ivarea Flack also noted a marriage between a John Anderson and a Sarah Flack in Pennsylvania in 1769, though it is unclear what if any connection this Sarah Flack had to the Flacks of Guilford and Rutherford.[78]

But before dismissing the "John Anderson of Guilford" conveyances as mere coincidence, we should note other connections between a John Anderson and John Flack of Rutherford or the Flacks generally. For example, one of Robert McQuiston's daughters, Sarah (1747–?), married Robert Cherry (?–ca. 1826) of Tryon in Rowan County in 1769.[79] Cherry purchased a tract along the Catawba in what would later be Lincoln County in 1771.[80] About 1783, he removed to Catheys Creek[81] where he was a neighbor of John Flack.

Robert Cherry witnessed the two Flack land transactions with John Anderson of Guilford in 1784,[82] and a John Anderson acted as one of the bondsman when Cherry married Sarah McQuiston.[83] In the 1790s, Cherry served on the commission which oversaw the intestate of John Flack of Rutherford.[84]

Like the Porters and the McQuistons, the Cherrys also may have been in Drumore Township, Lancaster County, PA, where we find a David and Robert "Chirry" in the 1763 tax list for that township.[85] In 1766, David and Robert Chirry of Drumore sold a 209 acre tract to a Thomas Porter (also of Drumore) which had been surveyed for a Robert Chirry in 1742;[86] in that same year, David Chirry witnessed a Drumore quit claim deed with a Samuel Porter.[87] Tryon/Rutherford deed books also make mention of a contemporary of Robert Cherry named David Cherry.[88]

Another interesting "twist" on the John Anderson of Guilford connection suggests a possible association between the Flacks of North Carolina and a John Flack (1758–1833) who was among the early settlers of Washington County, PA. Accord-

Appendix VI. Origins of the Flacks

ing to Beers, this John Flack, who came to Washington from Lancaster County, PA, first settled in Washington Village (1784), then removed to Buffalo Township (1788).[89] The timing of this move may suggest some connection with the John Flack or Fleck of Drumore Township noted above. Crumrine identifies a John Flack of Washington as an influential member of Upper Buffalo Presbyterian Church.[90]

In 1800, a man named John Anderson, "born in Guilford County, N.C., in April, 1768, and [who] received his education ... under the Rev. David Caldwell," was named pastor of Upper Buffalo.[91] Furthermore, wrote Beers, a daughter of the Rev. Anderson married the son of a John Flack.[92] Rankin identified this Rev. Anderson (d. 1840) as the grandson of a William Anderson, Sr.[93] who obtained a Granville grant on Kenady Creek, a branch of the Reedy Fork, in Guilford (then Orange) in 1758;[94] the Rev. John Anderson's mother (his father was William Anderson, Jr.) was of the Dennys of Lancaster with whom Robert McQuiston intermarried.[95] William Anderson, Sr. also had a son named John[96] who *may* be the same as the John Anderson of the John Flack-Rutherford land conveyances of 1784 and the Robert Cherry-Sarah McQuiston marriage bond.[97]

The marriage of yet another daughter of Robert McQuiston, Jane or Jeane (1745–?), also suggests a connection between Guilford and John Flack of Rutherford. Jane McQuiston first married a James Finley (?–ca. 1775) in Cumberland County, PA, in 1763, and the Finleys removed with Robert McQuiston to Rowan/Guilford.[98] Like Cherry, in 1772 Finley purchased land in Tryon/Lincoln along the Catawba River,[99] but ca. 1775 James Finley died.[100] His widow then married Robert Gilkey (?–ca. 1813),[101] a neighbor of John Flack's on Catheys Creek, who in 1787 bought several tracts there from Col. William Porter.[102]

Robert Gilkey served with Robert Cherry on the commission which settled Flack's intestate.[103] He was a patriot and captain of a company about the time of the Battle of King's Mountain, though his son, John Gilkey (1789–1887), stated in an 1881 interview with William Twitty that his father was with Gen. Gates in South Carolina at the time of that battle. He also stated that Robert Gilkey was a native of Ireland who came to America at the age of twelve and lived first in Lancaster County, PA, then Guilford, and then the Beatty's Ford area (where he lived during the War) before moving to Catheys Creek.[104] Robert Gilkey may have been related to William Gilkey of Salisbury Township, Lancaster County, PA, and the Gilkeys of nearby West Caln and Sadsbury Townships, Chester County, PA, on the east side of Octoraro Creek and bordering Lancaster.[105]

There is also a Rutherford will which may suggest a connection between John Flack of Rutherford and Guilford County. This is the will of George Black, which was proven before Rutherford court in 1789, in which John "Fleck" is named co-executor.[106] A Rowan/Guilford connection is suggested by the observation that a George Black was one of the early Nottingham colonists who obtained a Granville grant along Hunting Creek in 1762, and very near the Reedy Fork lands of Thomas Flack.[107] Shortly after George Black of Rowan sold his 504 acre tract to Thomas Donnell in January, 1767,[108] a George Black entered a 300 acre claim on Cane Creek in what was then Mecklenburg and would later be Rutherford.[109] Griffin referred to Black as an "influential citizen;[110] he was a patriot and one of the original signers of the Tryon Association.[111]

Appendix VI. Origins of the Flacks

Like Thomas Flack and George Black, John Flack too was a patriot. In 1781, he was appointed a justice of the peace in Rutherford[112]—thus we can at least document that he served in a civil capacity for the "Rebel" government. This was not without peril, as Jonathan Hampton (see below), who also served as a j.p. in Tryon/Rutherford during the Revolution, was nearly hung by Ferguson's men, in part it was said for using his authority as j.p. to marry one Thomas Fleming.[113] Flack probably received this appointment for his Whig sympathies and perhaps because he was better educated than most of his contemporaries—suggested by his estate inventory (returned in 1792) which indicated that he owned five books: one large Bible, two small ones, Joseph Alleine's or Allein's *Alarm to the Unconverted*, and Robert Russel's *Seven Sermons*.[114] Surviving account books of the Revolution also indicate that John Flack supplied various provisions to the militia in pursuit of Ferguson, including beef, a horse and a mare.[115]

It is certainly possible that Flack was at King's Mountain, or served in some capacity with the militia, and that his appointment as a j.p. was made in part as a reward for this service. Following his 1881 interview with John Gilkey, William L. Twitty wrote to Lyman Draper that "in the fight at King's Mt. ... [was] John Flack on the wh[ig] side & Wm. Flack (his brother) on the loyalist."[116] However, there are no primary sources to indicate that John Flack bore arms during the Revolution.

But soldier or no, John Flack was certainly a man of considerable influence in early Rutherford—the justices presided over the County court and as such were quite powerful in local affairs. He was referred to by the title "squire" or "esquire" in at least some records,[117] certainly due in part to his station in local government, but also suggesting the status of landed gentry. At the time of his death in early 1792, he had significant land holdings (approximately 580 acres, with a claim on 300 more) on Catheys and Mountain Creeks,[118] owned five Negro slaves,[119] and even some silver plate[120] (a luxury item which was probably unusual for the western North Carolina frontier, ca. 1790).

The first Tryon deeds on which Flack's name appears also suggest that he rapidly gained favor with the prominent Whigs of old Tryon/Rutherford soon after his arrival. The 1778 deed for the Catheys Creek tract, for example, was witnessed by Col. Andrew Hampton (?–1805) and his son Jonathan Hampton (1751–1843). Col. Andrew Hampton was among the earliest settlers on the Catawba and distinguished himself as commander of the Rutherford men at King's Mountain.[121] As noted above, Jonathan Hampton served as a j.p. during the Revolution. He was notorious for holding "the King's authority in great contempt," and was tried for treason by Ferguson when the latter entered Rutherford.[122]

In late 1778, Flack himself witnessed a conveyance by Col. John Walker to one James Cook (proved in January, 1779, court).[123] The names here again suggest Flack was an intimate of Rutherford patriots. Col. Walker (1728–1796) served as a Captain in the First Regiment of the Continental Line and, according to Griffin, "worked untiringly" for the Whig cause,[124] and there is evidence that Cook made provisions to the militia.[125] Witnessing this deed along with Flack were William Robertson and Col. William Porter. Lyman Draper recorded that a William Robertson was wounded at King's Mountain, "shot completely through the body,"[126] and Col. William Porter (ca. 1755–1817?) was a very prominent figure in early Rutherford, serving in the leg-

Appendix VI. Origins of the Flacks

islature for many years and a veteran of the King's Mountain campaign, where he probably commanded a company.[127] His brother, Maj. James Porter (ca. 1760–1840),[128] was also reported by Draper to have been at King's Mountain — and wounded — though Miles Philbeck's more recent work has established that he was wounded at Ramsour's Mill the Summer previous to King's Mountain.[129] A putative cousin, Col. Robert Porter, is also believed to have fought in the Battle.[130]

A close relationship between John Flack and Col. William Porter *may* be implied by the latter's appointment as co-executor of the former's intestate in 1792 (though Porter's status in the community probably also contributed to his appointment).[131] But Ivarea Flack made an even bolder claim for a Porter-Flack connection. She states that the first wife of John Flack of Rutherford was Jane Porter (ca. 1750–?), a sister of the brothers, Col. William Porter and Maj. James Porter, noted above, and a daughter of James Porter (ca. 1724–?), a native of Ireland who settled in Lancaster County, PA.[132] Unfortunately, as with many of Ms. Flack's assertions, there is no direct evidence to support the Jane Porter-John Flack marriage. In fact, more circumspect researchers indicate that William and James Porter's sister Jane (d. 1852) married a William Young.[133]

John Flack's first wife thus remains unknown, though we can say that he was probably married before the purchase of the Catheys Creek tract, for his eldest son, Andrew, was born in 1775.[134] This further suggests that he was married *before* he arrived in Tryon/Rutherford. At any rate, John Flack's first wife probably died about 1780, and perhaps shortly thereafter he took as his second wife Mary _____ (Ivarea Flack had it that her surname was McMurry).[135]

But to return to the Porters, what can we say of their origins? Miles Philbeck's careful work has established that the Porters of Tryon/Rutherford noted above were the sons of two brothers who settled in what Robert Ramsey called the "Irish" and "Trading Camp" settlements of Old Rowan,[136] between the late 1750s and the mid- to late-1760s. Robert Porter of Tryon/Rutherford *may* have been the son of William Porter (d. ca. 1760) of Second Creek, and William and James Porter of Tryon/Rutherford *were* the sons James Porter (d. ca. 1791) of Fourth Creek.[137]

The family of a Robert Porter (d. ca. 1811) of Tryon/Rutherford (believed by Griffin to have been the aforementioned cousin of James and William Porter[138]) was associated with the Flacks. Twitty reported that a Robert Porter, referred to as "the cousin of Capt. [William] Porter[,] ... lived on Catheys Creek near Mr. John Gilkey's place,"[139] which would also mean that he lived near the Flack home place. John Flack's eldest son, Andrew Flack, married Polly Porter, daughter of a Robert Porter, in 1796.[140] George Flack, the next-to-oldest son of John Flack, was named co-executor in the will of the same Robert Porter, proven in Rutherford court in July, 1811.[141] However, we must caution here that it seems there were at least *two* Robert Porters in Rutherford.[142]

There is considerable evidence linking the Porters with Lancaster County, PA. Philbeck holds that a Thomas Porter (1739–1800), who was an elder of and is buried at Third Creek Presbyterian Church, *may* have been a brother or cousin of William and James Porter of Rowan. This Thomas Porter, a cooper of Lancaster County, PA, purchased a 420 acre tract on Rowan's Walnut Branch, not far from James Porter, in 1765, and likely witnessed the will of James Porter proven in Rowan court in 1791.

Appendix VI. Origins of the Flacks

A Lancaster connection is further suggested by James Porter of Rutherford's sale in 1800 of two tracts in Iredell "granted to James Porter deceased" to a William Porter of Lancaster County, PA.[143] Ramsey also linked the Porters of Drumore and Sadsbury townships in Lancaster County, PA, with those in Rowan, stating that they were associated with Porters in Cecil County, MD, as early as 1716.[144]

But the Porters were a numerous and complex family, made especially so by the frequent repetition of Christian names. For example, in the Oath of Allegiance lists for Lancaster, taken in 1777 (which include a John "Flick"), one may find Porters with the same first names as those in Rutherford—Robert, James and William.[145] Lancaster wills also include numerous Porters who may be candidates for those who went to Rowan and Tryon/Rutherford or their relatives, again with Christian name correlates: a Robert Porter of Drumore Township, who died in 1745, had sons named Robert and James;[146] a John Porter of Drumore (will probated 1765) had sons named Thomas and William;[147] a James Porter who gave his residence as Cecil County, MD, and died in 1785 had sons named William and James;[148] and another James Porter of Drumore (will probated 1786) had a son named William.[149]

As noted above, John Flack himself died without a will in Rutherford in 1792 (as letters of administration for the estate were issued in October court, 1792). Though the record states that the second wife, Mary, and the children of the first, or their legal guardian, William Flack, "amicably agreed" in the settlement, the estate was complicated by children from two marriages, the legal requirements of the widow's dower, suits over debts owed by and to the estate and other difficulties. The estate was not finally settled until 1797, following "the petition of Andrew Flack [John Flack's eldest son] now of full age."[150]

* * *

Additional *possible* evidence in support of a Lancaster County connection to the Flacks of North Carolina *may* be found in the person of James Flack (1746–1835), who apparently came to Guilford County about the time Thomas Flack died (ca. 1780). It was Horace Flack who first suggested a "probable" connection between the Rutherford and Guilford Flacks and this James Flack, a soldier of the Continental line and a native of "Killserl," Ireland (we will say more about this below), who came to the New World, ca. 1768, and "was living in Lancaster County, Pennsylvania, when he volunteered for a Private in August 1776...."[151] About this same time he married Jean Glenn (ca. 1755–?), daughter of Hugh Glenn (ca. 1730–1807), also residents of Lancaster.[152] After serving several tours of duty in the middle states between 1776–77, James Flack "removed to Guilford County, North Carolina, and served a tour of three months in 1780."[153]

The statement "*removed* to Guilford County"[154] does *not* mean that he came here merely as a journeyman soldier, for this James Flack is the same who in 1780 purchased land near Big Troublesome Creek in present-day Rockingham County (then Guilford).[155] He sold his Rockingham lands in 1803[156] and probably soon thereafter removed to Madison County, Kentucky, joining his father-in-law and other in-laws,[157] for he was enumerated there in the 1810 census.[158] He applied for his pension in March, 1834,[159] and died shortly thereafter.

Appendix VI. Origins of the Flacks

Withal, however, it must be noted that the decision of James Flack of Lancaster to settle in Guilford/Rockingham may well have been a coincidence, for documentary evidence suggesting a relationship between James Flack and either the Thomas Flack family of Rowan/Guilford or the Flacks of Tryon/Rutherford is lacking. Until such is forthcoming, any suggestion that James Flack of Lancaster/Guilford/Rockingham was the fourth of the Flack "brothers" to come to North Carolina (the "Jefferson" in the Crawford tradition) must be regarded with a healthy skepticism.

James Flack of Rockingham also must not be confused with Thomas Flack's eldest son, James Flack of Guilford (1761–1840),[160] who during the Revolution served in the Guilford militia with his father,[161] as well as three tours of duty between 1779–1781,[162] and also eventually moved to Kentucky. Land records clearly indicate that he obtained a State grant for lands along the Reedy Fork in 1783, which bordered the line of his mother, the "Widow" Flack.[163] James Flack of Guilford married Nancy Ross, the daughter of a neighbor, in 1798,[164] sold his Guilford lands in 1812,[165] and moved to Todd County, Kentucky, probably soon thereafter, where he applied for a military pension in 1832.[166]

* * *

Since the Flacks of Rutherford were associated with the Presbyterian Church at Little Brittain,[167] and Thomas Flack of Guilford was also a Presbyterian, we would first assume that these men were of Scots-Irish heritage — and thus that they came first from the Scottish lowlands (where the followers of John Knox originated). This is consistent with the family tradition fist recorded by Dudley W. Crawford, and yet apparently confounded by the observation (1978) of the Scottish Tartans Society coordinator of research, Capt. T. Stuart Davidson, "that this name is not indigenous to Scotland." Davidson reported that he could "only find five of the name Flack(s) in the Telephone Directories for the whole of Scotland."[168]

Consistent with Capt. Davidson, George F. Black (*The Surnames of Scotland*, 1962) also makes no mention of the surname Flack, but he does identify the variant "Fleck" in Scotland. He recorded a Patryk Flek in Inverness in 1559, a minister named Andro Flecke in Dundee in 1650, Flecks in Edinburgh (1605) and Roberoun (1657), a William Fleck in Humbie "accused of sorcery in 1659," a Robert Fleck of Dumfries (1679) and a John Fleck of Little Milton, parish of Urr (nd).[169]

It is also interesting to note Edward MacLysaght's contention in his *The Surnames of Ireland* that Flack "*is* a Scottish name fairly numerous in Ulster." He wrote that "[i]t was formerly Affleck, a contraction of Auchinleck."[170] But Black held that the name was English, "perhaps of local origin from Flegg in co. Norfolk."[171] Barber also associated the name with Flegg and Flagg,[172] however, Hanks and Hodges believed it was "unlikely" to be a variant of "Flagg."[173] The name may well have continental German, Dutch or even Scandinavian origins[174] — but the surname's origins remain something of a puzzle.[175]

What does seem clear is that, in the British Isles, Flacks are found in certain parts of England in some abundance. For example, in his research some years ago, Charles Z. Flack, Sr., discovered an article by Waldo Chamberlain Sprague (1960) which identified a line of Flacks near Saffron Walden in the County of Essex, England, located just north of London, ca. 1575.[176] The discovery of the English connection led him to muse in a letter to his niece, "I had rather be English than Irish,"[177] and so he adopted Cotton Flack of Saffron Walden, who migrated to Boston about 1633,[178] as his first American ancestor.

In fact, many Flacks are indeed still said to be found in Essex,[179] and LDS records do strongly support the concentration of Flacks there as well as in nearby London, Cambridge, Hertford and Suffolk.[180] Hanks and Hodges also reported the name was "found mostly in Cambridgeshire."[181] The name's occurrence in Saffron Walden may be antedated, however, by the appearance of a Robert del Flac of County Kent (1276) in the *Hundred Rolls*, identified by Bardsley,[182] as well as Reaney and Wilson.[183]

But if Flack is an English surname, how came those of North Carolina to be associated with the culture of Scots-Irish Presbyterians? A likely explanation for this apparent Scots Irish-English paradox is the fact of English, as well as lowland Scots, immigration to the province of Ulster. This is well-documented by James G. Leyburn who writes that the colonization of Ulster was stimulated in part by King James' desire to relieve overcrowding in London,[184] and in the beginnings of the Plantation, it was English, not Scottish, participation which was deemed most important.[185] Leyburn observed,

> Many Americans who consider their ancestors to have been Scotch-Irish are actually descendants of English settlers, especially from the counties between London and Wales and from the northern counties of England, who migrated to Ulster and there became members of communities where the Scottish influence was predominant. When the movement to America began after 1717, many of these English Ulstermen joined their Scottish friends and neighbors in their removal to the New World.[186]

Flacks from England thus could have easily joined in the migration of English and Scots to Ulster in the early 17th century. In the generations which intervened between their settlement of Ulster and later move to America (perhaps 100 to 150 years), they likely were absorbed into the Presbyterian culture of the Scots.

The English origins of the Flacks of the New World are further supported by Leyburn's research on the ethnic make-up of the counties of the province. Leyburn wrote that Lord Chichester's English colony "so prospered that much of Southern Antrim became English in character."[187] Other counties, such as Armagh and Derry were "prevailingly English," and significant English settlement also took place in Fermanagh and Cavan.[188]

Other research links the Flacks to some of these same counties of Northern Ireland. Horace E. Flack, for example, noted that a Flack from Pennsylvania, who served in the Revolution, was born in county Antrim in 1750.[189] Dr. Robert Crawford Robertson, Legrand A. Flack and Dr. Charles Foster Glenn, suggested an association between the Flacks of Rutherford and county Kerry. Ralph R. Flack held, however, that county Kerry must be "positively wrong," as the Flacks were Presbyterians from Northern Ireland and county Kerry was in the South. He believed that they rather meant county Derry.[190] Though we do find probates for wills of James (1724) and Thomas Flack

(1759) in County Cork,[191] as well as a James Flack who was an attorney in Dublin in the mid-18th century,[192] most of the Irish Flacks do seem to be concentrated in Ulster.

Matheson found this to be so as late as 1890, though he did not associate them with any particular county in Northern Ireland.[193] A lineage chart (which begins in 1777) for a Flack family in the Ulster county of Armagh can be found in the Public Record Office of Northern Ireland,[194] but Flack roots there may run much deeper, as Hanna identified a Fergus Flack as a tenant on lands of a John Hamilton in that county as early as 1617.[195] Another source has it that many of the Flacks who settled St. Lawrence County, NY, in the early 19th century came from counties Monaghan and Cavan.[196] A Robert Flack who eventually settled in Washington County, Pennsylvania, is also said to have come from county Monaghan,[197] and LDS records associate Flacks with Drumgoon and Bailieborough parishes in Cavan.[198] Other LDS records place Flacks in counties Down and Tyrone.[199] Gravestone records for Dromore First Presbyterian Graveyard in county Down also identify Flacks, including those with the Christian names Thomas and John, both born in the early 19th century.[200] All of these counties were part of the province of Ulster.

Perhaps the best clue as to where the Flacks of Guilford/Rutherford *may* have come from is contained in the pension application of James Flack — i.e., if we accept the unproven assumption that he and the other Flacks of Guilford/Rutherford were related. The application explicitly states, "I was born in Killserl Ireland in 1746."[201] James Flack seems to have been illiterate (he signed both his 1803 Rockingham conveyance and the pension application itself with a mark); thus, we must consider this place-name "Killserl" as a *phonetic approximation* to the name of the place where James Flack came from. In a 1967 letter to Ralph Flack, an Ulster-Scot Historical Society researcher suggested that "Killserl" was likely Killysorrell, a town or townland of county Down.[202] Again, a correlation with one of the same counties with which Flacks are associated in other research. But then all this is guesswork.

* * *

In my opinion, collateral family evidence presented above strongly indicates that the Flacks of Rutherford were related to Thomas Flack of Guilford and *probably* also to John Flack or Fleck of Drumore Township, Lancaster County, PA. The John Flack of Lancaster association with the Rutherford Flacks is intriguing and important, but it may be impossible to establish the nature of the familial relationship. Could William and John Flack of Tryon/ Rutherford have been his sons? Or were they possibly cousins who may have tarried briefly in Lancaster before migrating down the "Great Wagon Road" to the Carolinas?

I lean toward the latter "cousin theory" because it is consistent with the Crawford tradition of 1) a cousin in Pennsylvania (i.e., John Flack of Lancaster) and 2) more or less direct movement of John and William Flack of Tryon/Rutherford from Ulster to Carolina in the 1760s — though this was evidently uncommon.[203] Lands were filling and prices were high in Pennsylvania in the mid-18th century — a principal cause of southward migration to the cheaper, more plentiful lands of Carolina.[204]

With respect to their Old World origins, I think we *can* safely assume that the

Flacks of Rutherford had roots in an Ulster county. However, the concentration of the surname in England strongly suggests that the Ulster Flacks (even if Lowland Scots) had English antecedents.

Of course, much of the foregoing research on the origins of the Flacks of Rutherford/Guilford has been both tentative and inconclusive, but hopefully the above will at least suggest some avenues for further inquiry. Clearly, the rebel Populist, Mills H. Flack, had a "revolutionary pedigree." But a definitive answer to the question of Flack origins has proven disappointingly elusive.

Perhaps the only thing I can say conclusively is that the answer will not be found in North Carolina records, though even here other possible associations between the Rutherford Flacks and the families of Thomas Flack of Guilford, James Flack of Rockingham, and possibly even Samuel Flake of Anson, deserve further scrutiny. Needless to say, Lancaster County records (and possibly those of Washington County, PA, as well) need much more careful investigation — herein I have largely relied upon transcriptions and abstracts rather than consulting original records.

Careful genealogical research, based upon primary source evidence, is always an unfinished task.

APPENDIX VII

Plato Durham, John Baxter Eaves and the Ku Klux Conspiracy in Rutherford

RUTHERFORD'S BRIEF KU KLUX ERA (1869–71) is perhaps now regarded as the most colorful episode in the County's history. For those who are acquainted with this period, it conjures images of the infamous illicit distiller, Amos Owens, of gatherings on Cherry Mountain to imbibe his "cherry bounce" whiskey, and of a "family feud" or "neighborhood squabble" of plain and largely ignorant men which got out of hand, was exaggerated by Rutherford's Radical Republican leadership for political purposes, and landed a "noble" and "innocent" Virginia gentleman with a gift for the hyperbolic rhetoric of the "unreconstructed," Randolph Abbott Shotwell, in Albany Penitentiary. It is a view which was endorsed by Shotwell himself,[1] J.G. de Roulhac Hamilton,[2] and more recently by Daniel Wayne Jolley.[3]

But this explanation of the Rutherford Klan ignores clear evidence of its racial and political purposes: dozens of well-documented whippings of whites and Negroes in the County who had nothing to do with the Cherry Mountain feud; consistent Klan warnings to victims of raids (both white and black) to cease voting the Radical ticket; and strong circumstantial evidence that Rutherford Klansmen received assistance from "ruling" class Klan politician-lawyers in neighboring Cleveland County.

Of contemporary historians, perhaps only Paul D. Escott, in his *Many Excellent People*, has unequivocally held that "prominent men — gentry and middle-class figures who were accustomed to holding office and wielding power — led the Klan"[4] in Rutherford. Even Allen Trelease (whose account of the Rutherford Klan is by far the most careful and thorough) endorsed the neighborhood feud thesis with his view of its activity in Rutherford as "a haphazard growth of independent dens which acted as they pleased ... greatly alarm[ing] the leadership in Cleveland County...."[5] But was the Klan indeed largely fragmented and leaderless, or might this assertion have been part of an elaborate deception to provide their leadership with deniability? Could a *too* literal interpretation of what alleged Klan leaders said lead us to ignore the "[underground] path to survival and success"[6] of the very secretive Invisible Empire?

In the following, I attempt to bring together a critique of the "family/neighborhood feud interpretation" with portraits of two now largely forgotten Reconstruction political leaders (and first cousins): Plato Durham of Cleveland County and John Baxter Eaves of Rutherford. Capt. Durham, a brave veteran of the Army of Northern Virginia, was certainly the dominant political figure in the Conservative-ruled "State of Cleveland" during Reconstruction. Bright and a leader of men, he was also an "unregenerate Rebel" who joined and supported the secretive Invisible Empire or Ku Klux Klan in its use of intimidation and violence to dismantle Radical Republicanism. Eaves, on the other hand, was a quiet and cautious leader of Republican Rutherford who used the prestige of his position and war record (he was also a CSA Captain) to help *fight* the Klan.

For the South, the Civil War and its legacy created bonds of shared experience and loyalty between neighbors and friends, fathers and sons, brothers and cousins—many of whom lived and fought and died together in the same regiments—which could not be sundered by defeat. These bonds lent themselves to the emergence of a leadership class of ex–Confederate officers who would become the political demigods of a defeated, resentful "nation" which sought relief from Yankee oppression, "black Republicanism" and the abominable threat of Negro social equality. In Cleveland County, former Confederate officers such as Capt. Durham and Col. Leroy M. McAfee would exploit their "enormous prestige"[7] to organize and direct the Klan; but in Rutherford, Republican Capt. John B. Eaves would use a similar prestige as a counterweight to assist in its destruction.

Eaves' dual career as ex–Confederate officer and Republican politician would also serve another purpose: as a bridge between Rutherford's Whig-Unionist past and the neo–Confederate patriotism celebrated by the "Lost Cause." Capt. Eaves was not at the center of Radical Republicanism in Rutherford—far from it—but was a man who steered away from conflict with the Klan and avoided the strong rhetoric of Rutherford Radicals such as State Legislator, James M. Justice. He rather filled the vacuum of Confederate hero in the "local hagiography," and at the same time he forged a "middle-ground" political career that would take him to State-wide prominence and only end in 1894—long after Rutherford's Radicals like George W. Logan and James M. Justice had bitten the proverbial political dust—when his "straight-out" Republicanism was rejected by the office-hungry Fusionists of his own party. Simply put, it was not the Radical Republicans who emerged from the political chaos of Reconstruction as the "political winners" in Rutherford, but rather Capt. Eaves.

Following the Ku Klux conspiracy, Plato Durham's political career was never the same. After being the leader of the State's Conservative minority in 1868, he was

Appendix VII. Durham, Eaves and the KKK Conspiracy

essentially marginalized by his party and his ambition to represent the 7th District in Congress was never realized — disintegrating in a futile attempt to defeat the Democratic "ring" candidate in an independent candidacy in 1874. He might yet have fulfilled his promise as a leader of North Carolina's "Restoration." But this promise was never realized. Tragically, Capt. Durham was cut down in his prime in 1875.

* * *

John Baxter Eaves was born in Spartanburg County, SC, on June 3rd, 1838.[8] His father, Spencer Eaves (1800–1882), son of Andrew Eaves (1776–1861) of the Floyd's Creek community, was a native of Rutherford and a well-to-do farmer and merchant.[9] Eaves' mother, Jane Baxter Eaves (1813–1873),[10] was the daughter of the venerable William Baxter, Sr. (1759–1852) of Rutherford's High Shoals section.[11] Some time after 1840, Spencer Eaves returned to Rutherford County,[12] eventually building or occupying a substantial house near the legendary old Red Tavern, not far from Burnt Chimney.[13] Henceforth, John Baxter Eaves would call Rutherford home.

Surviving records and family tradition indicate that Eaves' father, Spencer Eaves, was especially close to his Baxter in-laws,[14] who were Whigs in their politics,[15] two of whom would later be prominent opponents of the Civil War. John Baxter (1819–1886), William Baxter's eldest son by his second marriage, served both Rutherford and Henderson Counties in the State House in the 1840s and 50s (where he was elected speaker in 1852), then moved to Knoxville where he became one of East Tennessee's most eminent attorneys. He was a strong Unionist during the War, and President Hayes later rewarded him with an appointment (1877) to the federal bench in the U.S. 6th Circuit Court of Appeals.[16] John's younger brother, Elisha (1827–1899), moved to Arkansas in 1852 where he read law, raised a Union cavalry regiment, and served a year (1873–74) of travail as Reconstruction governor of that state. A dispute over his election to that office led to what is familiarly known in Arkansas history as the Brooks-Baxter War.[17]

Active between 1835 and the Civil War, the "loosely knit" Whigs of Western North Carolina rallied around the issue of internal improvements (better roads, transportation) as a means of

Captain John B. Eaves (ca. 1880), Republican leader in Rutherford from the 1870s–1890s. (North Carolina Office of Archives and History, Raleigh)

facilitating the economic development of an otherwise "backward, isolated" section of the State. Whig support in North Carolina was strongest among small farmers in the West and mercantile interests who tended to align themselves against the "aristocratic" slaveholders down East.[18] Rutherford remained a Whig stronghold until the Civil War,[19] long after the party's strength began to ebb elsewhere in the State. This in turn contributed to strong Unionist support in Rutherford during the War years and would serve as the foundation for the county's emergence as a Republican stronghold during Reconstruction.

The predominance of the Whigs in Rutherford, as well as Spencer Eaves' close relationship with the Baxters and vocation as a merchant,[20] combine to support the likelihood he was an "old-line" Whig in politics. Many Whigs were slaveowners (as were the Baxters and Eaves[21]) who adroitly managed to cultivate the seeming contradiction of Unionism. Though many western North Carolina Whigs (such as Zeb Vance) turned to the Democratic Party after the War, the strength of post–War mountain Republicanism was owed in large measure to the Whig tradition. Like his son, Spencer Eaves would become a Republican following the War.[22]

But Capt. Eaves also had his share of "secesh" relatives on the Baxter side — men who would rank among the most committed Conservatives in the State. One of Jane Eaves' sisters, Ester McDowell Baxter (1817–1868), married Micajah Durham (1804–1864), a farmer who operated an iron works near High Shoals.[23] Their most distinguished offspring was Capt. Plato Durham, Cleveland County's "leonine" hero of Reconstruction and the Invisible Empire, born on September 20th, 1840, and raised on his father's High Shoals farm.[24]

Clarence Griffin wrote that the elder Durham took a great interest in his community, building churches and school houses, was curious about science and culture, and assembled a considerable library — though he lacked formal education.[25] But Micajah Durham was also "a confirmed advocate of States' Rights," and he represented Rutherford at the Secession Convention in 1861–62.[26] George G. Eaves (1850–1940), a younger brother of John Baxter Eaves, recalled hearing "Cage" Durham give a speech on the eve of war at the old muster ground at Burnt Chimney in which he said that "the Yankees would not fight and that he could wipe up all the blood that would be spilled with his pocket handker-

Captain Plato Durham (ca. 1870) of Cleveland County, Klansman and outspoken leader of North Carolina Conservatives during Reconstruction. (North Carolina Office of Archives and History, Raleigh)

chief."[27] But by the Summer of 1862, when it had become apparent that the War would indeed be bloody and protracted, Durham (though an old man for military service) enlisted with his son Zachariah in Co. E of the 18th NC. He was himself killed at the Battle of the Wilderness on May 5th, 1864,[28] and two of his sons would also sacrifice their lives to the cause.[29] With a father like Cage Durham, it is little wonder that his son Plato would be "unreconstructed."

Plato Durham began the study of law under L.F. Churchill in Rutherfordton about 1858, and when war came in 1861, he was reading with his lawyer-uncle, John Baxter, in Knoxville.[30] He first enlisted there, but learning that three of his brothers had joined the "Cleveland Guards," he made his way home and, in June, 1861, enlisted as a private with Co. E of the 12th NC.[31] Brave in battle, then Lieut. Durham and his command were noted in a letter from Gen. R.E. Lee to President Davis following an engagement with a Federal picket on the Rapidan in October, 1863.[32] He would rise through the ranks to captain before surrendering with his company nearly four years later,[33] and veterans of the unit claimed they "fired the last muskets at Appomattox." Durham signed their paroles as commanding officer of the regiment.[34] As Allen Trelease put it, "Durham emerged from the war with an enviable record for gallantry and with a wholehearted dedication to the 'Lost Cause.'"[35] One might also add that Durham's war experience left him with a fearless contempt for the Yankee victor. It is said that when he returned from the War to his mother's High Shoals farm in the Summer of 1865, a Union soldier tried to steal his "fine saddle horse," but that he "unsheathed his sword, ... looked the Yankee in the eye [and] ... stated: 'The damn Yankee that touches this horse is a dead man.'"[36]

He soon again returned to the study of law, reading under Richmond Pearson at his private school at Richmond Hill in Asheville during the Fall of 1865, and completing his studies at the University of North Carolina during 1866-67.[37] He began his law practice in Shelby in 1866. A later biographer wrote, "Those who remember his power at the bar tell of his keen intellect which guided his clear and independent thinking."[38] A member of the joint select committee of Congress before which Durham would later give his Ku Klux testimony referred to him as "'the most intelligent witness, Mr. Durham.'"[39]

In 1866, Durham gained Cleveland's seat in the State House in the first election following the War. Courtship, marriage and family were also on his mind, but even here the War and its legacy dictated. Capt. Durham married Catherine Lenora Tracy (1845–1933), daughter of a King's Mountain physician, on April 9th, 1868 — exactly three years after Lee's surrender to Grant at Appomattox. Later, he would name two of his children after the great heroes of the Southern cause, military commanders Robert E. Lee and Stonewall Jackson.[40]

Durham's law partner, Maj. Herbert D. Lee (1830–1890), was a cousin of the former's grandmother, Catherine Lee Baxter (1792–1839).[41] Like Durham, Lee was also a native of Rutherford who had studied law under John Baxter.[42] When war came, Lee organized Rutherford's first company (Co. D, 16th NC)[43] and was permanently crippled by a hip wound received at the Battle of Fredericksburg in 1862.[44] He would later help establish (1874) the first bank in Shelby — known for many years (1879–1895) as H.D. Lee & Company, Bankers.[45] There he lived in the imposing "Banker's House," on North Lafayette St.— a classic Victorian manse in the Second

Empire style which still stands.[46] George G. Eaves recalled (1928) that H.D. Lee "was familiar at [the Spencer Eaves] home."[47]

Unlike his cousins, John Baxter Eaves seems to have shown no interest in the law, though he did attend the Rutherfordton Academy under Frank I. Wilson.[48] In the late 1850s, his father placed him in the mercantile business in Rutherfordton with William Miller,[49] thus forming the firm of Miller & Eaves.[50] In Rutherfordton, he resided at the Village Hotel with his brother Andrew, a druggist, and his lawyer-cousin, H.D. Lee. The 1860 census, taken in July of that year, shows that the twenty-two year old Eaves had property valued at $7000,[51] suggesting he had prospered well, though George Eaves recalled that once "John complained and seemed hurt because some of the family had done some trading in other stores in town."[52]

By the following spring the nation would be on the brink of war. His brother George wrote that Eaves "was opposed to secession but when the state seceded, he went in for the war and raised a company ... and mustered and organized them at Burnt Chimney."[53] The unit, Co. I of the 50th NC, was also known as the "Rutherford Regulars" or "Rutherford Regulators," and was raised and enlisted during March of 1862. Eaves was commissioned as captain and commanding officer that same month.[54] He and his men served in Virginia, eastern North Carolina, Georgia and South Carolina, and, in March, 1865, participated in both the battles of Averasboro and Bentonville.[55] Capt. Eaves was wounded at Averasboro (fought on March 16th)[56] and hospitalized in Greensboro with an "unspecified complaint" a few days later.[57]

Following the War, Eaves returned to Rutherford and rapidly ensconced himself in the County's Republican leadership. In August, 1865, he was named clerk of the county court, probably by Ceburn Harris, who, along with Nathan Scoggins, was appointed by Governor Holden to reorganize county government in the immediate aftermath of conflict. Eaves was "the last man to hold this position," as the old court of pleas and quarter sessions was eliminated by the constitution of 1868.[58]

A few months later, on Feb. 19th, 1866, Eaves married Johnnie Amelia Logan (1842–ca.1935),[59] the daughter of George W. Logan (1815–1889) of Chimney Rock. Logan had practiced as an attorney in Rutherfordton and held several minor county offices during the ante-bellum period. An opponent of secession, he gained prominence as a leader of the peace movement in Rutherford during the War and was elected to the Confederate Congress in 1863. In the dark days immediately after the War, the weight and responsibility for the County's Republican leadership largely fell upon its elder statesman, Logan. In 1868, following the passage of North Carolina's Radical Republican Constitution, George W. Logan was elected Superior Court Judge in the 9th Judicial District.[60]

Republicans swept all the offices in Rutherford in 1868, with Capt. Eaves elected to the Senate and James M. Justice (1835–1877)[61] taking the County's seat in the House. Justice's Conservative contemporaries, such as Shotwell and Durham, derisively portrayed him as a "$20 dollar lawyer,"[62] but his lengthy Congressional Ku Klux testimony suggests the former mechanic was rather articulate. He clearly competed with the Republican newspaper, *The Rutherford Star*, edited by J.B. Carpenter (1838–1926)[63] and Judge Logan's son, Robert W. Logan (1845–1923),[64] as Rutherford County's most outspoken voice for the Radical Republican causes of political equality for the Negro and denunciation of Conservatives and the Klan.

In stark contrast, Eaves was notably taciturn about his political views—though he was elected as a Republican to the State Senate, I find no substantive statements of his politics in surviving files of *The Star*. Eaves almost seems to have been *consciously* reluctant to speak out — though he and Justice did stump together at Republican rallies. For example, his address at an August, 1868, meeting in the Conservative stronghold of Shelby was described as "short but telling" and as "a few very appropriate and patriotic remarks," while Justice gave a Radical harangue of an hour and a half, causing Harvey Cabiness, Shelby lawyer, "Rebel Nullifier" and future Klansman to interrupt and draw a knife in anger — though peace was soon restored.[65]

Yet Eaves' majority in the April, 1868, Senate race was huge ("something over 900 votes"), much larger than the nonetheless impressive 590 vote Republican majority in Rutherford that Fall[66] and Justice's 259 vote majority in the 1870 elections.[67] In his later Congressional testimony, Justice explained the size of Eaves' victory thus: "I think he got a few conservative votes. He was a confederate captain, and his men pretty much all voted for him regardless of party."[68] Summing up Eaves' political career, Clarence Griffin also held that his popularity was largely owed to his captaincy in the 50th NC. "He was one of the most popular Confederate officers from Rutherford County," Griffin wrote, "and was beloved by every man of his command. After the war, in the viccisitude (sic) of reconstruction and turmoil of political oppression, these old comrades in arms turned to him frequently for assistance, which was freely given. And in political campaigns following the war, these same men, Democrat and Republican, honored him with their ballot."[69]

Though not on the ballot, Capt. Eaves was active during the Fall campaign of 1868, making speeches at Republican gatherings throughout the County.[70] A member of the Union League, he and his wife Johnnie boldly assisted Negro education by selling a small parcel of land in Rutherfordton to the Negro trustees of the Freedman's School, Louis McDowell and Nelson Bryan, in late December, 1868.[71] About 1869, Eaves accepted a Federal appointment as Assistant Assessor of Internal Revenue.[72] He also fulfilled his Senate duties, attending two sessions during 1868–69.[73] But he suddenly resigned from the Senate on November 30th, 1869, thus necessitating a special election.[74]

The Star failed to record a reason for Eaves' departure. He may have resigned for personal reasons or in order to better meet the obligations of his Federal appointment as tax assessor (he did take five leaves of absence during his two sessions in the Senate[75]). But Eaves was also part of the "Harris-Logan" group of western (chiefly Rutherford) Republicans who were angered in the Summer of 1869 by Governor William W. Holden's challenge to the constitutional authority of the State's Superintendent of Public Works, Rutherford's Ceburn L. Harris, to appoint the directors of State-owned railroads.[76] Many western Republicans coveted control of the railroads as essential to the internal improvement of the section — thus harking back to their old Whig roots—though, in its editorial column, *The Star* emphasized "consolidation" (or linking) of eastern and western rails over sectionalism.[77] But private stockholders (predominantly Democratic) favored Holden, he ultimately prevailed,[78] and Harris was "read out of the party."[79] By late 1869, *The Star* had completely broken with Holden[80]—who would soon be impeached. The coincidence of the Harris-Holden controversy with Eaves' resignation invites speculation that the two events

Appendix VII. Durham, Eaves and the KKK Conspiracy

were connected. Could the resignation have been a show of loyalty to local Republicans? Whatever the reason, the effect of the resignation was to cost Rutherford Republicans their Senate seat.[81]

* * *

In late 1868 and early 1869, stung by the passage of the state's "Negro equality constitution" and the loss of the Legislature, many Conservatives in the State turned to the Ku Klux Klan—a secret organization of white men which often used violent raids to intimidate its political opponents—as a vehicle to restore white supremacy and the control of the Democratic Party. As "Restoration" historian J.G. de Roulhac Hamilton put it, "the Ku Klux lifted the South from its slough of despond[ence] by the application of illegal force which overthrew Reconstruction and ultimately restored political power to the white race."[82] The actual role of the Ku Klux in the demise of Radical Reconstruction is debatable,[83] but it does seem clear that the Klan (in the guise of the "Invisible Empire") was organizing in Rutherford's neighbor, Cleveland County, probably by late 1868.

Cleveland was ripe for development of the Klan. In stark contrast to Rutherford, Cleveland was a Conservative/Democratic stronghold—sometimes even referred to in the columns of the *Rutherford Star* as the "State of Cleveland."[84] Robert W. Logan described it as "one of the strongest secession counties in the State."[85] The undisputed leader of the Conservatives there was the young and fiery Capt. Durham, who emerged as the Radical Republican regime's most outspoken critic during the Constitutional Convention of January and February, 1868. When the overwhelmingly Republican delegation passed a blasphemous "Negro equality" constitution, "Durham moved that the Capital bell be tolled while the signatures of the delegates were being affixed."[86]

Conservatives there were particularly sensitive to fears of the Negro. In 1868, Rutherford's Rep. Justice, in a speech before Negroes in Cleveland, managed to incite a riot, leaving the county, in Durham's words, "in a state of perfect terror." This episode triggered concern for armed attacks by "Loyal League" Negro militias, which were presumably organized and drilling in several places in Cleveland. Durham also stated that the "common white people" were enraged against the county's Negro population because they believed *political* equality would lead to *social* equality—"there are already instances in the county of Cleveland in which poor white girls are having negro children." Fears were furthered by reports of rapes and barn burnings by Negroes.[87] Jolley found that an alleged Negro rapist was lynched in Shelby's "Court Square."[88]

There was also a palpable sense among the County's Conservative leaders that the Radical Republican government was corrupt. Durham ran for U.S. Congress in his district that Fall and was apparently elected by eighteen votes in a close race with the Republican nominee, A.H. Jones.[89] But the election was awarded to Jones three months later—by a majority of one vote.[90] Hamilton claims that Durham was the victim of a conspiracy sown at the highest councils of Gov. Holden's Radical government to fraudulently alter the returns.[91] Many Clevelanders would come to feel that Judge Logan and the Radicals of Rutherford were no less corrupt than Holden and his minions. In 1870, Durham again ran for the 7th District Congressional seat but was forced to withdraw because he could not take the "test oath."[92]

Durham and other Conservatives in Cleveland were therefore embittered and angry, had likely lost trust in the "ordinary ... devices" of politics,[93] and were thus especially vulnerable to the Klan's appeal as a secret vigilante organization which might remedy the wrongs of what they considered an unjust Reconstruction. The development of Cleveland's Invisible Empire seems to have followed the Tennessee model — described by Trelease as a sort of para-military terrorist organization where ex–Confederate officers commandeered the Klan for their own purposes.[94] When Durham made a reluctant confession to his Ku Klux involvement during his Congressional testimony, he described it as "an organization for mutual protection and defense" against Negro militia or a Cleveland version of the Kirk-Holden War.[95]

Dr. Franklin has also emphasized the role of "former confederates" in what he called the "Counter Reconstruction."[96] In Cleveland, virtually all Klan leaders were ex–Confederate officers. As noted above, Durham had been the Captain of Co. E, 12th NC Regiment;[97] another presumed member (who later fled the State), Cleveland Sheriff B.F. Logan, served as 1st Lieutenant under Durham;[98] Maj. H.D. Lee had organized Co. D of the 16th NC before being promoted to the Field & Staff command of that unit;[99] Col. Leroy M. McAfee commanded the distinguished 49th NC;[100] Harvey D. Cabiness, a Shelby lawyer (and, ironically, a brother-in-law of Judge Logan), served in Co. D of the 15th NC as a 1st Lieutenant, as well as in the 49th NC, Co. B[101]— he would later be active in recruiting Klansmen in Rutherford.

Presumably the Klan's first contact in Cleveland was a message relayed to Col. McAfee — with the assistance of none other than the "many-talented" Thomas Dixon, McAfee's nephew and then only a small boy — but this story is perhaps apocryphal.[102] In his Congressional testimony, Durham offered that McAfee was the "chief" of the County. Others named Durham himself, but, though he did admit joining the organization in late 1868 or early 1869, he denied he was chief. Regardless, as events unfolded in Rutherford in 1871, it seems clear that it was Durham, not McAfee, who played the lead role. Total Klan membership in Cleveland may have been as high as 600–1000; James Justice said, "I think nine-tenths of the democrats in that county [Cleveland] are Ku-Klux."[103]

These figures may well be exaggerated, but it is clear that Cleveland's Invisible Empire was active in raiding, whipping and abusing Negroes, Radicals and "loose" women in that county between 1869 and 1871. Victims were often accused of very minor offenses: a Negro who had allegedly committed a petty theft or insulted a white person, a woman with a bad reputation, or perhaps a white man who had publicly supported the Radical party. As the targets of these raids imply, the Klan's purposes were typically racial, political and "moral"; the Invisible Empire was an arbiter of justice, yes, but a justice of the "old order."

In August, 1871, Durham "conservatively" estimated that the Klan had made twenty-five raids in Cleveland (or, in the parlance of the time, committed "outrages"),[104] but there were likely many more. The indictment of Klansmen in Cleveland Superior Court in the Fall of 1869 suggests that raiding was well underway by that time,[105] though Justice held that outrages there began even earlier, soon after the presidential election of 1868.[106] In August, 1870, an outbreak of Ku Klux whip-

Appendix VII. Durham, Eaves and the KKK Conspiracy

pings and beatings was reported in the "Blanton old precinct,"[107] and the following December the home of Col. John W. Logan in the Sandy Run section was raided.[108] The week after the Logan raid, *The Star* reported "that the Ku Klux outlaws [in Cleveland] are still riding every night, and committing numerous outrages whereever (sic) they go,"[109] and this continued throughout the winter with raiding parties numbering as many as 200–300 roaming the county.[110] Sometimes the Klan got the worst of it, as during a raid upon a Cleveland Negro named Ned McBrayer in December, 1869, when a Klansman named Bush Putnam was mortally wounded with an axe.[111] Both Justice and Eaves were afraid to go to Cleveland on business, and Eaves testified in July, 1871, that "citizens there are ... completely under the control of men who ride in the night."[112]

A consumptive Col. Leroy Mangum McAfee (ca. 1870), legislator and Klan leader in Cleveland. (North Carolina Office of Archives and History, Raleigh)

It was apparently the Winter of 1869–70 that the Ku Klux finally came to Rutherford. The first proof of Klan activity in the County was the discovery of a written Ku Klux pledge at Rock Springs Campground in October, 1869,[113] but there were no Klan raids reported until one made upon an old Negro man named Nelson Birge, probably in early February.[114] Far more important for the course of events in Rutherford was the next, known as the McGaughey (spelled also as MaGaha and McGahey) raid.

On the night of February 22nd, 1870, with a light dusting of snow upon the frozen ground, a group of Klansman from the Cherry Mountain section of Rutherford, led by one Decatur DePriest, the chief of the County's first Klan "den,"[115] raided Ibbey Jenkins, Almon Owens,[116] and the home of James McGaughey, a farmer who resided in the same area. McGaughey was not at home at the time of the raid, but his wife was greatly frightened and "shoved about" by men who broke down their door, forced their way in, and threatened to kill her husband and son. Two days later McGaughey, in company with a group of friends and neighbors which included one Aaron V. Biggerstaff (1811– ?), killed Decatur DePriest. Testimony in a subsequent trial indicated that Aaron Biggerstaff fired shots into the home of Klansman Samuel Biggerstaff, his half-brother, with whom there had for some time been ill-feeling,[117] though the latter Biggerstaff was unharmed.[118]

Aaron V. Biggerstaff, described by *The Western Vindicator* as a "grissly haired old rustic ... born to fight and snarl and bicker all the way from the cradle to the grave,"[119] became the fulcrum upon which the story of the Klan in Rutherford turned.

A strong Unionist and "a very decided Republican," he was said to have assisted the escape of fugitive Yankee prisoners who passed through Rutherford County during the War. When a Federal contingent invaded the County during Stoneman's raid in April, 1865, he received papers from General Palmer which protected his stock from plunder—but not that of his Conservative neighbors. One Klansman testified that Biggerstaff was actively trying to suppress the Klan, and Congressman Blair would later characterize McGaughey, Biggerstaff and company as a "band of Republicans."[120]

At Superior Court in Rutherfordton in the Spring of 1870, Republican Judge George W. Logan presiding, six Klansmen were indicted (though the case apparently never came to trial[121]) for the raid of Feb. 22nd: William DePriest, William Baber, Amos Owens, Olin O. Carson, R.A. McEntire and Julius Fortune.[122] James McGaughey (who was also indicted for the murder of DePriest) was apparently "lying out," and eventually fled to Tennessee, though, in June, *The Star* reported that he fired shots at men who attempted to arrest him at his home.[123] Aaron V. Biggerstaff, Webb Toney, William Holland and A. Ramsey were indicted for felonious trespass in the assault upon the home of Samuel Biggerstaff,[124] but when tried in Fall 1870 court Judge Logan gave them only light fines—in Biggerstaff's case, a mere $20.[125] Their defense attorney had been none other than Rutherford's Radical legislator, James M. Justice.[126]

The Conservative bar was furious with the judgment in the Biggerstaff case, and considered it politically motivated. H.W. Guion, a Mecklenburg County attorney who would later testify before Congress during its Ku Klux investigation, described Biggerstaff as "a particular political friend of Judge Logan, [who] had taken his part very warmly, and given him the aid of his judicial powers." Capt. Durham argued that corruption led Judge Logan to essentially "[discharge] Aaron Biggerstaff for an assault with a deadly weapon with a deliberate purpose to kill ... a penitentiary offense," and, as a consequence of the Biggerstaff case, "the most intelligent portion of the community ... have come to the belief that justice cannot be had in the courts in the western part of North Carolina." It seems it was immediately following the Biggerstaff trial (in the Fall of 1870) that Klan activity again began to heat up in Rutherford. The Klan was also angered by rumors that Biggerstaff had assisted DePriest's killer, McGaughey, in escaping.[127]

Of these first Rutherford Klansmen who formed a den on Cherry Mountain, by far the most famous (or infamous) today is Amos W. Owens (1820?– 1906?).[128] Melvin L. "Corn Cracker" White of Shelby, Owens' admirer and turn-of-the-century biographer, described him as the "leading spirit" of the Klan in Rutherford.[129] During the War, he had served under Maj. H.D. Lee in Co. D of the 16th NC, then in Co. I of the 56th NC,[130] but his fame was owed to his "cherry bounce" whiskey, a wicked mixture of fermented cherries made at his "castle" atop Cherry Mountain.

This "lovely concoction" probably explains the Klan's "neighborhood feud" on Cherry Mountain, insofar as it was such, for Owens and other Cherry Mountain men may well have formed their den at least in part to gain protection for illegal distilling. One Rutherford den was reputed to have its own still, and, as Klansman James L. Grant testified, the Ku Klux "would put down the revenue, so that they could just run their stills publicly, and would not be interrupted." But this "feud" nonetheless cleaved along *political* lines—the "revenuers" were Federal officials and mostly Republicans. The fear that their Unionist/Radical neighbors would disclose the locations of their stills to revenue officers—at the same time likely gaining protection for their own stills, as Biggerstaff had done for his stock during the War—may well have led to the McGaughey raid.[131] Moreover, Biggerstaff's subsequent involvement with McGaughey and the "Republican raids" upon Samuel Biggerstaff and Decatur Depriest probably had more to do with the focus of Klan wrath upon him than illegal distilling.

Klan activity in Rutherford was neither limited to the MaGaughey-Biggerstaff difficulty nor the Cherry Mountain community. There were many raids which had nothing to do with a feud over illicit distilling (as elsewhere, typically Negroes, Radicals and "unchaste" women were victims, see Table I). Eaves' estimate of about thirty to forty Klan raids in Rutherford up to the time of the first Biggerstaff raid in April, 1871, is probably fairly accurate, but Carpenter claimed there may have been as many as 100–200 when he testified that June. Though the Cherry Mountain section near the Cleveland line was very active, many of the Klan outrages in the County allegedly occurred in the southern section bordering South Carolina; furthermore, Klansmen who participated in these raids were often members of dens in Cleveland and South Carolina, not Rutherford. But eventually, seven or eight dens would be formed in Rutherford, with a total membership of about 300.[132]

Eaves, Carpenter and Justice all emphasized that the Klan raids were motivated by a political purpose: to discourage Radicals from voting. Even Biggerstaff said he was made to promise to never again vote the Republican ticket. This was of course denied by Durham in his later testimony. But at Rutherford Court in the last week of March, 1871, Maj. Lee was alleged to have warned "that Rutherford ... would certainly suffer more than any other county in the State, on account of its republican majority being so large." With Capt. Eaves, the Major was rather more circumspect. During a family visit that March at Eaves' home in Rutherfordton (probably during court week), Lee told Eaves to steer clear of the Klan and advised him to take a stance neither for it nor against it. Maj. Lee told him that was his own position, and, in answer to Eaves' remonstrance to take a bold stand against the Klan, he insisted he could do nothing.[133]

But beyond mere politics, Cleveland's Klan leadership *may* have also feared that the continuing investigation into the McGaughey raid of February, 1870—eventually moved to McDowell County—could reveal their identities. This seems to have been the meaning of an exchange between J.B. Harrill and Capt. Durham which the former alleged occurred on the Shelby road one day about the time of Spring court. Harrill testified that Durham told him: "Beatty Carpenter, George Logan, and them fellows, must be killed if they did not stop taking up [i.e., arresting] men and doing the way they were doing."[134]

Most of the Shelby bar was in fact in Rutherfordton that week, but their schedule of cases was light.[135] The leadership of Cleveland's Invisible Empire (Durham, McAfee, Lee and Cabiness) thus seized the moment to actively initiate Klansmen and organize the movement in Rutherford;[136] when *The Star* made notice of "hundreds" of Klan initiations, it also mentioned that "the officiating officers who conducted the initiation[s] were *leaders* of the *Democratic Party* of this county and of the county of Cleveland."[137] Their most significant recruit was Lt. Randolph A. Shotwell (1844–1885), who was appointed "Grand Chief" of the county, ostensibly

Table I. A Partial List of Ku Klux Raid Victims in Rutherford (1870–71)

Note: The following list is based upon newspaper articles, the Ku Klux testimony and the Shotwell Papers, and was checked against the 1870 U.S. Census for Rutherford County (with townships of victims indicated where believed known[a]). Generally, this data suggests that raiding was concentrated in the Logan Store (8) area, to the east of Cherry Mountain; in Coolsprings (6), located in the approximate center of the county near what was then Burnt Chimney (now Forest City); and in Colfax (4) township, in the central-eastern section of the County, near the Cleveland line. This is consistent with higher frequency neighborhood activity associated with the Cherry Mountain and Burnt Chimney dens, as well as "spillover" from Cleveland. About equal numbers of Negroes (22) and whites (21) were raided. The lack of documented cases from southern sections of the County suggests that either raiding there was poorly reported or exaggerated. At least some alleged victims whom I could not find in the census may have been from other counties.

Name(s)	Race	*Township*
Beam, Adeline[b]	N	—
Biggerstaff, Aaron & Fam. (x2)[c]	W	Logan Store
Bradley, T. (Thomas?) P. & Fam.	N	High Shoals
Brooks, Elizabeth	W	Cool Springs
Birge or Burge, Nelson	N	Cool Springs
Camp, ____ (woman)	N	—
Carpenter, Henry	N	Cool Springs
Doggett, George	N	—
Doggett, Martin	N	Cool Springs
Downey, Mrs.[d]	W	—
Downey, T.J.	W	Cool Springs
Gillespie, ____ [e]	W	—
Hall, Lightner (or Leitner)[f]	W	—
Hamilton, Mose (Pose?)	N	Rutherfordton?
Harrill, ____ Family	N	—
Harvey, Allen & Family	W	Cool Springs
Hawkins, Martin & Wife	W	—
Holland, William	W	Logan Store
Houser, Ben	N	Logan Store
Houser, Henry	N	—
Jackson, Mrs.	W	—
Jenkins, Ibby (Ibba?)	N	Logan Store
Justice, James M.	W	Rutherfordton
Logan, Dick (Richard)	N	Logan Store?
Logan, Henry	–	—
Lovelace, Mr. W. (Wm.?) & wife	W	Colfax

[a] Correlations of raiding victims with the US Census is sometimes conjectural.
[b] Possibly of Gaston County.
[c] Well-publicized cases (such as Biggerstaff and Justice) are not sourced, though a census citation is provided; x2 = raided twice
[d] Possibly T.J. Downey's sister, Elizabeth Brooks, already noted.
[e] Shotwell said Gillespie was a justice of the peace.
[f] Probably of Polk County.

(Table I cont.)

Name(s)	Race	Township
McGaha, James & Wife	W	Logan Store
Miller, Granville (x2)	N	Rutherfordton
Nodine, John	W	___
Owens, Almon	W	Logan Store
Owens, Nancy	W	Logan Store
Pearson, Martin & Family	N	Colfax
Pearson, York & Family	N	___
Simmons, Mrs.	_	___
Star Office (Logan & Carpenter)	W[g]	___
Taylor, M. (Miller?) E. & Family	W	Hickory Grub
Tessanear (sp?), Joseph	W?	___
Toms, Joe	N	___
Toms, Robert (Bob)	N	Colfax
unknown girl	N	___
unknown girl	N	___
Walker, Morgan	N	___
Warren, Ann	W	___
Watts, Jonas	N	___
Womach or Womack, Elizabeth	W	Colfax

[g] *No victims were present during The Star raid, but the editors were white.*

SOURCES: *Testimony*, pp. 22–23, 27–28, 104–109, 114, 134, 138–139, 204–205, 219, 223–224, 447, 555–558, 586–587; *Shotwell Papers*, vol. II, pp. 366–367, 386, 391–392, 426–427; *The Rutherford Star*, 25 March 1871, p. 3; 29 April 1871, pp. 2, 3; 27 May 1871, p. 2; and 22 July 1871, p. 2.

to try to reign in unruly, independent dens—though he was probably already a member of the order.[138]

For students of Rutherford's Ku Klux period, Shotwell will need little introduction. A native of Virginia, in 1864 he was appointed Lieutenant from ranks in his Co. L, 8th Virginia, for his gallantry at the Battle of Gettysburg. He was later captured and imprisoned at Point Lookout and Fort Delaware. Following the War, he came to Rutherfordton (where his father was a Presbyterian minister) and attracted considerable notoriety for an ultra–Conservative rag he founded (1868) and edited called *The Western Vindicator*. Shotwell then briefly sojourned in Asheville where he established *The North Carolina Citizen* and was nearly killed in a street affray with Virgil S. Lusk, a Republican of some note. He then returned to Rutherfordton, and though he was presumably reading law, he seems to have been "at loose ends"—subject, by his own admission, to "frequent potations."[139]

Shotwell probably had nothing to do with the so-called first Biggerstaff raid, which would follow shortly after Spring court and the Klan initiations in Rutherfordton. Our question is more to what extent were the Klan leaders of Cleveland culpable? Clearly, the Cherry Mountain men had reason to be angry. Aaron Biggerstaff and his compatriots had received a mere "wrist tapping" from Judge Logan for the

"Republican raid" against Samuel Biggerstaff, but a grand jury was still hearing testimony against the Klan in the McGaughey raid. Furthermore, there had been no vengeance for the killing of Decatur Depriest and protecting McGaughey.[140] The Klan had raided for far lesser offenses. But could Durham and other Klan leaders of Cleveland, disgusted with Judge Logan's perversion of justice, eager to reduce Rutherford's Republican majority in district elections and concerned to protect their identities, have decided to make common cause with the Cherry Mountain men? Or were Durham, et al., genuinely trying to gain control of the organization in Rutherford and put an end to further violence?

Definitive answers to these questions are elusive, but what we do know is that Plato Durham himself was at Cherry Mountain when the first Biggerstaff raid was planned, and that a large contingent of Cleveland Klansmen participated in the raid. On Saturday, April 8th, Capt. Durham addressed a crowd of about sixty men at Cherry Mountain which included "details from several klans"—no doubt himself imbibing a bit of Owens' famous "juice." David Schenck would state in his Congressional testimony that Durham had "*heard* that they were assembling there to inaugurate a raid on Aaron Biggerstaff, and he went there to prevent it."[141] In an affidavit he later filed with the Federal Circuit Court in Raleigh, Durham was contradictory, admitting that "at the time the conspiracy was formed at which Aaron Biggerstaff was directed to be whipped, [he] had been present," but also claiming "[that] the question of whipping Biggerstaff was not considered until after [he] left."[142] At any rate, "a portion of the Klan [swore] that he advised them to go." Durham was eventually "indicted ... for being present when the conspiracy was made up or formed to whip Biggerstaff."[143]

Around midnight, April 8th, 1871, a Klan raiding party of 50–200 men, many in disguise, arrived at the home of Aaron V. Biggerstaff and violently broke down the door. Mary Ann Norville (Biggerstaff's daughter) said that she immediately rushed upstairs. Amos Owens, attired in a red gown with horns, followed, "struck me ... and then he pitched me over the banister, down-stairs." Old man Biggerstaff was twice taken into the road in front of the house and beaten with sticks, guns, etc., all over his body, "so hard that my flesh was numbed and flew off sometimes with the blows." He may have received as many as 200 lashes, and his attackers even attempted to set his head afire with turpentine. After they fetched him back into the house the second time, Owens said, "Let's gash him," and he removed a knife seven inches long for this purpose. But the leader of the raid concluded Biggerstaff had had enough and the party soon left. One of the Klansmen claimed he was the ghost of Decatur DePriest.[144]

There was broad agreement that most of the raiders came from Cleveland County, at least part of whom were led by Martin Horde, in whose den Biggerstaff was tried by committee before the raid by order of John Wiley, also of Cleveland. Even the known Rutherford participants point to Cleveland involvement. J.B. Harrill, for instance, testified that Amos Owens "went down there" and was "the main cause of the Cleveland crowd coming." Though Harrill minimized the role of Rutherford men, claiming that of the Klansmen who participated only Owens was actually from Biggerstaff's neighborhood, the apparently reorganized Cherry Mountain den, headed by John C. Withrow, was also in the raid.[145] Withrow, who resided on his father's farm in Rutherford, just across the Cleveland line, had served in the 49th NC under McAfee and in the same company with Harvey Cabiness.[146] One Congressional witness even claimed Cleveland Sheriff B.F. Logan (who accompanied Durham to Cherry Mountain) was in the Biggerstaff raid.[147] Could Owens and Withrow have gone to their old commanders for help? Or, might the Shelby politician-lawyers have used the Cherry Mountain men as instruments in the administration of Klan justice?

When Judge Logan received word of the raid upon Biggerstaff, he immediately began issuing warrants for the arrest of Klansmen who were identified by the latter and his family. He was so alarmed that he had local militia sent out to picket the roads and detailed a posse (which included a Negro unit). The Judge delayed his appearance at Shelby's Spring court for several days[148] greatly angering the bar (who lost their fees) and the "citizens of Cleveland."[149] Logan also wrote a letter to Gov. Caldwell in which he said he could not hold court or administer the law in Cleveland due to Klan activity.[150] When this letter was published, David Schenck, a Lincolnton attorney who would later admit to membership in the Invisible Empire, wrote a letter denouncing Logan as corrupt and incompetent. In May, Logan disbarred Schenck for contempt, ignoring that this was an express violation of the law, and providing for many further proof of Logan's incompetence. Schenck was reinstated by the North Carolina Supreme Court. In June, thirty-two members of the North Carolina bar (some Republican) petitioned the legislature to remove Logan.[151]

As warrants were issued, arrests made, and the battle between Logan and the bar raged, Rutherford was further shocked by the multiple murders of a bi-racial family in the Northern part of the County near Union Mills. On the night of April 26th, three men, Govan and Columbus Adair, and Martin Baynard or Benard, brutally murdered a Negro (and Republican) named Silas Weston, three of his children, and burned their house. They left for dead a white woman with whom Weston lived, one Polly Steadman, but Steadman survived to identify her attackers. The community was at first concerned that the murders were the work of Ku Klux, but it is generally believed that the Adairs (who were also Republicans) were attempting to prevent Weston from testifying against them in a case of stolen brandy which was pending in McDowell court.[152]

Following the raid upon the Biggerstaff home, U.S. Marshal Joseph G. Hester arrived in Rutherford (with a small contingent of eight to ten "blue coats"), augmented Judge Logan's investigation, and even re-arrested men whom the latter had freed on bond. In connection with Hester's continuing efforts, on May 12th Biggerstaff and members of his family were summoned to meet the former at the head of the railroad in Cherryville to give evidence before the U.S. Commissioner in Charlotte in the attack of April 8th. Eaves testified that en route they passed a man on the road named Toms who may have alerted Klansmen of their intention to give evidence.[153] The Biggerstaff party made camp at a place called Grassy Branch, in northern Cleveland County, about ten to twelve miles from their home in Rutherford. In the early morning hours, they were attacked by a group of about ten to fifteen Ku Klux. They struck William Holland with a gun, put a rope around Biggerstaff's neck, and "told us that if we would go home, not give evidence, and not vote the radical ticket agin (sic), they would not kill us."[154] Biggerstaff and party returned to Rutherford and at first refused to answer another subpoena to report to the U.S. Commissioner in Shelby.[155] The Cherry Mountain den led by John C. Withrow was responsible for this second raid.[156] Could there have been orders from Cleveland to silence "Old Pukey"?

The people of Rutherford were now becoming extremely alarmed.[157] The Red Tavern, near the home of Capt. Eaves' father, Spencer Eaves, was a rendezvous point for the Burnt Chimney den, and the old man was said to be "greatly in fear." Biggerstaff, his family and twelve to fifteen others, including Negroes from Cleveland and the southern part of Rutherford, moved to Rutherfordton for protection,[158] where residents (including Capt. Eaves) began guarding the town at night. This was continued for several weeks, but was stopped in late May or early June because of a lull in the violence, continuing arrests and assurances from Conservatives that they were trying to stop Klan outrages.[159] But despite the lull, Eaves and his family, who resided next to Jim Justice, "moved out ... just before the [Rutherfordton] raid" to a house on the outskirts of town.[160] Given that the men believed the violence had stopped and had ceased guarding the town, it seems strange that Eaves moved. Could he have had definite warning of a raid? Might he have recalled the warning of his cousin, Maj. Lee, to steer a middle course away from conflict with the Klan?

Clearly his neighbor, Rep. James M. Justice, had *not* pursued a middle course. Justice had repeatedly used "harsh language" against the Klan for at least a year, and in the aftermath of the Biggerstaff raids he had carried his incendiary rhetoric into the courtroom where he was acting as a prosecuting attorney against the Klan. On the Tuesday before the raid on Rutherfordton, Ku Klux from William Webster's den near the State line were being tried for raiding a man named Gillespie and others.[161] Here Justice took the opportunity to boldly compare the leadership of the Klan with secession leaders who "encouraged the war of the rebellion in 1861, in which they did not themselves go, but pressed forward the poor plow-boys of the country." Now these "same secession leaders," continued Justice, "had organized this midnight and exceedingly dangerous organization, and were pushing the poor men, the laboring men, forward to commit these deeds, and ... when the day of the trial came their secession leaders would step behind the curtain and say 'I had nothing to do with it,' and leave the poor boys to suffer.'"[162]

In yet another tirade during the hearing of the same case, Justice had even said Klan leaders should be hanged. When Rutherfordton was raided on that stormy night in June, a soaked and bleeding Justice, clothed only in his nightshirt, was reminded by his assailants that he was "in favor of hanging leaders." "Now, you are a leader on the other side," he was told, "and what objection can you make to your being hung, as you advocate the doctrine of hanging leaders?" Moreover, there was the question of just what Justice, Logan and other Radicals were learning about the identities of the Klan leadership. Biggerstaff and others were identifying their Klan attackers, and Klansmen such as Thomas J. Downey were believed to be "puking" or informing upon their comrades. Justice's assailants would demand the names of the "seven traitors."[163]

Shotwell said that "very substantial and respectable citizens ... declared that some action *must* be taken" against Justice and those who were talking.[164] Might these "substantial and respectable citizens" have included Capt. Durham and the rest of the Klan leadership in Cleveland? Could Cleveland's leader of the Invisible Empire, this son of Rutherford's fire-eating "Cage" Durham (who had joined the Confederate Army at fifty-eight and given his life at the Battle of the Wilderness), idly stand by while Justice insulted the honor of his martyred father? Could he, McAfee and others risk the exposure of the Cleveland leadership in court testimony?

On Saturday night, June 10th, at a gathering on Cherry Mountain, the decision to make the Rutherfordton raid was made. According to later Congressional testimony, the purpose of the raid was to kill Justice, Biggerstaff and Downey. Klansmen would also testify that the raid was led by Lt. Shotwell. In his diary, he denied foreknowledge of the Rutherfordton raid, stating he had not even been on Cherry Mountain that weekend[165] (his brother Addison was there[166]), but "Professor Shotwell" would all but admit that he led the raiders into town in a newspaper article published in 1878.[167]

On the next night, Sunday, June 11th (amidst intermittent downpours), Shotwell, perhaps accompanied by Ladson Mills, Jr., Rutherfordton's "Village chief," met a group of about seventy-five mounted men, many of whom were in disguise, at Cox's Shop, located just a couple of miles below Rutherfordton. Shotwell probably led them to Justice's home and pointed at the door,[168] then retired to a room in the old Gen. Bryan house,[169] located near the center of town, while the Ku Klux did their work. Included were some of William Webster's men (whose den, as noted above, was then on trial), as well as Withrow's den from Cherry Mountain and a contingent from Burnt Chimney.[170]

But the Rutherfordton raid seems to have been largely the work of South Carolina men. Most of the party of Klansmen that attacked the Village that night (forty to fifty) were from the Horse Creek and Bald Rock dens, situated just across the border in Spartanburg County. According to J.B. Harrill, they had been fetched by Webster (though Harrill implied Shotwell had had a hand as well).[171] It seems most likely that the leader of these men was Capt. J. Banks Lyle (5th SC Infantry),[172] county Chief of Spartanburg County. The Limestone Springs area, where Lyle operated a boy's academy, was described by Trelease as a hotbed of Klan raiding and "the worst section" in Spartanburg.[173] But would Lyle have made a risky inter-state raid upon the town of Rutherfordton at the behest of a lowly den leader or a neophyte County chief? Or, does the participation of the Spartanburg men suggest coordination at a higher level? A Columbia, SC, grand jury would later find evidence of a "Grand Klan [meeting], held in Spartanburg County, at which there were representatives from the various Klans of Spartanburg, York, Union and Chester counties in this state, besides a number from North Carolina" establishing that "leading men of these counties" were "directing its operations ... in detail."[174] Trelease believed this Grand Klan was "under the nominal leadership of ... Lyle."[175] Their proximity would suggest the participation of the Cleveland Klan leaders in this so-called "Grand Klan." Could *they* have requested Lyle's assistance?

At any rate, Klansmen burst open Justice's door, assaulted him, and took the poor man through the streets of the village to a point just outside town where the Klansmen had gathered. "Oh you rascal, we've got you now," they said. Wet and bleeding, Justice was undoubtedly terrified, for the Klansmen led him to think that he would be executed forthwith. He was harangued for some time for his politics and, observing a wound on his head, one of Justice's attackers told him: "'It's the damned nigger equality blood that is running out, and it will do you good.'" But, finally, a magnanimous Klansman (perhaps Capt. Lyle) seemed to take Justice's part, and, after the latter agreed to mend his political ways, they let him go. Meanwhile, other Klansmen tore up the office of *The Star*, paid "puker" T.J. Downey "a visit," and made vain searches for Biggerstaff (then hiding in Rutherfordton) and Judge Logan's son Robert Logan, who edited the Star with J.B. Carpenter. Both Carpenter and Judge Logan were out-of-town.[176]

As noted above, Capt. Eaves (who had been Justice's next-door neighbor) moved to the back side of town, a quarter to a half mile from Justice, just a week before the events of June 11th. He did not learn what happened that night in Rutherfordton until the following morning, when he was informed by a servant. He went to Justice's home, found him in bed, and, perhaps remembering the words of his cousin, Maj. Lee, advised his Radical colleague "not to make any expression whatever." Eaves also said he feared another attack, but, interestingly, Justice's brother, W.D. Justice, a Democrat, who was also present, told Eaves, "'I don't believe you are in danger.'"[177]

What Justice meant by this statement is unclear. Did he allude to Eaves' prestige as a former Confederate officer? Or his numerous relations in the Klan?[178] "'Well,'" Capt. Eaves responded (perhaps defensively), "'I don't know anything about that.'" Making common cause with his fallen Republican "brother," Eaves said further, "I expect to hold on to the plank he goes down on," and he made this point by remaining with Justice until troops arrived in Rutherfordton, even resorting to the jail for protection.[179] Yet, there *was* a perception that Eaves was different from the run of Rutherford's Radicals. Shotwell put Eaves in "the better class of Republicans,"[180] and at no point in the Congressional testimony is there mention of a specific threat against him.[181]

This is perhaps surprising given Eaves' likely association with the most notorious of the Rutherford Klan's "pukes" or informers, Thomas J. Downey. Downey, who had served as a private during the War under Eaves,[182] and entered Den No. 3 headed by one-legged CSA veteran Jesse R. DePriest (16th NC, Co. G),[183] said that his former captain "told [him] to go into it [the Klan], if I could with safety." "I told Captain Eves (sic) about it," said Downey. "I corresponded with him all this time."[184] Thus, Eaves seems to have had a hand in at least encouraging, if not planting, Downey as an informer. Shotwell, who constantly railed against this "puker" in his diary, believed Downey began betraying the Klan in early May after his sister, Elizabeth Brooks, a woman of "doubtful virtuous habits," had been outraged. At the subsequent trial for this raid, Downey allegedly shared information about the Klan with the prosecution.[185] Shotwell later wrote that he believed some action against Downey was necessary because "if Downey's treason were allowed to pass unpunished, others would follow."[186] Consequently, for his "betrayal" in court during the trial for the Brooks outrage, Downey received a warning from the Klan the night of the Rutherfordton raid. But Downey insisted in his testimony before Congress that before speaking with Judge Logan (shortly after the Rutherfordton raid) he had communicated *only* with Capt. Eaves.[187] If Eaves did in fact receive warning of the Rutherfordton raid, it may well have come from Downey.

Eaves himself testified that he talked to "*two* of the first who confessed," but

Appendix VII. Durham, Eaves and the KKK Conspiracy

did not name them. "I reckon they said more to me and I to them than anybody else," he said.[188] If Downey was one of these informers, the other was probably John B. Harrill (1848–1930), a young farmer who also worked as a butcher in Rutherfordton with Gaither Trout (50th NC, Co. I,[189] and a fellow Klansman).[190] Harrill, whom Shotwell described as "a young fellow of some dash, but unscrupulous character,"[191] had been initiated by a man named Richard Martin from Cleveland, and seems first to have been a member of Den No. 3 under DePriest, then a member of Burnt Chimney den, led by Matt McBrayer.[192] Though too young for the War, he was the son of Alfred W. Harrill, who had served in the 50th NC under Capt. Eaves.[193] Harrill claimed that his father dissuaded him from participating in the Rutherfordton raid, but Justice named him as one of his attackers and Downey identified Harrill and Trout among the Klansmen who raided him.[194] At any rate, not long after the Rutherfordton raid, Harrill fled to Georgia.[195] Durham and Shotwell believed that Harrill's father then made a clemency deal with Judge Logan in exchange for his son's testimony.[196] While there is no direct evidence that Eaves had anything to do with securing Harrill's testimony against the Klan, when Eaves testified before Congress, it was Harrill's affidavit that he brought with him.[197]

Just as Eaves worked to undermine the Klan in Rutherford, the Cleveland leadership provided support to the hundreds who would eventually be indicted, arrested and jailed.[198] So many Klansmen were confined in the tiny Rutherfordton gaol that *The Star* jokingly referred to it as the "Democratic Hotel."[199] Many, such as Withrow and Lyle, fled[200] and thus evaded prosecution, while Shotwell, Owens and others were arrested and later tried in the U.S. Circuit Court in Raleigh under the Enforcement Acts. But Durham and the "State of Cleveland" did not abandon them. Robert Lee Durham wrote many years later that his father "threw every ounce of the weight of his abilities, effort, time and money in their defense";[201] and before the Klan trials in Raleigh in September, 1871, citizens of Cleveland raised approximately $45,000 in bond for defendants, though most were from Rutherford.[202] Shotwell even tells us of an effort Durham led to raise $4,000 to bribe two jurors during the trials.[203] Maj. Lee's $1,000 mortgage loan to his former soldier, Amos Owens, about this time,[204] may well have had something to do with this endeavor. But it was to no avail. The proud Virginian, Randolph A. Shotwell, was marched through the streets of Raleigh in chains on his way to Albany Penitentiary.

Things were now beginning to unravel. More and more Klansmen were talking, Durham's testimony before Congress on August 2nd was clearly evasive, and the specter of arrest and indictment began to hang over the Cleveland leadership itself. Durham and McAfee were both indicted that Fall,[205] and Cleveland Sheriff B.F. Logan was reported to have joined those who absconded in order to avoid arrest.[206] But rumors of a deal to suspend the Ku Klux prosecutions were floated as early as October, 1871,[207] and none of Cleveland's Klan leaders were ever brought to trial. There is some suggestion that Durham managed to strike a deal with President Grant in exchange for the former's *non*-support of Liberal Republican and Democratic Party nominee Horace Greeley in the election of 1872, as the prosecutions effectively ended the next Spring (see below).[208] The fate of McAfee, Logan and other Ku Kluxers of Cleveland was perhaps as Marcus Erwin explained with respect to Durham in 1874. "The prosecution against him, as I understand it," wrote Erwin,

Appendix VII. Durham, Eaves and the KKK Conspiracy

John Baxter Harrill (right), Klansman and "puker" or informer (ca. 1890). To the left is his brother, Housen Harrill. (Helen Flack Cole)

"has been *nol prossed* by order of the Attorney General ... of the United States, executing justice in mercy, being satisfied with having broken up, for a time at least, the dangerous conspiracy with which Mr. Durham admits he was associated."[209] By late 1872, McAfee was very ill with consumption;[210] he would remove to Yorkville (now York), South Carolina, where he died in September, 1873.[211] Logan continued as Cleveland sheriff until 1880.[212]

Publicly, at least, the Cleveland men defiantly thumped their chests at the prosecutions. In December, 1871, 1st Lt. Albion Howe, commanding U.S. Troops in Shelby, reported that leaders there "openly declared that 'the thing was all over, and nobody was going to be prosecuted anymore for this business.'" Howe reported further that the *Cleaveland Banner* (edited in part by a brother of Durham) had "at times advocat[ed] open, armed resistence," contrasting it with the more moderate *Vindicator* of Rutherfordton.[213] On Christmas day, armed and mounted Klansmen in disguise defiantly marched through the streets of Shelby, and Howe heard one of the riders to say, "'Captain Durham told us to ride and we should not be hurt.'"[214]

* * *

Appendix VII. Durham, Eaves and the KKK Conspiracy

Though the sheer number of documented raids in Rutherford is enough to dispel the notion that the Klan conspiracy there can be reduced to a neighborhood feud on Cherry Mountain, the extent to which Durham and the Cleveland leadership were culpable is far less clear — undoubtedly this was why Durham's case was entered *nolle prosequi*, i.e., dropped for lack of sufficient evidence.

But in the narrative above we have provided considerable *circumstantial* evidence for involvement of Durham and the other Klan leaders of Cleveland, especially with respect to the first Biggerstaff raid. Perhaps most damning, this raid occurred *after* the March, 1871, Rutherford court week initiations and *after* Durham's address to the Cherry Mountain men on the day of the raid. These facts must be received against the claim that the purposes of the initiations and Durham's visit to Cherry Mountain were to *restrain* the Klan — the effect seems to have been just the opposite. The Ku Klux testimony also makes it clear that a large body of Cleveland men participated in the first Biggerstaff raid; and the apparent leaders of the Cherry Mountain men who raided Biggerstaff, Owens and Withrow, had served in CSA infantry regiments under Col. McAfee and Maj. Lee. Surely we must ask: Would the Klansmen of Cleveland and Cherry Mountain have so blatantly disregarded the counsel of the charismatic Capt. Plato Durham had the first Biggerstaff raid been against his wishes? Withrow's Cherry Mountain den also participated in the subsequent Grassy Branch and Rutherfordton raids in which Biggerstaff was a target. This observation *could* be offered in support of the neighborhood feud thesis, but it could just as easily suggest the "underground" shadow of the ex–Confederate Cleveland leadership.

As to *motive*, the feud theory is again *apparently* sustained by the difficulty in reconciling the seeming insignificance of Aaron V. Biggerstaff with the involvement of Durham, et al. Why on earth would they target this simple mountain man? But here it is important to note that Biggerstaff, though his Unionist sympathies were well-known in his neighborhood, was *not* an original "mark" of the Klan, but became such only *after* his involvement in the "Republican raids" upon Decatur DePriest and Samuel Biggerstaff and *after* the "wrist-tapping" he received from Judge Logan in the Fall of 1870. He was marked by the Klan as a matter of honor and "justice" — and perhaps to send a message to Judge Logan that a "corrupt" and politicized "Republican judiciary" would not be tolerated. Furthermore, insofar as a long-standing Cherry Mountain feud over Biggerstaff's complicity in the theft of stock by Yankee soldiers at the War's end did give rise to the raids, it is easy to see how Durham would have been sympathetic. Capt. Durham's *own* horse was said to have been a target of Yankee marauders. But Durham's motives and the seeming isolation of Biggerstaff as a Klan victim can also be understood in broader contexts: the necessity to protect the identities of the Klan leaders of Cleveland; and the potential benefits from Republican voter intimidation that would accrue to Durham's congressional ambitions. Again, the raids upon Biggerstaff and his family were but few among many.

Durham's contemporaries *did* at least partly blame him (along with McAfee) for the wave of Klan activity in Rutherford and Cleveland. The Republicans were naturally loud in their condemnation, while the Democrats were generally silent. But the silent wrath of his own party was probably the most painful. For though he avoided formal punishment, justice *was* meted out for Durham: as a sort of subtle

Appendix VII. Durham, Eaves and the KKK Conspiracy

exile from the State's Conservative hierarchy — an exile that an impenitent Durham would *continue* to invite by his own actions.

After the initial furor over the Ku Klux investigations died down, Capt. Durham, as indicated above, continued to work to end the prosecutions — which had grown to an estimated 1,400 pending indictments in July, 1872.[215] To this end, it is probable that he secured an audience with President Grant that Fall, in which the latter agreed to end the proceedings against the Ku Klux — possibly in exchange for Durham's agreement not to support the Liberal Republican candidate (and also the Democratic Party's nominee) for President, Horace Greeley.[216] When, on the eve of the 1872 presidential contest, Durham, in a "remarkable ... apostasy" repudiated the Greeley ticket in the *Cleaveland Banner*,[217] the *Greensboro Patriot* quipped, "[it] would have been a little more consistent if he had done so earlier and *before he visited Washington.*"[218] Nonetheless, Durham prevailed and the Ku Klux investigations effectively came to a halt in April, 1873.[219]

Durham settled back into the practice of law (which he continued in partnership with H.D. Lee until March, 1875[220]) and the management of *The Cleaveland Banner* (of which he had became editor in October, 1872[221]) in Shelby. But there was also this *burden* of his "exile," and at least one fellow Klansman observed that it had taken a toll. Following his pardon and release from Albany Penitentiary in August, 1873, Randolph Shotwell paid Durham a visit in Shelby, but found the once bold leader of the Invisible Empire "very nervous and irritable ... drinking more freely than his deep, impassioned yet reserved nature could bear." He also felt Durham was affected by "the *meanness* and *ingratitude* of politicians."[222] Shotwell refers here to the view that the "old men," or leadership, of the Democratic Party (e.g., Zebulon Vance) had reaped the benefits of the Klan (such as the intimidation of Radical voters), yet had distanced themselves from the organization when the prosecutions had started.[223] The Klan's youthful leaders such as Durham and McAfee had as a consequence found themselves politically isolated (or, in the case of Shotwell, imprisoned), and Durham's continued bitterness would translate into one, final "politically reckless"[224] act against his own party.

This was his quixotic quest for the 7th District Congressional seat in 1874. Gen. Robert B. Vance, Zeb Vance's brother, had won the office in 1872, receiving the Democratic nomination over James C. Harper, the man to whom Durham had essentially given this office in 1870 when he withdrew (at the behest of the "older and wiser heads" of the party leadership) because he could not take the "test oath."[225] But, in 1874, and in the absence of a Republican challenger, Durham determined to mount an independent candidacy to challenge the incumbent, "ring candidate" Vance. Surprisingly, it seems the former Klansman hoped to draw support from "candidateless" Republicans — and the *Rutherford Star* in fact gave Durham tacit support.[226] However, Vance had overwhelming support through most of the district and especially his home county, Buncombe. Durham carried only Cleveland and Rutherford counties, and Vance won the election by nearly a two to one margin.[227]

Capt. Durham was still a very young man (only thirty-four) and the Restoration was but two years away — during the contest of 1874, R.B. Vance had even suggested that the 7th District seat could well be Durham's for the taking in two years.[228] He might yet have been "rehabilitated," and as Cleveland's representative at the

Appendix VII. Durham, Eaves and the KKK Conspiracy

Constitutional Convention of October, 1875, he acquitted himself well.[229] But just a few weeks later, he contracted pneumonia at Lincoln court, and, "after a fortnight of suffering," and surrounded by family and friends, the bold, angry young Durham "[sank] into the oblivion of the grave" on November 9th, 1875. His funeral was said to have been the largest ever attended in Shelby.[230]

Papers across the State mourned his passing. The *Southern Home* drew attention to his role during the dark days of 1868 when "a young man, unknown outside of his county, sprang suddenly into the highest esteem and admiration of nearly the whole white population of the State — drawing all eyes and warming all hearts by his bold, steadfast, honorable bearing at the head of a pitiful minority in an insolent assemblage of scalawags and carpet baggers, pretending to be the Constitutional Convention of North Carolina."[231] The *Daily Sentinel* of Raleigh wrote, "His faults have been entombed with his clay, but the memory of his noble qualities survives."[232] Raleigh's *Daily News* remarked that "whatever of personal peculiarity marked his course, there was that in him of talent, and energy, and purity of purpose that ensured his future eminence as a statesman had his life been spared."[233]

* * *

In contrast to poor Durham, most of John Baxter Eaves' political career still lay ahead. The dearth of surviving Rutherford newspaper files makes it difficult to follow his career between about 1875 and 1888 with any precision, but the basic outlines can be ascertained. Eaves held the position of Assistant Assessor of Internal Revenue until about 1873,[234] and was reported in the employ of the Revenue Service again in the U.S. Census of 1880.[235] In the early 1880s, he participated in the planning of Rutherford's railroads, serving as chairman of the Rutherford & Spartanburg Railroad Commission,[236] and, as State Senator in 1883, introducing the bill to incorporate the Rutherford Railroad Construction Company[237] over which he would be president.[238] The sheer quantity of Rutherford deeds in the names of Eaves and his wife suggest that he was also deeply involved in land speculation.[239]

But most importantly, Capt. Eaves became the successor to Rutherford's Whig/Unionist heritage and emerged as the leader of the Republican Party in Rutherford. This was perhaps in part because none of Rutherford's other Republican leaders from the Reconstruction era remained. His father-in-law, George W. Logan, lost his 9th District judgeship to David Schenck in 1874 and retired to his hotel at Chimney Rock.[240] James M. Justice left the House in 1872; he represented Rutherford at the Constitutional Convention of 1875, but in 1877 he was killed in a fall.[241] J.B. Carpenter left politics for the ministry.[242] The political career of prominent Rutherford Republican and former State Public Works Director, Ceburn L. Harris, also essentially ended with Reconstruction.[243] Eaves was the lone survivor and stepped in to fill the vacuum in party leadership. In 1878, he wrested the County's Senate seat away from Democratic control, and save for the Democratic year of 1884 (when an independent third-party candidate was in the field and he lost to T.B. Twitty),[244] Eaves would hold the office continuously for the next decade, gaining election in 1880, 1882 and 1886.[245]

Why did he survive? Was it because he had kept his mouth shut and was thus less vulnerable to charges of Radical Negro equalitarianism in the years following the Restoration? Or was it perhaps because he belonged to the class of ex–Confederate officers who were looked to for leadership throughout the South? Might the answer lay in the loyalty of the men who served under him and who padded his majorities? Or did Eaves simply inherit a county with a strong Republican tradition?

Given the paucity of source material, it is admittedly very difficult to definitely ascertain the reasons for Eaves' success. Probably all of these factors came into play. But, among those which he could control, surely the quiet, middle course he took during Reconstruction and his "Confederate image" were key. The contrast between the hyperbole of Justice and the silence of Eaves is striking; this silence allowed him to distance his politics from his father-in-law's Radical agenda.[246] Furthermore, we should not minimize the seemingly apolitical prestige of Eaves' status as an ex–Confederate officer, for many of Rutherford's company commanders either would not return from the War or left Rutherford soon thereafter.[247] He therefore filled the role of local Confederate hero just as he filled a similar role in the Republican Party's local leadership. As I have suggested above, Eaves likely used the weight of his prestige as Confederate officer to undermine the Klan in Rutherford through informers or "pukers." But the importance of Rutherford's old Whig/Unionist base — which Eaves would nuture rather than invent — should not be minimized either. This base of support would eventually make it possible for Fusion to succeed in the county during the Populist era — and, perhaps with some irony, destroy the career of Eaves, who was himself an opponent of Fusion. But in the meantime, it was Capt. Eaves who emerged as the real "winner" of Republican Reconstruction in Rutherford.

Outside Rutherford, Capt. Eaves was best known as chairman of the Republican Party's State Executive Committee (1888–94), and for his brief tenure as revenue collector in the western district of North Carolina. He first won the chairmanship at the party's 1888 convention in Raleigh, buoyed by the support of Henderson County's Hamilton Ewart, a leader of western Republicans.[248] That October, as the election neared, Eaves attracted criticism in Democratic papers for circulars signed under his name which were intended to deter voter fraud.[249] But en route by rail to the "'nogeration" of Benjamin Harrison in March, 1889, *The Daily News* of Charlotte observed that "Eaves had a regular ovation all along the line, having been met at nearly all the stations by delegations of whites and blacks, all anxious to give him a parting reminder of their desire for certain offices."[250]

Eaves' own appointment as collector of revenue the following year embroiled him in the first of several intra-party conflicts which would plague him throughout his career as State chair. As the State government remained in the control of the Democrats during these years, the most coveted offices in the Republican Party were federal appointments — and especially so were the district revenue collectorships. Those offices had fallen out of Republican hands during Grover Cleveland's administration, but with Benjamin Harrison's victory in 1888 they now returned to Republican control.

Eaves was "temporarily commissioned" collector for the 5th (or western) District (subject to Senate approval), with an office in Statesville, NC, by President Harrison in June, 1889.[251] But this greatly disappointed Dr. John J. Mott,[252] an Iredell County Republican and long-time fixture in the Party, who had previously held this position. Though Mott's son was employed in the same district office[253] (along with future Senator, Jeter Pritchard, who was appointed deputy collector[254]), he was bitterly unhappy with the way Eaves ran things.[255] He thus began a campaign to undermine Eaves' appointment (which still had to be approved by the Senate), describing the Rutherford man in one letter to President Harrison as a "petty boss" and "utterly spoiled by his promotion."[256] Regardless of the motives or merits of Mott's arguments, he ultimately succeeded. Eaves' appointment was defeated in a Senate floor vote on June 18th, 1890.[257]

Despite the loss of the collectorship, Eaves would remain a force in the party for four more years. At the 1890 Republican state convention he was re-elected as chairman of the State Executive Committee by acclamation,[258] and, in a show of solidarity, he was also belatedly endorsed by the convention for the collectorship.[259] The *Asheville Citizen* claimed "the bitter contest" between Eaves and Mott was reconciled.[260] But Republican candidates performed poorly in the election that year and factional conflict again heated up.

Ceburn L. Harris's son, J.C.L. Harris (1847–1918) of Raleigh,[261] laid the blame for defeat upon the "disgraceful reign of John Baxter Eaves," asserting that the latter's delay in calling the convention in 1890 (owing to his focus upon the quest for the collectorship) had given the party little time to organize. He ridiculed Eaves as a "creature" of dishonest revenue agents, opining the Rutherford man was incompetent to fill the office of collector. The strong endorsement he received at the convention was, according to Harris, merely a result of Eaves' success in packing the meeting with his own supporters. Of the latter's pursuit of the nomination for U.S. Senate at the Republican Party's legislative caucus in early 1891, Harris charged Eaves had used undue influence among Negro legislators and defied the counsel of friends to "promote harmony" by dropping the matter. "Upon what meat has this our Caesar fed that he has grown so great?," asked Harris.[262]

It was Jeter Pritchard to whom Eaves lost the Republican nomination for Senate[263] (an office which Pritchard would attain in 1897). Pritchard, who represented the party's business wing, stirred further intra-party strife when he led the organization of a new Protective Tariff League in Asheville in July, 1891. Eaves opposed emphasis upon the tariff because he felt it drew attention away from local issues important to Republicans, especially the popular election of county government officials.[264] In particular, the power of the legislature (controlled by "the Democracy") to appoint justices of the peace (who in turn appointed county commissioners) deprived Negro Republicans of self-government — and blacks were an essential component of the Eaves coalition. Though Ben R. Justesen's characterization of Eaves' commitment to the Negro as an "'absolute freedom and equality' [of blacks] with whites within the party"[265] is somewhat exaggerated — I believe Eaves was a cautious paternalist[266] — he nonetheless seems to have been willing to share power with the Negro in exchange for his support. When Pritchard began talk of the tariff, Eaves sensed a reorganization of "white Republicans of the State upon a Democratic platform" — i.e., a movement toward (or at least an accommodation to) white supremacy. Pritchard denied these charges,[267] but factional bickering persisted.

The struggle continued as the 1892 election approached and the divisions between Eaves' faction and the "lily white" coalition of Pritchard, Harris, Dr. Mott and Daniel Russell deepened. Eaves' opponents urged cooperation with the Populists' third-party effort and Republican withdrawal from races for state and county offices in order to ease white fears of Negro rule — especially in "black belt" counties down east.[268] But Capt. Eaves remained an unflinching straight-out Republican. Using martial prose, he pleaded with his party in 1891: "Stand by your colors; if the enemy take them in an honest struggle, all well, but we will not ourselves trail them in the dust."[269]

Eaves would successfully resist intra-party pressure to fuse with the Populists in 1892. In an April convention in Raleigh, he was again elected State chair of the Executive Committee,[270] and that summer there was even talk of an Eaves nomination for governor.[271] "Eaves' Convention" finally met in early September and nominated a State ticket.[272] A Negro candidate for attorney general was considered, though Eaves probably "vetoed the idea" because it would "[hand] the race issue openly to the Democrats."[273] But he continued to cultivate Negro support. Eaves perhaps believed that the animus of Negro rule would be offset by the effect of the Populist insurgency upon the Democratic vote. He wrote confidently to President Harrison that Republican victory was possible.[274]

But though one researcher has described the Republican electoral outcome in 1892 as a "respectable showing,"[275] the Democrats nonetheless won again. As 1894 approached, the observation that the combined Republican and Populist votes would have exceeded the Democratic vote[276] gave impetus to "[the] singular appeal of fusion ... an opportunity to defeat the Democratic hegemony."[277] Eaves and his supporters continued "to uphold ... the integrity of the party,"[278] noting the incongruity of Populist and Republican economic issues and Populist disregard of (and even outright opposition to) the Negro.[279] When Eaves refused to call a meeting of Republican leaders to discuss cooperation with the Populists, his opponents took matters into their own hands and solidified an agreement on the eve of the Populist convention.[280] Eaves' "both sides against the middle" opponents *this time embraced* the county government issue, undermining his Negro base. Simultaneously, they forged an accommodation on Populist economic issues, favoring international bi-metalism and the unlimited coinage of American silver.[281] Capt. J.B. Eaves, the stalwart opponent of Fusion was thus finally defeated and lost his chairmanship, or, as the *Charlotte Daily Observer* put it, "was whipped and surrendered."[282] When he spoke against the "joint stock company formed for the purpose of controlling the offices in the State" at Rutherford Courthouse in October, 1898,[283] it must have been with mixed emotion that Eaves condemned his own party.

Like Durham, Eaves was greatly mourned when he died after a week's illness in June, 1900. Though the tiny stone which marks his grave in Rutherfordton City Cemetery belies this popularity, it is perhaps fitting that this quiet ex–Confederate should in death call so little attention to himself.

Notes

Preface

1. *History of the General Assembly of North Carolina, January 9–March 13, 1895, Inclusive* (Raleigh: E.M. Uzzell, Printer and Binder, 1895), p. 94.
2. Quoted in Marie-Louise von Franz, *C.G. Jung: His Myth in Our Time* (New York: G.P. Putnam's Sons, 1975), p. 89.

Introduction

1. Clarence W. Griffin, *Essays on North Carolina History* (Forest City, NC: The Forest City Courier, 1951), pp. 146–149.
2. Griffin, *Essays*, p. 149; and Clarence W. Griffin, *The History of Old Tryon and Rutherford Counties* (Asheville, NC: The Miller Printing Company, 1937), p. 380.
3. Mrs. Grover C. Haynes, Sr., *Raleigh Rutherford Haynes: A History of His Life and Achievements* (Asheville, NC: Miller Printing Company, 1954), pp. 11–16; and B.E. Washburn, *Rutherford County and Its Hospital* (Spindale, NC: The Spindale Press, 1960), pp. 13–14.
4. Griffin, *Essays*, p. 150.
5. Department of Commerce and Labor, Bureau of the Census, *Thirteenth Census of the United States, Taken in the Year 1910, Abstract of the Census, Statistics of Population, Agriculture, Manufactures, and Mining for the United States, the States, and Principal Cities, with Supplement for North Carolina, Containing Statistics for the State, Counties, Cities, and Other Divisions* (Washington, D.C.: Government Printing Office, 1913), p. 656; and R.E. Price, *Rutherford County: Economic and Social* (Durham, NC: The Seeman Printery, 1918), pp. 28–30.
6. Edward L. Ayers, *The Promise of the New South* (New York: Oxford University Press, 1992), pp. 235 ff.
7. Ibid., p. 221.
8. Ibid., p. 265.
9. Helen G. Edmonds, *The Negro and Fusion Politics in North Carolina, 1894–1901* (Chapel Hill: The University of North Carolina Press, 1951), p. 23.
10. Alliancemen distinguished between the productive farmer whose labor created a tangible product (e.g., food) and the non-productive (e.g., the merchant) who used accumulated capital to generate more wealth. See Bruce Palmer's discussion in *"Man Over Money": The Southern Populist Critique of American Capitalism* (Chapel Hill: The University of North Carolina Press, 1980), pp. 11, 15.
11. Ayers, *Promise*, p. 281.
12. "Jute bags" were used by cotton farmers to bag their cotton. When, in 1888, a cartel cornered the jute market and drove up prices, the Alliance organized a successful boycott by substituting cotton bagging. See Robert C. McMath, Jr., *Populist Vanguard: A History of the Southern Farmers' Alliance* (New York: W.W. Norton & Company, 1977), pp. 54–59.

145

13. Under the "subtreasury plan," which was never adopted, the Federal government would have provided farmers with storage warehouses for nonperishable crops, allowing them to borrow against their value (thus abating the problem of credit) and to sell the crops at anytime (thus avoiding the low prices of the harvest-time glut). See Palmer's discussion on pp. 104–110, and McMath's on pp. 90–91.

14. Lawrence Goodwyn, *The Populist Moment: A Short History of the Agrarian Revolt in America* (New York: Oxford University Press, 1978), p. 199, emphasis added.

15. Joel Williamson, *The Crucible of Race: Black-White Relations in the American South Since Emancipation* (New York: Oxford University Press, 1984), pp. 226–229. An abridged version of this work, *A Rage for Order: Black-White Relations in the American South Since Emancipation*, was published by Oxford University Press in 1986.

16. Glenda Elizabeth Gilmore, *Gender & Jim Crow: Women and the Politics of White Supremacy in North Carolina, 1896–1920* (Chapel Hill: The University of North Carolina Press, 1996), pp. 66–67.

17. W.J. Cash, *The Mind of the South* (New York: Vintage Books, 1941), p. 172.

18. Quoted in the preface to *Democracy Betrayed: The Wilmington Race Riot of 1898 and Its Legacy*, edited by David S. Cecelski and Timothy B. Tyson (Chapel Hill: The University of North Carolina Press, 1998), p. xiv.

19. C. Vann Woodward, *Tom Watson: Agrarian Rebel* (New York: Oxford University Press, 1963), p. 220.

20. C. Vann Woodward, *Origins of the New South, 1877–1913* (Baton Rouge: Louisiana State University Press, 1971), p. 276.

21. C. Vann Woodward, *The Strange Career of Jim Crow*, 3rd revised ed. (New York: Oxford University Press, 1974), p. 61.

22. Woodward, *Origins*, p. 277.

23. Woodward, *Watson*, p. 223.

24. Williamson, *Crucible*, p. 28.

25. May F. Jones, ed., *Memoirs and Speeches of Locke Craig, Governor of North Carolina, 1913–1917: A History—Political and Otherwise from Scrapbooks and Old Manuscripts* (Asheville, NC: Hackney and Moale Company, 1923), p. 55.

26. Maj. Lawson P. Erwin (1835–1901) was associated with numerous Rutherford papers during his lifetime and very active in local politics. See Griffin's sketch, *History*, p. 296.

27. Edmonds, p. 141.

28. Oliver H. Orr, Jr., *Charles Brantley Aycock* (Chapel Hill: The University of North Carolina Press, 1961), p. 126.

29. Also known as "White Government Leagues" or "White Government Unions." See Edmonds, pp. 142–143; Gilmore, pp. 91, 98–99, 108–109; Jeffery J. Crow and Robert F. Durden, *Maverick Republican in the Old North State: A Political Biography of Daniel L. Russell* (Baton Rouge: Louisiana State University Press, 1977), p. 125; and Orr, p. 131.

30. The "Red Shirts," which first appeared in South Carolina in 1876, amounted to a sort of "racial" militia. For their role in North Carolina in 1898 and 1900, see Edmonds, pp. 148–150; Josephus Daniels, *Editor in Politics* (Chapel Hill: The University of North Carolina Press, 1941), pp. 292–294; Crow and Durden, pp. 128, 133–135; and Orr, pp. 131–132.

31. Woodward, *Origins*, p. 349.

32. See Joseph Lacy Seawell, *The First Lynching was the First Overt Act for American Liberty*, revised and reprinted from *Wayside Tales from Carolina* (n.p.: n.p., July, 1927), pp. 10–14; James Elbert Cutler, *Lynch-Law* (New York: Longmans, Green, and Co., 1905), pp. 17–18, quoted in Walter Samuel Lockhart III, "Lynching in North Carolina: 1888–1906," M.A. Thesis, Univ. of North Carolina, 1972, p. 10; and Walter White, *Rope & Faggot: A Biography of Judge Lynch* (New York: Alfred A. Knopf, 1929), pp. 83–84.

33. Griffin, *History*, pp. 68–70; Lyman C. Draper, *King's Mountain and Its Heroes: History of the Battle of King's Mountain, October 7th, 1780, and the Events which Led to It* (Johnson City, TN: The Overmountain Press, 1996, originally published in 1881), pp. 330–345.

34. Williamson, *Crucible*, p. 18.

35. Allen Trelease, *White Terror: The Ku Klux Klan Conspiracy and Southern Reconstruction* (New York: Harper & Row, Publishers, 1971), p. xlii.

36. William Faulkner, *Intruder in the Dust* (New York: Signet Books, 1958), pp. 20 ff.

37. See W. Fitzhugh Brundage's classification of lynch mobs in *Lynching in the New South: Georgia and Virginia, 1880–1930* (Urbana: University of Illinois Press, 1993), pp. 18 ff.

38. Trelease, pp. xx, xxi, xxvi and xliii.

39. J.G. de Roulhac Hamilton, ed., with the collaboration of Rebecca Cameron, *The Papers of Randolph Shotwell*, vol. II (Raleigh, NC: The North Carolina Historical Commission, 1931), p. 343.

40. Williamson, *Crucible*, pp. 116, 183–184.

41. Jacquelyn Dowd Hall, *Revolt Against Chivalry: Jessie Daniel Ames and the Women's Campaign Against Lynching* (New York: Columbia University Press, 1979), p. 148.

42. Williamson, *Crucible*, pp. 114–115, 311–312, 314.

43. Stewart E. Tolnay and E.M. Beck, *A Festival of Violence: An Analysis of Southern Lynchings, 1882–1930* (Urbana: University of Illinois Press, 1995), p. 271.
44. Williamson, *Crucible*, pp. 57–59.
45. Ibid., pp. 58, 115–116; Woodward, p. 355.
46. Hall, p. 146.
47. Leon Litwack, *Trouble in Mind: Black Southerners in the Age of Jim Crow* (New York: Alfred A. Knopf, 1998), pp. 197 ff.
48. Williamson, *Crucible*, pp. 111 ff.
49. Ibid., p. 308.
50. Hall, p. 148.
51. Williamson, *Crucible*, p. 308.
52. Hall, p. 148.
53. Williamson, *Crucible*, p. 115. Williamson's reference to the *protection* of white women sounds very much like Alexander Manly, a Negro and editor of the *Record* of Wilmington, who inflamed white indignation during North Carolina's white supremacy campaign of 1898 when he suggested that white women occasionally had affairs with black men and that "white men are careless in the matter of protecting their women...." Quoted from Daniels, p. 286. Might Williamson's sexual repression theory be a subconscious echo of Manly?
54. Ibid., pp. 114–115, 311–312, 314.
55. Williamson, *Crucible*, p. 308.
56. See Tolnay and Beck, pp. 46–50. According to these researchers, for the period 1882–1930 murder was the crime most strongly associated with lynching as a sanction; however, before the turn of the century, rape was indeed the more common trigger in the South. Tolnay and Beck found that the highest correlation between rape and lynchings was 40.6% in the border states between 1882 and 1899. In general, Williamson's "about a third" estimate is accurate.
57. Williamson, *Crucible*, p. 184.
58. Brundage, *New South*, pp. 12, 67.
59. Tolnay and Beck, p. 255.
60. Donald G. Matthews, "The Southern Rite of Human Sacrifice," *The Journal of Southern Religion* 3 (2000). http://jsr.as.wvu.edu/mathews.htm, part III, p. 5.
61. Brundage, *New South*, p. 67.
62. Ibid., p. 12.
63. Arthur F. Raper found that lynchings tended to correlate with poorer counties where tenancy was high. See his oft-cited study, *The Tragedy of Lynching* (Chapel Hill: The University of North Carolina Press, 1933), p. 6.
64. In his *Honor and Violence in the Old South*, abridged ed. (New York: Oxford University Press, 1986), p. 210, Bertram Wyatt-Brown wrote, "The chief aim [of a lynching] was the protection of traditional values and conventions against forces outside as well as within the community. They were simple group dramas in which evil was defeated, good was reinstated. By that means virtues were reconfirmed, boundaries of conduct set...." The protection of these values and the community was deeply rooted in a Southern code of honor which superceded legality and sanctioned violence in its defense.
65. Donald Matthews argues that "'blood sacrifice' ... was an essential part of Southern culture ... because it was central to the Christian narrative of salvation." He equates the lynched Negro to Christ upon the cross. See his "Southern Rite of Human Sacrifice," part II, pp. 3 ff.
66. Several empirical studies have taken up the possible association between Populism and lynching, but results have been mixed. In a study on Louisiana during the Populist era (1889–1896), Inverarity found that parishes with strong indicators of "mechanical solidarity" (for example, a high percentage of blacks and thus by inference the threat of "Negro rule") tended to correlate positively with a higher incidence of "repressive justice"—i.e., lynchings. See James M. Inverarity, "Populism and Lynching in Louisiana, 1889–1896," *American Sociological Review*, 41 (April 1976), pp. 274–275. Olzack, in another study, presented data which showed that "the Populist challenge *per se* ... appears to have sparked increases in lynching." See Susan Olzack, "The Political Context of Competition: Lynching and Urban Racial Violence, 1886–1914," *Social Forces*, 69 (December 1990), p. 415.

Sarah A. Soule, on the other hand, in her "Populism and Black Lynching in Georgia, 1890–1900," *Social Forces*, 71 (December 1992), p. 444, found "that the Populist movement did not increase rates of black lynching." Similarly, Tolnay and Beck identified an inverse relationship between counties with stronger Republican and Populist parties and lynchings. See their *Festival of Violence*, pp. 195–199. See also their discussion of the literature on pp. 169–170.
67. The best review of various explanations for racial lynching in the South is probably Fitzhugh Brundage's in his *Lynching in the New South*, pp. 8 ff. See also Brundage's "Introduction" to *Under Sentence of Death: Lynching in the South* (Chapel Hill: The University of North Carolina Press, 1997), pp. 1–20. Tolnay and Beck review various theories in Chapter 8 (pp. 239–258) of their *Festival of Violence*. Their dismissal of the association of lynching with political motivations and Redeemer/Populist Party politics (pp. 249–250) is, of course, at variance with my views about the Forest City lynching. In

addition, the literature review in Donald G. Matthews' recent "The Southern Rite of Human Sacrifice," part I, pp. 1 ff., is useful.

68. Litwack, pp. 203, 213, 215, 234, 246, 265, 282, 284.

69. Ibid., pp. 280 ff.

70. With respect to this need for spectacle and torture, one can find parallels between lynching in the New South and Michel Foucault's analysis of the functionality of *public* executions in 18th century France in *Discipline and Punish*. "Atrocity," he wrote, "is that part of the crime that the punishment turns back as torture in order to display it in the full light of day...." "Not only must people know, they must see with their own eyes. Because they must be made to be afraid; but also because they must be the witnesses, the guarantors, of the punishment, and because they must to a certain extent take part in it." The people thus participated in the ritual affirmation of the power of the sovereign, displayed in the corporeal punishment of the condemned. See Michel Foucault, "The spectacle of the scaffold (Chap. 2)," *Discipline and Punish: The Birth of the Prison*, trans. by Alan Sheridan (New York: Vintage Books, 1979), especially pp. 54–59. One might suggest that in the New South the power of the sovereign was synonymous with the power of "the fathers."

71. Litwack, p. 290.

72. Tolnay and Beck, pp. 271–272.

73. Quoted in Williamson, *Crucible*, p. 95; also quoted in H. Leon Prather, Sr., "We Have Taken a City," in Cecelski and Tyson, p. 23; LeeAnn Whites, "Love, Hate, Rape, Lynching: Rebecca Latimer Felton and the Gender Politics of Racial Violence," Cecelski, et al., p. 149; and Richard Yarborough, "Violence, Manhood, and Black Heroism: The Wilmington Race Riot in Two Turn-of-the-century African American Novels," Cecelski, et al., p. 228.

74. Litwack, p. 207.

75. Crow and Durden, p. 127.

76. Williamson, *Crucible*, p. 79.

77. Prather in Cecelski, et al., p. 35.

78. Williamson, *Crucible*, p. 209.

79. Brundage, *New South*, pp. 50–52.

80. Forest City First Baptist Church (1848), Forest City, NC, Records, 1888–1991, 10 vols., vol. 1, pp. 14 ff. (microform, reel #1).

81. Brundage, *New South*, p. 76.

82. Ibid., p. 50.

83. Ibid., p. 52.

84. Wyatt-Brown, p. 16.

85. Edward L. Ayers, *Vengeance & Justice: Crime and Punishment in the 19th-Century American South* (New York: Oxford University Press, 1984), p. 26.

86. Brundage, *New South*, p. 80.

87. Palmer, p. 220.

88. Ibid., pp. 126–133.

89. Brundage, *New South*, p. 70.

90. Ralph R. Flack, unpublished manuscript, 1968 (HFC).

91. *The Sun* (Rutherfordton), 28 July 1904, p. 5.

92. Ibid.; and personal knowledge.

93. Gilmore, p. 118.

94. Cash, pp. 120–121.

95. Quoted from *The Winston-Salem Journal*, 17 September 1903, p. 1.

96. Lockhardt, pp. 84–98, 151–165.

97. Litwack, pp. 258–259.

98. Ibid., pp. 247 ff.

99. Ibid., p. 259.

1. Mills Higgins Flack

1. To date, the best study of the origins of the Rutherford Flacks is Horace E. Flack's *The Flack Family* ([Lenoir, NC]: Helen Flack Cole, 1972). Also see the Ralph R. Flack Papers (ICC).

2. Rutherford County, NC, Record of Wills, 1791–1813, vol. B, pp. 86–87 (microform).

3. Seventh Census of the United States, 1850: Rutherford County, NC, Agricultural Schedule, pp. 441–442 (microform).

4. Ibid.; and Seventh Census of the United States, 1850: Rutherford County, NC, Slave Schedule, p. 57 (microform).

5. Ivarea Flack, *Flack Family Heritage 1975* (Rutherfordton, NC: Liberty Press, 1975), p. 8; also in Helen Mason Lu and Gwen Blomquist Neumann, *North Carolina Spectator and Western Advertiser (1830–1835) Rutherford County, North Carolina Abstracts* (Dallas, TX: the authors, 1982), p. 12.

6. See Ivarea Flack, pp. 8–9. It seems obvious that Mills Higgins Flack was named for his maternal grandfather since the latter's name was Mills Higgins.

7. Rutherford County, NC, Record of Wills, 1782–1868, vol. E, p. 380 (microform).

8. Griffin, *History*, p. 238.

9. Seventh Census of the United States, 1850: Rutherford County, NC, Population Schedule, p. 276 (microform).

10. Collins & Goodwin, *Biographical Sketches of the Members of the General Assembly of North Carolina, 1895* (Raleigh: Edwards & Broughton, 1895), p. 51. William S. Powell's *North Carolina Through Four Centuries* (Chapel Hill: The University of North Carolina Press, 1989), pp. 290–

Notes—Chapter 1

291, briefly discusses the common schools of Mills Flack's day.

11. *Biographical Sketches*, p. 51.
12. Griffin, *History*, p. 345.
13. *The Western Vindicator* (Rutherfordton), 23 March 1899, p. 1.
14. For example, see Griffin, *History*, p. 585.
15. As the crow flies, it was over six miles from the Flack lands on Catheys Creek to Brittain Church. However, it should be noted that inscribed upon Andrew Flack, Jr's tombstone (he died in 1890) is the following statement: "He was a pious man and a Presbyterian." Thus, perhaps the Flacks still attended Brittain during his youth. But since George Flack, his father, was buried at Mountain Creek when he died in 1860, I have to assume that the Flacks were by that time members of the latter congregation. At any rate, it is at least *possible* that Mills Flack was raised as a Presbyterian. This problem may well be impossible to solve as the early Mountain Creek Baptist and Brittain Presbyterian records seem to have been either lost or destroyed.
16. Hemphill Family Heritage Committee, *Hemphills in North Carolina* (Collegedale, TN: The College Press, 1981), pp. 51–53.
17. [Clarence W. Griffin], *The First Baptist Church of Forest City, N.C.* (Forest City, NC: The Forest City Courier, 1939), p. 12; see also op. cit., Forest City First Baptist Church Records, vol. 1, pp. 17 ff.
18. Seventh Census of the United States, 1850: Rutherford County, NC, Slave Schedule, p. 57 (microform).
19. Eighth Census of the United States, 1860: Rutherford County, NC, Slave Schedule, p. 20 (microform).
20. It is also interesting to note that the births of slaves were recorded in the George Flack family bible. See "George Flack Family Bible," *Bulletin of the Genealogical Society of Old Tryon County, North Carolina*, 1 (August 1973), p. 27.
21. Brent H. Holcomb, compiler, *Marriages of Rutherford County, North Carolina, 1779–1868* (Baltimore: Genealogical Publishing Co., Inc., 1986), p. 44; Ivarea Flack, pp. 8, 36–37, 45.
22. Ivarea Flack, p. 36; *Hemphills in North Carolina*, pp. 54, 56–57, 71. The George Flack farm was located "in the forks of Cove and Cedar Creeks." See Ralph R. Flack, unpublished manuscript, 1968 (HFC). Parts of this work were published as *Memories*, ed. by Helen Flack Cole ([Lenoir, NC]: n.p., 1978).
23. Op. cit., Rutherford Wills, vol. E, p. 380.
24. Ivarea Flack, p. 45.
25. Frances H. Casstevens, *The Civil War and Yadkin County, North Carolina: A History* (Jefferson, NC: McFarland & Co., Inc., Publishers, 1997), pp. 72–75; Burton J. Hendrick, *Statesmen of the Lost Cause* (New York: The Literary Guild of America, 1939), pp. 352–362; Richard E. Yates, *The Confederacy and Zeb Vance*, Confederate Centennial Studies, 8 (Tuscaloosa, AL: Confederate Publishing Company, Inc., 1958), pp. 45–47.
26. Hendrick, p. 355.
27. Yates, p. 29.
28. Stephen E. Bradley, ed., *North Carolina Confederate Militia Officers Roster as Contained in the Adjutant-General's Officers Roster* (Wilmington, NC: Broadfoot Publishing Co., 1992), p. 275. In a later biography, Flack identified his unit as "the Seventy-sixth Regiment, N.C. Militia." See *Biographical Sketches*, p. 51.
29. Griffin, *History*, pp. 258–259. Ceburn L. Harris (1822–1908) was a prominent Republican in Rutherford and the State during Reconstruction. It seems likely that he was a Union man during the War, and it is possible that Mills Flack shared similar Unionist sentiments, though this is pure conjecture. See Griffin's sketch of Harris, pp. 319–320. It was for Flack's service in the 69th Battalion, NC Home Guard, that Katie Harrill Flack would eventually receive a widow's pension. Katie applied for her widow's pension three times before it was finally approved in 1928. See NC Confederate Widow's Pension Records, 1900 (NC Office of Archives and History, Raleigh, NC).
30. Rutherford County, NC, Minutes, Court of Pleas and Quarter Sessions, 1850–1868, 2 vols. (microform). Capt. Flack's company is first mentioned during Spring Term 1862 (vol. 2, p. 4) and last mentioned March Court 1865 (vol. 2, p. 140).
31. Casstevens, p. 72; and Gerald Wilson Cook, *The Last Tarheel Militia 1861–1865* (Winston-Salem, NC: the author, 1987), p. 4.
32. Cook, p. 6.
33. See Yates' discussion, pp. 62–67.
34. Cook, p. 3.
35. Many of the Confederacy's first volunteer units were drawn from the militia. See Cook, p. 3; and Casstevens, p. 72.
36. Stephen E. Bradley, Jr., abs., *North Carolina Confederate Militia and Home Guard Records. Volume 3: Home Guard Letter Book, 1863–1865* (Virginia Beach, VA: The author, 1995), p. 79.
37. Ibid., pp. 42–43, 79; Dr. Stephen E. Bradley, Jr., abs., *North Carolina Confederate Militia and Home Guard Records. Volume 1: Militia Letter Book, 1862–1864* (Virginia Beach, VA: the author, 1995), pp. 50, 56, 86.

Notes — Chapter 1

38. Op. cit., Bradley, *Letter Book*, vol. 3, pp. 42–43, 70, 79.
39. Ibid., p. 29.
40. John C. Inscoe and Gordon B. McKinney, *The Heart of Confederate Appalachia: Western North Carolina in the Civil War* (Chapel Hill: The University of North Carolina Press, 2000), p. 206.
41. See Daniel Wayne Jolley, "The Ku Klux Klan in Rutherford County, North Carolina, 1870–1871," M.A. Thesis, Univ. of North Carolina, 1994, pp. 7–8; and J.G. de Roulhac Hamilton, *Reconstruction in North Carolina* (Gloucester, Mass.: Peter Smith, 1964, a rpt. of the Columbia University ed. of 1914), p. 395.
42. Flack was a representative of Morgan Township at a Conservative meeting held amidst Ku Klux turmoil in Rutherford on June 19th, 1871. See *The Western Vindicator* (Rutherfordton), 26 June 1871, p. 2.
43. Op. cit., Rutherford Court of Pleas and Quarter Sessions, vol. 2, pp. 3 ff.
44. Ibid., vol. 2, p. 127.
45. Dr. Stephen E. Bradley, Jr., abs., *North Carolina Confederate Militia and Home Guard Records. Volume 2: Militia Letter Book, 1864–1865, and Home Guard Orders* (Virginia Beach, VA: The author, 1995), p. 34; op. cit., Bradley, *Letter Book*, vol. 3, pp. 42.
46. Op. cit., Bradley, *Letter Book*, vol. 3, pp. 39, 101, 119.
47. D.F. Morrow, *Then and Now: Reminiscences and Historical Romance, 1856–1865* (Macon, Ga.: J.W. Burke Company, 1926), pp. 54 ff. Inscoe and McKinney also noted bushwhacker attacks in Rutherford. See their *Heart of Confederate Appalachia*, p. 240.
48. Ninth Census of the United States, 1870: Rutherford County, NC, Population Schedule, p. 139 (microform); Ninth Census of the United States, 1870: Rutherford County, NC, Agricultural Schedule, p. 3 (microform).
49. Ibid.; and Tenth Census of the United States, 1880: Rutherford County, NC, Agricultural Schedule, p. 9 (microform).
50. Ivarea Flack, pp. 45–52. Posey's middle name, "Maggie," was evidently a tribute to his mother.
51. Ibid., pp. 8, 37, 45.
52. Ralph R. Flack Papers (HFC).
53. *Hemphills in North Carolina*, pp. 51–56, 71, 189, and 207.
54. Published Montford Cove church records indicate that, following her marriage to Sam Bruce, Sarah briefly (1860–1862) resided in "the West." See *Hemphills in North Carolina*, p. 52. By 1870, she resided with a child (but without Sam Bruce) next to her father in Montford Cove. See Ninth Census of the United States, 1870: Rutherford County, NC, Population Schedule, p. 133 (microform).
55. Rutherford County, NC, Bastardy Bonds, 1872–1878, 1 vol., p. 25 (microform).
56. *Hemphills in North Carolina*, p. 207; and Ralph R. Flack, unpublished manuscript, 1968 (HFC).
57. The records of Montford Cove Baptist Church still exist, but regrettably I was unable to examine them. These records could reliably establish if Mills Flack was a member of the church and might also shed light on the affair with Sarah Bruce. If Flack and Bruce were members, they were likely expelled for fornication.
58. Clipping in the Ralph R. Flack Papers (HFC).
59. Ibid.
60. Ivarea Flack, pp. 51–54.
61. See note 74.
62. Ralph R. Flack, unpublished manuscript, 1968 (HFC).
63. Ibid.
64. I have been unable to locate the original deed for this land but I believe it is the 87 acre tract referred to in Rutherford County, NC, Record of Deeds, vol. 100, pp. 24–25 (microform), and in an auction notice in *The Rutherfordton Tribune*, 29 August 1901, p. 3.
65. Op. cit., Tenth Census, 1880: Rutherford County, NC, Agricultural Schedule, p. 9.
66. Ralph R. Flack, unpublished manuscript, 1968 (HFC).
67. Rutherford County, NC, Record of Deeds, vol. 62, pp. 15–17 (microform).
68. Griffin, *History*, p. 358.
69. Rutherford County, NC, Record of Deeds, vol. 58, pp. 72–73.
70. Genealogical Society of Old Tryon County, *The Heritage of Rutherford County, North Carolina, Volume I, 1984* (Winston-Salem, NC: Hunter Publishing Co., 1984), p. 27.
71. Ibid., pp. 19, 25, 27; Griffin, *History*, pp. 595–596.
72. Op. cit., Forest City First Baptist Church Records, vol. 1, pp. 14 ff.
73. Ibid., p. 14.
74. Ibid., pp. 18–23. The Cool Springs records were in the possession of the church's clerk, Martin J. Harrill, who was the brother of the Rev. Housen D. Harrill.
75. The fathers of Housen D. Harrill and Katie Harrill were cousins.
76. Op. cit., Forest City Baptist Church Records, vol. 1, pp. 19–20, 22.
77. Ibid., p. 28.
78. Ibid., p. 43. Within one year of the issuance of the letters of dismission, Mills Flack

appears back in the Forest City Baptist Church records.

79. Ibid., pp. 43 ff.
80. Ibid., pp. 67 ff.
81. The sale of the Cove Creek lands can be documented by three deeds, all transactions between Flack and Richard Ledbetter. The first sale, of 18 3/4 acres, was made in April, 1890; the second sale, of 41 1/2 acres, took place in December, 1893; the final transaction, of three parcels totaling 278 1/2 acres, and presumably the last of the Cove Creek lands, was made in December, 1897. Flack was paid a total of $1,950 for the Cove Creek tracts. See Rutherford County, NC, Record of Deeds, vols. 63, pp. 268–269; 67, pp. 126–127; and 71, pp. 177–178.
82. See *The Rutherfordton Tribune*, 29 August 1901, p. 3; and Rutherford County, NC, Special Proceedings, 1901–1914, vol. C, pp. 208–214 (microform). Flack owed $500 to $600 at the time of his death.
83. Quoted from Laura F. Edwards' "Captives of Wilmington: The Riot and Historical Memories of Political Conflict, 1865–1898," in *Democracy Betrayed*, p. 131.
84. Ibid.
85. Ralph R. Flack, *Memories*, p. 3.
86. Woodward, *Origins*, p. 185.
87. Charles Reagan Wilson, et al., eds., *The Encyclopedia of Southern Culture* (Chapel Hill: The University of North Carolina Press, 1989), pp. 29–31.
88. Woodward, *Origins*, pp. 180–181.
89. Palmer, pp. 10 ff., quoted from p. 23.
90. Theodore Mitchell, *Political Education in the Southern Farmers' Alliance, 1887–1900* (Madison: The University of Wisconsin Press, 1987), pp. 82–84.
91. The farmer's/Populist movement of the late 1880s and 1890s has been the subject of considerable attention from historians. In addition to the works by Palmer and Mitchell, see Goodwyn's *Populist Moment* (1978); McMath's *Populist Vanguard* (1977); Woodward's *Tom Watson* (1963); and Ayers' *Promise of the New South* (1992), pp. 214–282.
The Populist Movement in North Carolina is briefly treated in Powell's *North Carolina Through Four Centuries* (1989), pp. 422–431; and Paul D. Escott, *Many Excellent People: Power and Privilege in North Carolina, 1850–1900* (Chapel Hill: The University of North Carolina Press, 1985), pp. 241–262.
92. Ayers, *Promise*, pp. 263, 282. I think there is a sense in which the agrarian movement also anticipated the conflicts between "town people" and "mill people," which would develop in the up-country of South Carolina, culminating in Bleasism. See the very excellent work by David Carlton, *Mill and Town in South Carolina, 1880–1920* (Baton Rouge: Louisiana State University Press, 1982). The post-Reconstruction strength of the Republican Party in Rutherford may also be indicative of class conflict.
93. Ayers, *Promise*, p. 221.
94. The only full-length biography of Polk is Stuart Noblin's *Leonidas LaFayette Polk: Agrarian Crusader* (Chapel Hill: The University of North Carolina Press, 1949). His editorship of *The Progressive Farmer* and role in the establishment of the agricultural college are discussed on pp. 147–182.
95. McMath, p. 40.
96. Ibid., p. xi.
97. Ibid., pp. 33 ff.
98. Ayers, *Promise*, pp. 220, 225.
99. *The Progressive Farmer* (Raleigh), 10 July 1888, p. 3; *New Era* (Shelby), 30 June 1888, p. 1; 7 July 1888, p. 1; and 14 July 1888, p. 1.
100. According to Griffin, Col. J.L. McDowell (1829–1890) served a term as a county commissioner, beginning in 1880. See Griffin, *History*, p. 352.
101. *New Era* (Shelby), 28 July 1888, p. 3.
102. Marion Butler Papers, #114, subseries 2.3.1, Farmers' State Alliance, Quarterly Reports, 1891–95 (Southern Historical Collection, Wilson Library, University of North Carolina at Chapel Hill).
103. *Biographical Sketches*, p. 51. It seems likely that Flack would have been a member of a sub-alliance in or near Forest City, perhaps L.C. Hardin's. See Records of the North Carolina Farmer's State Alliance, Secretary's Records, Sub-Alliances Register, 1893–1898, pp. 155–156 (NC Office of Archives and History, Raleigh, NC). It is possible that Flack ascended to the presidency of the County Alliance at the time of Col. McDowell's death in March, 1890.
104. *The Progressive Farmer* (Raleigh), 14 August 1888, p. 6. This letter may have been written by Barnabas A. Baber (1822–1899).
105. McMath, p. 48; Goodwyn, pp. 55 ff.
106. Ayers, *Promise*, pp. 237–238; McMath, pp. 54–59; Goodwyn, pp. 87–89.
107. Goodwyn, pp. 55 ff.; McMath, pp. 48–52.
108. McMath, p. 51.
109. Goodwyn, pp. 75 ff.
110. Ibid., p. 77.
111. Ibid., p. 84; McMath, pp. 30–32.
112. For example, see McMath's discussion, pp. 88 ff., of the platform issued from the important St. Louis convention in December, 1889, which introduced the sub-treasury plan as an Alliance issue.

113. *The Progressive Farmer* (Raleigh), 5 February 1889, p. 3; *New Era* (Shelby), 8 February 1889, p. 3.
114. New Era (Shelby), 22 February 1889, p. 2.
115. Ibid., 1 October 1889, p. 4.
116. Ibid., 5 February 1889, p. 3.
117. Ibid., 8 October 1889, p. 2. This may be the L.C. Hardin (ca. 1871–ca. 1844) buried at Sandy Mush. Also see note 94.
118. Ibid.
119. Ibid., 1 October 1889, p. 4.
120. Ibid., 10 December 1889, p. 1.
121. Goodwyn defines "the movement culture" as a "mass democratic insurgency ... antithetical to the social, economic, and political values of the received hierarchical culture." For him, this is the meaning of Populism. See note, p. 165.
122. McMath, pp. 107–108. Mitchell's work, cited above, is of course devoted to political education in the Alliance.
123. *The Progressive Farmer* (Raleigh), 28 July 1891, p. 1.
124. Ibid., 12 January 1892, p. 4.
125. Ibid., 31 May 1892, p. 4.
126. Mitchell, pp. 50–51.
127. McMath, pp. 72–76; Mitchell, pp. 50–51, 95.
128. McMath, p. 73.
129. *The Progressive Farmer* (Raleigh), 23 October 1894, p. 1.
130. Goodwyn, pp. 134, 164; Noblin, pp. 266–267; *The News and Observer* (Raleigh), 9 March 1895, p. 2. Goodwyn, on p. 164, quoted Polk: "the gigantic struggle of today between the classes and the masses."
131. Mitchell, pp. 86–92.
132. Palmer, p. 24.
133. *Biographical Sketches*, p. 51.
134. Quoted in Orr's *Charles Brantley Aycock*, p. 105.
135. Mitchell, p. 91.
136. Richard Hofstadter, *The Age of Reform From Bryan to F.D.R.* (New York: Vintage Books, 1955/1960), pp. 70–81.
137. Clement Dowd, *Life of Zebulon B. Vance* (Charlotte, NC: Observer Printing & Publishing House, 1897), pp. 281–291. The sub-treasury controversy may not have hurt Vance in Rutherford either. In the Fall of 1890, T.B. Justice wrote the Senator, "Vance holds his own in Rutherford, Alliance or no Alliance." See the Zebulon B. Vance Papers, #3952, T.B. Justice to Zebulon B. Vance, 27 September 1890 (Southern Historical Collection, Wilson Library, University of North Carolina at Chapel Hill).
138. *The Progressive Farmer* (Raleigh), 9 February 1892, p. 1.
139. Ibid., 23 August 1892, p. 4.
140. Ibid., 27 September 1892, p. 2.
141. Ibid., 4 October 1892, p. 4. Dr. Oliver Hicks (1842–1910) was remembered and discussed by Benjamin E. Washburn in his *To Everything a Season: Rutherfordton Long, Long Ago* (Spindale, NC: The Spindale Press, nd), pp. 21–22.
142. For example, Macune. Goodwyn, p. 67, wrote that Macune "consistently opposed Alliance political activism and feared the emergence of the third party."
143. Goodwyn, pp. 163–164.
144. *The Daily Charlotte Observer*, 19 July 1892, p. 1.
145. Ibid., 10 August 1892, p. 1.
146. Ibid., 25 August 1892, p. 2.
147. Ibid., 9 September 1892, p. 1. Michael Hoke Justice (1844–1919) served four terms as a state senator and was a superior court judge from 1901 until his death. He was one of Rutherford's most important figures during the late 19th and early 20th centuries. See Griffin's sketch, *History*, pp. 345–346.
Though Justice was probably Rutherford's most outspoken opponent of "Negro rule" during the white supremacy campaigns of 1898 and 1900, it is interesting to note the following anecdotes from an account of his funeral: "John Michael, a colored carpenter and mason offered to construct a concrete vault free of charge, on account of the many acts of kindness shown him by the [J]udge. He had always promised the [J]udge to see that he had a part in burying him. 'Uncle Simon Wright,' an aged colored man who has worked around the Justice home for many years was seen standing at the grave after most of the crowd had gone and remarked: 'The best friend that I have in this world is gone.' These two instances only show the love and esteem in which Judge Justice was held, by both races and conditions of mankind." See *The Sun* (Rutherfordton), 20 February, 1919, p. 1.
148. Ibid., 20 September 1892, p. 1.
149. Ibid., 29 September 1892, p. 1.
150. Ibid., 13 October 1892, p. 3.
151. *The Progressive Farmer* (Raleigh), 1 November 1892, p. 4.
152. *The Daily Charlotte Observer*, 9 November 1892, p. 4.
153. Griffin, *History*, p. 362.

2. The Fusion Era

1. Ayers, *Promise*, p. 285.
2. Edmonds, p. 27.

Notes—Chapter 2

3. Ibid., p. 36.
4. Ibid., p. 27; see also Ayers, *Promise*, p. 290.
5. Edmonds, p. 29.
6. Capt. John Baxter Eaves (1838–1900) is sketched in Griffin, *History*, pp. 318–319. Griffin writes very flatteringly of Eaves, who served five terms as Rutherford's State senator, sought the G.O.P. nomination for U.S. Senate in 1891, and was even mentioned for governor. For more on Eaves, see Appendix VII.
7. *The Daily Charlotte Observer*, 29 August 1894, p. 1.
8. Ibid., 31 August 1894, p. 1.
9. Ibid., 21 & 31 August 1894, p. 1.
10. Joseph F. Steelman, "Republican Party Strategists and the Issue of Fusion with Populists in North Carolina, 1893–1894," *The North Carolina Historical Review*, 47 (July 1970), p. 252.
11. Edmonds, pp. 34–36.
12. "E. Lane" may be E.P. Lane (1861–1924).
13. *The Daily Charlotte Observer*, 2 October 1894, p. 2.
14. Ibid. A. D'K. Wallace (1848–1928) would become Rutherford's most prominent Populist. Though, in 1896, he was defeated for State Senate by M.H. Justice, during the administration of Daniel Russell, he was appointed as chief clerk to Secretary of State Cyrus Thompson. See Griffin's sketch in *History*, p. 574. See also his obituaries in the *Forest City Courier*, 19 April 1928, p. 5; and *The Rutherford County News*, 19 April 1928, p. 1. M.O. Dickerson, Jr. (1860–1935), was Rutherford's clerk of court for many years. He also merited a biographical sketch in Griffin's *History*, p. 376.
15. For example, during the gubernatorial campaign of 1892, Populist candidate Wyatt P. Exum and Aycock were involved in a well-publicized fight. See Orr, pp. 93–94.
16. Griffin, *History*, p. 363. It should be noted that Griffin either misidentified or failed to identify the party affiliation of several of the elected Fusion era Populists in Rutherford. On the election of 1894, he said, "In the County a complete set of Republican officials was elected." However, in addition to Flack, W.O. Baber, elected treasurer in 1894, and Franklin Moore, elected coroner in that year, were Populists, not Republicans. See the Populist nominations in *The Daily Charlotte Observer*, 2 October 1894, p. 2. Also see Appendix II. There are brief sketches of Moore (1831–1909) and Baber (1848–1897) in Griffin's *History*, pp. 301–302, 374.
17. Probably the most important work on North Carolina's Fusion era remains Helen G. Edmonds' *The Negro and Fusion Politics in North Carolina, 1894–1901*. Josephus Daniels provides a highly partisan (Democratic), but nonetheless interesting, account of the Populists and the Fusion legislature of 1895 in his *Editor in Politics*, pp. 120–156. For a still more extreme Democratic view of the Fusion assembly, see op. cit., *History of the General Assembly*.
18. *The News and Observer* (Raleigh), 26 January 1895, p. 2.
19. *History of the General Assembly*, pp. 98–100.
20. Edmonds, p. 41.
21. *The News and Observer* (Raleigh), 15 January 1895, p. 2.
22. Ibid., 13 February 1895, p. 2.
23. Ibid., 21 February, p. 2.
24. Today the University of North Carolina at Greensboro.
25. *The News and Observer* (Raleigh), 9 March 1895, p. 2.
26. See the sketch of Ewart (1849–1918) in William S. Powell, ed., *Dictionary of North Carolina Biography*, vol. 2, D–G (Chapel Hill: The University of North Carolina Press, 1986), p. 173.
27. Amos Owens, the famous "blockader" of Cherry Mountain, was known far and wide for his "cherry bounce" whiskey. For more on Owens, see Appendix VII.
28. *The News and Observer* (Raleigh), 9 March 1895, p. 2.
29. Ibid.
30. "It was the revolutionary 'farmers' legislature of 1891 that ... established a normal college for white girls," writes Hugh Talmage Lefler and Albert Ray Newsome in *North Carolina: The History of a Southern State*, Chapel Hill: The University of North Carolina Press, 1954, p. 513. See also the discussion in Noblin, pp. 183–189.
31. See Ayers, *Promise*, pp. 227, 246.
32. See Chap. 2.
33. Negroes were banned from membership in the whites only Farmers' Alliance, but organized a parallel Alliance of their own. See, for example, Ayers, *Promise*, pp. 234–237. The white landowners who dominated the Populist Party proved at best ambivalent toward the Negro, anxious to use his votes to obtain elected office but ultimately unable to resist the call of white supremacy. "The Populist experiment in interracial harmony," wrote C. Vann Woodward, "precarious at best and handicapped from the start by suspicion and prejudice, was another casualty of the political crisis of the 'nineties. While the movement was at the peak of zeal the two races had surprised each other and astonished their opponents by the harmony they achieved and the good will with which they

co-operated. When it became apparent that their opponents would stop at nothing to divide them, however, ... the bi-racial partnership of Populism began to dissolve in frustration and bitterness." Quoted from Woodward's *The Strange Career of Jim Crow*, p. 80.

34. Flack is mentioned only in the roll call vote for the Confederate Monument in Raleigh, which he voted against. See *History of the General Assembly*, p. 94. Flack's committee assignments during his term in the House included the Judiciary, Education, Federal Regulations and Printing Committees. Most of the bills he introduced were of a local nature, such as the "Act for the Relief of J.R. Wells, Disabled Confederate Veteran of Rutherford County," or the "Act to Establish the Commercial Bank of Rutherfordton." However, he did introduce bills of statewide import, such as an "Act to Abolish County Boards of Education." See the *Journal of the House of Representatives of the General Assembly of the State of North Carolina, at its Session of 1895*, (Winston, NC: M.I. & J.C. Stewart, Public Printers and Binders, 1895), pp. 26 ff.

35. Marion Butler Papers, #114, subseries 1.2, A. D'K. Wallace to Marion Butler, 20 May 1896 (Southern Historical Collection, Wilson Library, University of North Carolina at Chapel Hill).

36. Ibid.

37. Edmonds, p. 55.

38. *The Daily Charlotte Observer*, 8 September 1896, p. 2.

39. Advocates of "free silver" believed the unlimited coinage of silver would expand the money supply and thus help to reduce the indebtedness of cash-poor farmers. See Palmer's discussion, pp. 100–104.

40. *The Daily Charlotte Observer*, 8 September 1896, p. 2.

41. Ibid., 31 October 1896, p. 2.

42. Griffin, *History*, p. 363.

43. Ibid. Purgason (1856–1949) is sketched on p. 374.

44. *The Charlotte Daily Observer*, 7 November 1896, p. 2; Griffin, pp. 363–364. The office of coroner remained in the hands of the Populists in 1896 (won by W.A. Webb), along with the House seat won by Lindsey Purgason, though the Populist candidate for treasurer, W.O. Baber, was defeated by the Democrat C.L. Miller. A county commissioner elected in that year, S.F. Wall, was also a Populist.

45. Ibid., 2 October 1896, p. 1.

46. Ibid., 7 November 1896, p. 2.

47. Edmonds, p. 59.

48. *The Western Vindicator* (Rutherfordton), 28 April 1898, p. 3.

49. Ibid., 5 May 1898, p. 3.

50. Crow and Durden, pp. 122–125.

51. Edmonds, p. 144.

52. *The Daily Charlotte Observer*, 7 September 1898, p. 3. For a biographical sketch of Sheriff McFarland (1858–1930), see Griffin's *History*, p. 373.

53. *The Western Vindicator* (Rutherfordton), 25 August 1898, p. 4. Note: *Vindicator* dates are sometimes difficult to determine. Either many leaves from the paper were mixed up in microfilming, or the typesetter often failed to change the date from one issue to another.

54. *The Daily Charlotte Observer*, 7 September 1898, p. 3.

55. Ibid.

56. Edmonds, p. 62.

57. *The Western Vindicator* (Rutherfordton), 8 September 1898, p. 3; *The Daily Charlotte Observer*, 7 September 1898, p. 3.

58. Ibid., 27 September 1898, p. 2. Griffin, *History*, p. 364, wrote that "[the] Legislature of 1897 required the county boards of education to be appointed by the county commissioners, clerk of court and register of deeds. In compliance with this law, this group met June 7, 1897, and appointed three Republicans, W.P. Watson, A.F. Morgan and Nathan Scoggin[s]." It was this Republican board with whom the Negroes in Rutherford were at odds.

59. *The Western Vindicator* (Rutherfordton), 28 July 1898, p. 1.

60. Ibid., 4 August 1898, p. 1.

61. Ibid., 11 August 1898, p. 4. Carrier refers to Admiral William Thomas Sampson (1840–1902), commander of the North Atlantic squadron during the Spanish-American War and an expert on ordnance.

62. Ibid., p. 3.

63. Ibid., 25 August 1898, p. 3; *The Daily Charlotte Observer*, 25 August 1898, p. 3.

64. *The Daily Charlotte Observer*, 13 September 1898, p. 2.

65. Ibid.

66. *The Western Vindicator* (Rutherfordton), 8 September 1898, p. 1.

67. Ibid., 15 September 1898, p. 1.

68. Ibid., 22 September 1898, p. 1.

69. Ibid., 20 October 1898, p. 3.

70. Ibid., 25 August 1898, p. 1.

71. Ibid., 1 September 1898, p. 2.

72. Ibid., 20 October 1898, p. 1.

73. Ibid., 13 October 1898, p. 1; *The Daily Charlotte Observer*, 18 October 1898, p. 2. I assume this is the L.E. Green (1846–1920) buried at Bethel Baptist Church in Ellenboro.

74. Orr, pp. 122–126.

75. *The News and Observer* (Raleigh), 20

September 1898, p. 5; *The Daily Charlotte Observer*, 22 September 1898, p. 4. Wallace wrote to the *News and Observer*: "On the 9th of this month I carried her to Dr. Kirby, and placed her in his charge. After I had returned home and spent a sleepless night with my desolate little ones, I tried to nerve myself for the heavy duties before me by resorting to that 'fool's solace'—whisky." Mrs. Wallace died not long after this in January, 1899.

76. Ibid., 27 September 1898, p. 2; *The Western Vindicator* (Rutherfordton), 29 September 1898, p. 4.

77. *The Western Vindicator* (Rutherfordton), 29 September 1898, p. 4.

78. This can be inferred from the lack of any returns for Negro candidates in the post-election reports.

79. *The Daily Charlotte Observer*, 12 October 1898, p. 2.

80. *The Western Vindicator* (Rutherfordton), 13 October 1898, p. 3.

81. *The Daily Charlotte Observer*, 12 October 1898, p. 2.

82. Ibid. Spurlin was a Ku Kluxer. See Griffin, *History*, p. 330.

83. *The Western Vindicator* (Rutherfordton), 13 October 1898, p. 3.

84. *The Daily Charlotte Observer*, 12 October 1898, p. 2.

85. Ibid.

86. Ibid., 4 October 1898, p. 8; see also *The Western Vindicator* (Rutherfordton), 29 September 1898, p. 3.

87. *The Daily Charlotte Observer*, 5 October 1898, p. 4.

88. Ibid., 18 October 1898, p. 2.

89. Ibid.

90. *The Western Vindicator* (Rutherfordton), 20 October 1898, p. 4.

91. *The Daily Charlotte Observer*, 2 November 1898, p. 2.

92. Ibid., 10 November 1898, p. 1.

93. Ibid.

94. For discussion of the Manly editorial and white reaction, see Daniels, pp. 285–292; Gilmore, pp. 105–107; and Prather in *Democracy Betrayed*, p. 23.

95. The Wilmington Race Riot has been analyzed by many historians. H. Leon Prather's short treatment in *Democracy Betrayed*, pp. 15–41, is excellent. His *We Have Taken a City: Wilmington Racial Massacre and Coupe of 1898* (Cranbury, NJ: Associated University Presses, 1984) is the only book-length, scholarly study. *Democracy Betrayed: The Wilmington Race Riot of 1898 and Its Legacy*, ed. by Cecelski and Tyson, is a collection of essays devoted chiefly to various aspects of the riot and the era in which it took place. Other brief treatments of the Wilmington Riot and its historical context include Gilmore, pp. 108–117; Williamson's *Crucible of Race*, pp. 195–201; and Crow and Durden, pp. 129–135.

96. Alfred Moore Waddell, *Some Memories of My Life* (Raleigh: Edwards & Broughton, 1908), p. 243.

97. *The Daily Charlotte Observer*, 16 June 1900, p.1; 17 June 1900, p. 4; and 20 June 1900, p. 2.

98. Orr, p. 138.

99. Ibid., p. 139.

100. Powell, p. 438. See also Gilmore, p. 120. Orr discusses the significance of the amendment to Aycock on pages 149–156 of his biography.

101. Orr, p. 140.

102. Edmonds, pp. 199–200.

103. Ibid., p. 199; Gilmore, p. 121.

104. Edmonds, p. 205.

105. Ibid., p. 204; Orr, pp. 158–159.

106. Gilmore, p. 121.

107. Edmonds, p. 204; Orr, pp. 166–167.

108. *The Charlotte Daily Observer*, 3 July 1900, p. 2.

109. Ibid., 10 July 1900, p. 2.

110. Ibid., 14 July 1900, p. 3.

111. Ibid., 26 June 1900, p. 8; 3 July 1900, p. 2; 10 July 1900, p. 2; 15 July 1900, p. 10; 21 July 1900, p. 3; and 31 July 1900, p. 7.

112. Ibid., 28 July 1900, p. 2.

113. Ibid.

114. Ibid.

115. Ibid., 19 July 1900, p. 2.

116. Ibid., 7 August 1900, p. 7.

117. Williamson, *Crucible of Race*, pp. 201–209.

118. Ibid., p. 207.

119. William Ivy Hair's *Carnival of Fury: Robert Charles and the New Orleans Race Riot of 1900* (Baton Rouge: Louisiana State University Press, 1976) is the most important treatment of Robert Charles and the New Orleans Race Riot.

120. Powell, p. 438.

121. *The Daily Charlotte Observer*, 4 August 1900, p. 2.

3. The Forest City Lynching

1. Twelfth Census of the United States, 1900: Rutherford County, NC, Population Schedule, enumeration district 134, sheet 16, line 55 (microform).

Notes — Chapter 3

2. Rutherford County, NC, Minutes of the Superior Court, 1894–1902, 2 vols., p. 269 (microform).
3. *Charlotte Daily Observer*, 29 August 1900, p. 1.
4. Woodward, *Origins*, p. 354.
5. Williamson, p. 58.
6. Ibid., p. 50.
7. *Charlotte Daily Observer*, 29 August 1900, p. 1.
8. Rutherford County, NC, Record of Widow's Yearly Allowance, 1889–1962, vols. A–L (microform).
9. Wilson, et al., eds., *The Encyclopedia of Southern Culture*, pp. 29–31.
10. Otho Remus Flack (1877–1946) was Mills Flack's first child by his second wife Katie Harrill Flack. He was a section foreman for the Seaboard Airline Railroad for many years, and later in life became a Baptist minister. See Ivarea Flack, p. 52; and obituaries in the *Forest City Courier*, 28 February 1946, p. 5, and *The Rutherford County News* (Rutherfordton), 28 February 1946, p. 1.
11. *Charlotte Daily Observer*, 29 August 1900, p. 1.
12. Edwards, in Cecelski et al., p. 119.
13. Gilmore, pp. 102–103.
14. Gilmore, in Cecelski et al., p. 81.
15. Hair, *Carnival of Fury*, p. 14.
16. Ayers, *Vengeance & Justice*, p. 235.
17. Gilmore, in Cecelski et al., p. 81.
18. Ibid.
19. *Charlotte Daily Observer*, 31 August 1900, p. 7.
20. Ibid.
21. Ibid. I assume here that a similar article made its way into Rutherfordton and Forest City papers (now missing).
22. Ibid. Of course, if Raney Mills did not give her husband the gun with which Flack was killed, if Avery Mills "had the pistol in his pocket to kill crows," as she said, then the incident and Flack's culpability are cast in a very different light. However, it seems inconceivable that Otho Flack would have impugned the memory of Mills Flack and the family's honor unless Flack had indeed shot an unarmed man.
23. Raney Mills was pardoned by Gov. Aycock on the recommendation of the Judge in her Cleveland County trial, William S. O'Brien Robinson. See below.
24. *News and Observer* (Raleigh), 29 August 1900, p. 1.
25. Ibid.
26. Ibid.
27. *Charlotte Daily Observer*, 29 August 1900, p. 1.

28. The identity of this boy is an interesting matter for speculation. It was very likely one of Mills Flack's grandchildren, and possibly one of the sons of Andrew Braxton Flack, either Ralph R. Flack, then age fifteen, or perhaps Mays Cleveland Flack, age twelve. In his childhood memoir, Ralph R. Flack referred to himself as a "regular hoe hand" by the age of eleven or twelve. See his *Memories*, p. 3.
29. Raney Mills' affidavit, which was submitted to the Rutherford County Fall Court in November, 1900, argued that her trial be moved from Rutherford in part because of the prestige and influence of Mills Flack and his family.
30. *Charlotte Daily Observer*, 29 August 1900, p. 1.
31. In his brief biographical sketch of Mills Flack, Griffin does note that he was "murdered by a Negro." See his *History*, p. 373. However, he makes no mention of the lynching in any of his works. Nor does Washburn, who focused on the turn-of-the-century in *To Everything a Season*—though, of course, his work was principally a memoir of Rutherfordton.
32. It seems likely that the *Charlotte Daily Observer* reporter was an editor or reporter for one of the Rutherford County papers of that day, who, by some arrangement, wired reports of Rutherford news to Charlotte. In any event, Rutherford County news was a regular feature in the Charlotte paper.

Most of the other articles about the lynching which appeared in state papers are clearly based upon the *Daily Observer* story of the first day. These include: *The Charlotte News*, 29 August 1900, p. 4; *The Journal* (Winston-Salem), 29 August 1900, p. 1; the *Asheville Daily Gazette*, 29 August 1900, p. 1; *The Concord Times*, 30 August 1900, p. 2; *The Caucasian* (Raleigh), 30 August 1900, p. 3; *The Landmark* (Statesville), 31 August 1900, p. 2; *The Union Republican* (Winston-Salem), 6 September 1900, p. 4; and *The Burke County News* (Morganton), 7 September 1900, p. 3.

33. The loss of local papers is indeed unfortunate. The Rutherfordton correspondent for the *Charlotte Daily Observer* wired on September 6th, "The lynching last week is still the talk, especially with the papers. The Press editor has had all kinds of threats made against him by Forest City parties because of the editorials this and last week." See the *Charlotte Daily Observer*, 7 September 1900, p. 3. "The Press" would appear to refer to the *Rutherford Press*, a Republican paper which was succeeded by the *Rutherfordton Tribune* in 1901.
34. J. Cicero Greene (1865–1935?) founded the Forest City Ledger about 1889, and served

several terms as Mayor of Forest City in the 1890s. See Griffin's sketch, *History*, pp. 577–578. *The Western Vindicator*, 5 May 1898, p. 3, carried an advertisement for "Julius C. Green, Funeral Director." In an unpublished manuscript (HFC), Ralph R. Flack stated that "Green must have been the first person to sell caskets in Forest City. He played the organ at the Methodist Church for a long time."

35. *Charlotte Daily Observer*, 29 August 1900, p. 1. The original bill of complaint and warrant survive in Rutherford County, NC, Criminal Action Papers, 086.326.1 (NC Office of Archives and History, Raleigh, NC).

36. Sam Hamrick (1849–?), occupation "Police Chief," can be found in the Twelfth Census of the United States: Rutherford County, NC, enumeration district 134, sheet 16, line 84 (microform).

37. William C. Hardin (1866?–1937) spent most of his career in law enforcement in Rutherford County. He was the County Sheriff from 1924–1930. See Griffin's sketch, *History*, pp. 511–512.

38. *Charlotte Daily Observer*, 29 August 1900, p. 1.

39. Ibid.

40. Elijah A. Martin (1856–1928) was Rutherford County Sheriff from 1898–1908. See Griffin's sketch, *History*, p. 376.

41. James D. Justice (ca. 1864–?), occupation surveyor, can be located in the Thirteenth Census of the United States, 1910: Rutherford County, NC, Population Schedule, enumeration district 142, sheet 1, line 79 (microform).

42. *Charlotte Daily Observer*, 29 August 1900, p. 1.

43. Op. cit., Superior Court Minutes, p. 269.

44. According to Griffin, Forest City's population was 1090 in 1900. See his *History*, p. 380.

45. *Charlotte Daily Observer*, 29 August 1900, p. 1.

46. O. Carson Erwin (1873–ca. 1942) was a surveyor, but distinguished himself by taking an active part in politics and civic affairs throughout his life. See Griffin's sketch, *History*, pp. 509–510.

47. *Charlotte Daily Observer*, 29 August 1900, p. 1.

48. The scene is, of course, the author's conjecture.

49. *Charlotte Daily Observer*, 29 August 1900, p. 1.

50. Charles Z. Flack, Sr., unpublished manuscript, ca. 1985 (HFC).

51. Op. cit., Superior Court Minutes, p. 269.

52. *Charlotte Daily Observer*, 29 August 1900, p. 1.

53. Ibid. Most of North Carolina's thirty-three lynchings during the period studied (1888–1906) by Walter Samuel Lockhart were hangings, though he did identify eight events in which victims were dispatched by gunshot and an additional three which combined hanging and bullets. See Lockhart, p. 32.

54. Ibid.

55. Ibid.

56. Tolnay and Beck demonstrate that August was the peak month for lynchings which occurred in the South during the period 1882–1930. See Tolnay and Beck, p. 33. However, though this was true for the South generally, Lockhart identified March and September as the peak months for lynchings in North Carolina. See Lockhart, p. 22.

57. Jacquelyn Dowd Hall, p. 140.

58. Brundage, *Lynching in the New South*, p. 73.

59. Ibid., pp. 36 ff.

60. Ibid., pp. 40–41.

61. Lockhart, p. 26; Brundage, *Lynching in the New South*, p. 37.

62. Lockhart, p. 32.

63. Jacquelyn Dowd Hall, p. 140.

64. Brundage, *Lynching in the New South*, p. 36.

65. Jacquelyn Dowd Hall, p. 140.

66. Roberta Senechal de la Roche, "The Sociogenesis of Lynching," in Brundage, ed., *Under Sentence of Death*, pp. 48–76. See also Brundage, *Lynching in the New South*, p. 37.

67. Senechal de la Roche, pp. 52 ff.

68. I borrow the metaphor Huber uses in his fine case study of the Chatham County lynchings of 1885. See Patrick J. Huber, "'Caught Up in the Violent Whirlwind of Lynching': The 1885 Quadruple Lynching in Chatham County, North Carolina," *The North Carolina Historical Review*, 75 (April 1998), pp. 135–160.

69. I refer to Bryan's famous speech at the 1896 Democratic Convention.

70. Brundage, *Lynching in the New South*, p. 48.

71. Ibid., p. 76.

72. Ibid., pp. 41 ff.

73. Even in the photograph, a blanket, which was probably used to cover the body, lies next to it.

74. *Charlotte Daily Observer*, 31 August 1900, p. 7.

75. Trelease, p. 341.

76. This was the typical black response after a "mass mob" lynching. See Brundage, *Lynching in the New South*, pp. 47 ff.

77. *Charlotte Daily Observer*, 31 August 1900, p. 7.

78. Ibid.
79. Ibid.
80. Ibid., 29 August 1900, p. 1.
81. Ibid., 31 August 1900, p. 7.
82. Lockhart, p. 29.
83. Williamson, p. 126.
84. Thomas J. Shaw (1861–?), a native of Montgomery County, NC, moved to Greensboro in 1893, where he practiced law with A.M. Scales until his election as Superior Court Judge in 1899. He served in that capacity until 1907. For a brief biography, see *North Carolina: Rebuilding an Ancient Commonwealth*, vol. III (New York: The American Historical Society, Inc., 1928), pp. 6–7.
85. *Charlotte Daily Observer*, 19 November 1900, p. 3.
86. Charles Z. Flack, Sr., unpublished manuscript, ca. 1985 (HFC). However, as records for the Town of Forest City are missing for this period, it is impossible to document the issuance of warrants—see Griffin, *Essays*, p. 157.
87. *Charlotte Daily Observer*, 29 August, 1900, p. 1. See also Brundage, *Lynching in the New South*, p. 44. The coroner was Perry H. Hardin (1848–1925). He is mentioned in Griffin's *History*, pp. 353, 362 and 365.
88. *News and Observer* (Raleigh), 29 August 1900, p. 1.
89. Brundage, *Lynching in the New South*, p. 37.
90. Nelda Maxwell, granddaughter of Mills Flack, in a letter to the author (25 April 1998) wrote, "I believe it is pretty accurate to say that Lee Flack, oldest child of Mills' first marriage, and Otho Flack, oldest child of his second marriage[,] were 'out of town' for a while." However, Lee Roswell Flack (1860–1904) seems an unlikely participant because he resided in Shelby, according to the U.S. Census taken in June, 1900. See Twelfth Census of the United States, 1900: Cleveland County, NC, Population Schedule, enumeration district 56, sheet 11, line 79 (microform). Of course, it is possible that he was in Forest City the day of the incident, and court records do show that he was out-of-state (in Maryland?, the hand is difficult to read) by January, 1901. See op. cit., Special Proceedings, p. 210. On the other hand, Lee Roswell may have been elsewhere for work. The headquarters of the sewing machine business with which he was associated was in Washington, D.C. (he was there when he died in 1904). See *The Sun* (Rutherfordton), 28 July 1904, p. 5.

Otho Flack's (1877–1946) participation was more likely—perhaps his feelings of guilt spurred the day-after confessional that his father had shot Avery Mills first. Moreover, the court records indicate that he also lived out-of-state (again, in Maryland?) in January, 1901. See op. cit., Special Proceedings, p. 210. Of course, it is also possible that work had led him to leave the county.

In an earlier letter written by Ms. Maxwell to Helen Flack Cole (10 May 1985), the former indicated that her mother, Chinara Flack Wilson, never admitted that *any* of Mills Flacks' sons participated in the lynching, and suggested that they left town "only [because] the finger of suspicion pointed to them." However, since we know that the lynching occurred in broad daylight in the presence of law enforcement officers (something Ms. Maxwell never knew), we can only conclude that if any of the Flack boys left town, it was indeed because they numbered among the murderers of Avery Mills.

The executor of Flack's estate was his eldest son, Andrew Braxton Flack (1862–1948), who was employed by the County as a tax collector. In a 23 April 1985 letter to Helen Flack Cole, Charles Z. Flack, Sr. indicated that Andrew B. Flack was in the Golden Valley section collecting taxes on the day of Mills Flack's death. This, combined with the fact that he had signed an administrator's bond for Flack's estate on September 19th, just three weeks after the lynching, would indicate that he could not have been party to the mob. See the administrator's bond in Rutherford County, NC, Record of Administrators, 1896–1913, vol. 1, pp. 118–119 (microform).

However, in the same letter of 1985, Charles Z. Flack, Sr. recalled that another son of Mills H. Flack, Posey Maggie Flack (1875–1932), *did* participate in the lynching. The U.S. Census of 1900 indicates that Posey and his wife Gaetana resided in Cool Springs Township, Forest City, in June, 1900. See the Twelfth Census of the United States, 1900: Rutherford County, NC, Population Schedule, enumeration district 134, sheet 16, line 35 (microform). By January, 1901, he lived in South Carolina—again, work is an alternative explanation. See op. cit., Special Proceedings, p. 210.

Helen Flack Cole remembered that Logan ("Log") A. Moore (1868–1913), a brother-and-law of her mother, Emma Harrill Flack, was involved in the lynching. However, as Moore co-signed the administrator's bond for Mills Flack's estate with Andrew Braxton Flack, it seems unlikely that he was involved.

Of course, the story that participants in the lynch mob were forced to leave the County could be apocryphal. As indicated above, Lockhart's research on North Carolina lynchings found that criminal investigations were rare—

certainly white lynch mobs during the Radical era typically had little to fear from the authorities. However, the persistence of the story in family memory (supported by the account of the hardships of Katie Flack and her daughters left by themselves to tend the farm) would suggest that it has some basis in fact.

At least one other son of Mills Flack could have participated in the lynching. This was Samuel Mills Flack (1868–1942). The U.S. Census of 1900 indicates that he and his family resided in Cool Springs Township, Forest City, in June, 1900. See the Twelfth Census of the United States, 1900: Rutherford County, NC, Population Schedule, enumeration district 134, sheet 5, line 5 (microform). However, he was not among the Flack boys who were out-of-state in January, 1901. See op. cit., Special Proceedings, p. 210.

91. Information in a letter to the author from Ms. Nelda Wilson Maxwell, 25 April 1998.

92. Ibid.

93. Op. cit., Special Proceedings, p. 209. See also *The Rutherfordton Tribune*, 29 August 1901, p. 3.

94. *The Rutherfordton Tribune*, 29 August 1901, p. 3.

95. Op. cit., Special Proceedings, pp. 212–213.

96. Rutherford County, NC, Record of Estate Settlements, 1868–1920, vol. A, pp. 418–419 (microform). See also op. cit., Special Proceedings, pp. 213–214.

97. *Charlotte Daily Observer*, 29 August 1900, p. 1.

98. Ibid., 29 August 1900, p. 1.

99. Ibid., 2 September 1900, p. 8. The County Commissioners minutes of September 27, 1900, record payment for guarding Raney Mills for two nights. See Rutherford County, NC, Minutes, Board of County Commissioners, 1900–1901, p. 354 (microform).

100. *The Landmark* (Statesville), 4 September 1900, p. 3.

101. Op. cit., Superior Court Minutes, p. 269; op. cit., Board of County Commissioners, pp. 354, 357.

Raney Mills' court affidavit stated "that the authorities of said Rutherford County, sent her to McDowell County, where she remained a month...." It is not clear, but it seems likely that she gave birth to her second child there. The County Commissioners' minutes of September 27th record Sheriff E.A. Martin's reimbursement for conveying a "negro, to Marion jail," and the minutes of October 1st record payment to the Sheriff for "bringing Raney Mills from Marion."

102. Ibid., p. 357.

103. As with the scene of the lynching, this is the author's conjecture.

104. Op. cit., Superior Court Minutes, p. 209.

105. Ibid., pp. 268–270. This affidavit can also be found in op. cit., Criminal Action Papers, 086.326.1.

106. Ibid., pp. 244–245.

107. Ibid., pp. 269–270.

108. Ibid., pp. 244–245.

109. Ibid., p. 245.

110. Huber, pp. 135–136.

111. Cleveland County, NC, Minutes, Superior Court, Criminal, 1900–1906, vol. 4, p. 52 (microform).

112. *The Rutherfordton Tribune*, 8 May 1901, p. 3.

113. William S. O'Brien Robinson (1852–1927) served as Superior Court judge from 1894–1902. He was a Republican from Wayne County, as was Aycock. See *History of North Carolina: North Carolina Biography*, vol. VI (Chicago: The Lewis Publishing Co., 1919), p. 262, for a brief biographical sketch.

114. Pardons, Daniel L. Russell to Charles B. Aycock, 1899–1902, G.O. 48, p. 125 (NC Office of Archives and History, Raleigh, NC).

115. Reasons for Pardons, Charles B. Aycock to Robert B. Glenn, 1901–1907, G.O. 53, p. 22, no. 25 (NC Office of Archives and History, Raleigh, NC).

116. Op. cit., *North Carolina Biography*, p. 262.

117. See Daniels, p. 477.

118. Quoted in R.D.W. Conner, *The Life and Speeches of Charles Brantley Aycock* (Garden City, NY: Doubleday, Page & Co., 1912), p. 102.

119. Orr, p. 272.

120. Ibid.

121. Ibid., pp. 273, 277.

122. Conner, p. 100.

123. Orr, p. 119.

4. Epilog: Dishonor

1. Interview with Ms. Helen Flack Cole, 25 April 1998. Examination of Ralph R. Flack's personal papers also turned up no references to circumstances of the death of Mills H. Flack—despite the fact that Ralph Flack compiled a memoir of his childhood and youth which circumscribes the period in question and includes much on turn-of- the-century Forest City.

2. Information in a letter to Ms. Helen Flack Cole from Charles Z. Flack, Sr., 23 April 1985.

3. Information in a letter to Ms. Helen Flack Cole from Ms. Nelda Wilson Maxwell, 12 September 1989.
4. *The Forest City Courier*, 28 February 1946, p. 5; *The Rutherford County News*, 28 February 1946, p. 1; Ivarea Flack, p. 52
5. Interview with Ms. Helen Flack Cole, 1998.
6. For analysis of the emergence of the "Bible Belt," see Williamson's analysis, *Crucible of Race*, pp. 310–317.
7. Information in a letter to the author from Ms. Nelda Wilson Maxwell, 25 April 1998.
8. *Charlotte Daily Observer*, 29 August 1900, p. 1; *Charlotte Daily Observer*, 31 August 1900, p. 7.
9. Ibid., 31 August 1900, p. 7.
10. Brundage, p. 70.
11. Dickson D. Bruce, Jr., *Violence and Culture in the Antebellum South* (Austin, TX: University of Texas Press, 1979), p. 91.
12. *Charlotte Daily Observer*, 7 September 1900, p. 3. Griffin states that the *Press* became the *Tribune* in January, 1900, but I believe the correct date is January, 1901. See Griffin, *History*, p. 567.
13. *Charlotte Daily Observer*, 2 September 1900, p. 8; op. cit., Superior Court Minutes, pp. 244–245, 268–271.
14. Wyatt-Brown, p. 64.
15. Ralph R. Flack, unpublished manuscript, 1968 (HFC).
16. Wyatt-Brown, pp. 66–67.
17. Clipping, Ralph R. Flack Papers (HFC); *The Sun* (Rutherfordton), 28 July 1904, p. 5; Griffin, *Essays*, p. 158.
18. Griffin, *History*, p. 602; Griffin, *Essays*, p. 159.
19. I recognize that I have removed this scene from the context of meaning which Dickey was really trying to communicate in *Deliverance* (Boston: Houghton Mifflin, 1970), which is the problem of "authenticity" or "identity." Also, I do not in any way mean to suggest sympathy for the "crackers." I have merely attempted an allegory on the silence of justice for African-Americans during the lynching era.

But there is a way to use *Deliverance* to understand the depths of the grip that existence had upon Avery Mills. *Deliverance* is about deliverance from an identity shaped by the world to an identity shaped by the self (a generative or creative identity). But the achievement of a generative identity necessitates "heroism." Dickey's protagonist, Ed Gentry, is caught in the soulless grip of middle-class suburban materialism, which, rather than challenging us to heroism, tends to deaden us to the pursuit of it. But meeting the challenges of being "set upon" by ruthless men in an exceedingly wild and unpredictable natural circumstance ultimately has the effect of lifting Ed Gentry from his "somnambulance" and helping him to restore a measure of purpose and meaning to his life — at the end of the book, he has renewed his avocation as an artist.

The hold of the world upon Avery Mills is altogether more extreme, however, compounded by poverty, the peonage system of tenancy, and of course race. His existence was hardly better than that of his ancestors in bondage — and perhaps made even worse by the expectation of so-called freedom. Few men could have found authenticity in the face of such circumstance. The shooting of Mills H. Flack in a pointless argument over the ownership of some fruit, became perhaps, in a very real sense, Avery's final, desperate and quite hopeless act in a quest for meaning which could bear *no* fruit.

20. Goodwyn, p. 294.
21. Ibid., pp. 317–320.

Appendix VI. Research

1. Secretary of State, NC, Land Grant Office, Warrants, Plats, etc., Mecklenburg County, shuck no. 099 (microform). A warrant was issued and the land was surveyed, but the land was not granted as surveyed. It seems probable, however, that much of this same survey tract *was* granted to Flack in 1775 as part of the State grant of that year; the survey (made in 1774) for that grant refers to "his own improvement," suggesting he was living on this land before the grant was made, and the surveys of both 1768 and 1774 refer to the lands of Givens and Smart. See Secretary of State, NC, Land Grant Office, Warrants, Plats, etc., Tryon County, shuck no. 1245 (microform).
2. Tryon County, NC, Record of Deeds, 1769–1778, 4 vols. See vol. 1, pp. 103–105 (microform).
3. Griffin, *History*, pp. 83 ff. In his capacity as a j.p., Flack appears frequently in the Rutherford Court records of the 1780s and early 1790s.
4. I have found no *primary* source documentation for familial relationships between any of the Flack men who settled in Rutherford and Guilford. Thus, in the remainder of this paper, I have used quotation marks where stating relationships between the putative Flack brothers/cousins.

5. See D.W. Crawford, "Genealogy of the Flack Families in State and County," *Forest City Courier*, 8 September 1927, p. 1; and "Large Crowd Attends the Flack Reunion at Chimney Rock Thurs.," *The Rutherford County News*, 8 September 1927, p. 7. The name Jefferson must be incorrect, for, as a first name, Jefferson probably did not come into common use until the late 18th or early 19th century — I presume in honor of Thomas Jefferson. A son of Andrew Flack (1775–ca. 1865), the eldest son of John Flack, was named John Jefferson Flack (1807–1890). See Ivarea Flack, p. 64. Also see Horace E. Flack, p. 1.

6. Crawford wrote as follows: "The first Flacks to come to this country came from Northern Ireland about the year 1769. This party consisted of four brothers and two cousins. One of the cousins settled in New York and the other in Pennsylvania. The four brothers came to North Carolina...." Legrand A. Flack also identified a cousin who went to Pennsylvania, probably following Crawford (manuscript note in Ralph R. Flack Papers (HFC)). This tradition is also consistent with Ramsey's view, following McLanahan, that "the Scotch-Irish migrated as families." See Robert W. Ramsey, *Carolina Cradle: Settlement of the Northwest Carolina Frontier, 1747–1762* (Chapel Hill: The University of North Carolina Press, 1964), pp. 191–192.

7. Horace Flack, p. 3.

8. Historical Society of Pennsylvania, *Abstracts of Bucks County, Pennsylvania Wills, 1785–1825* (Westminster, MD: Family Line Publications, 1998), p. 90. See also the Flack Family Genealogy Forum, post by Marie Forehan. http://www.genforum.genealogy.com/flack/messages/135.html (1 May 2002).

9. Ivarea Flack, p. [1].

10. *Bucks County Wills*, p. 90.

11. Op. cit., Forehan post; Terry A. McNealy and Frances Wise Waite, compilers, *Bucks County Tax Records 1693–1778* (Doylestown, PA: Bucks County Genealogical Society, 1982), p. 78.

12. Op. cit., Forehan post.

13. See Ivarea Flack, pp. 114 ff., for information on these old men of the Flack Clan in 1927.

14. This is attributable to their scant examination of Guilford records, which apparently went no further than the 1790 census for that county — where Andrew Flack was the only head of household named Flack. See Dept. of Commerce and Labor, Bureau of the Census, *Heads of Families at the First Census of the United States Taken in the Year 1790, North Carolina* (Washington, DC: Government Printing Office, 1908), p. 152. The relationship between Thomas and Andrew Flack of Guilford can be inferred from the wills of Elisha and Jane McQuiston Flack. See Guilford County, NC, Record of Wills, 1771–1859, vol. A, files 0123 & 0124 (microform).

15. Walter Clark, collector and editor, *The State Records of North Carolina, vol. XXII. Miscellaneous*. (Wilmington, NC: Broadfoot Publishing Company, 1994), pp. 379–380.

16. Presumably, Andrew Hampton's son, Jonathan Hampton, was born at Dutchman's Creek, near the Catawba River (then Anson County), in 1751; land transactions and the diary of Moravian Bishop Spangenburg clearly place an Andrew Hampton there at this time. However, his activity in the militia as well as land transactions suggest that Andrew Hampton of Granville remained in that place well into the 1760s. The identification of Andrew Hampton of Granville with Andrew Hampton of Anson/Mecklenburg/Tryon/Rutherford seems to be based upon the observation that both "signed [their] name as Andw Hampton with a raised 'w'." See Carolyn Parker Maurice, *The Hampton Family: The History and Genealogy of Some of the Descendants of the Immigrant John Hamton who Migrated From New Jersey to Maryland to North Carolina to Kentucky to Illinois to Kansas to Indian Territory, Oklahoma* (Placitas, New Mexico: the author, 1993), pp. 7 ff., and Col. Robert B. Cox's notes in the same, p. 6 (discontinuous pagination).

17. *1755 Granville County, North Carolina Tax List, North Carolina Tax Series* (Signal Mountain, TN: Mountain Press, nd), p. 4.

18. Weynette Parks Haun, *Johnston County, North Carolina Land Warrants, Surveys & Miscellaneous Land Papers (Secretary of State Papers), 1737–1899* (Durham, NC: the author, 1993), pp. 34–35; also in Margaret M. Hoffman, *The Granville District of North Carolina: Abstracts of Miscellaneous Land Office Records*, vol. 5 (N.p.: the author, 1995), p. 53.

19. Brent Holcomb, *Anson County, NC Deed Abstracts, vol. II: 1757–1766 & 1763 Tax List* ([Clinton, SC]: the author, 1975), pp. 87–88.

20. Ibid., p. 63; *1763 Anson County, North Carolina Tax List, North Carolina Tax Series* (Signal Mountain, TN: Mountain Press, nd), p. 3.

21. Walter Clark, collector and editor, *The State Records of North Carolina, vol. XI, Miscellaneous* (Wilmington, NC: Broadfoot Publishing Company, 1993), p. 655.

22. See the Flake Family Genealogy Forum, post by D. Ellerton. http://www.genforum.genealogy.com/flake/messages/ 241.html (1 May 2002).

23. General William Alexander Smith and W. Thomas Smith, compilers, *Family Tree Book*

Notes — Appendix VI

Genealogical and Biographical: Listing the Relatives of General William Alexander Smith and W. Thomas Smith. Data for The Flake Tables gathered by Mrs. Julia Flake Burns and by Osmer D. Flake (Los Angeles: W. Thomas Smith, 1922), pp. 48, 145–148.

24. May Wilson McBee, *Anson County, North Carolina, Abstracts of Early Records, vol. 1* (N.p.: the author, 1950), pp. 24–25.

25. Weynette Parks Haun, *North Carolina Revolutionary Army Accounts: Secretary of State, Treasurer's & Comptroller's Papers, Journal "A", (Public Accounts) 1775–1776* (Durham, NC: the author, 1988), p. 101.

26. Walter Clark, collector and editor, *The State Records of North Carolina, vol. XIII* (Wilmington, NC: Broadfoot Publishing Company, 1993), pp. 150–151, 158–159.

27. Op. cit., Smith and Smith, pp. 147–148.

28. See the Flake Family Genealogy Forum, post by William F. Joiner. http://www.genforum.genealogy.com/flake/messages/179.html (1 May 2002).

29. Thomas Flack's indenture for a grant from Lord Granville of 181 acres "on both sides of the Walnut Branch" is dated 21 December 1761 and was recorded in the Rowan County Clerk's office on 22 July 1762. See Secretary of State, NC, Granville Proprietary Land Office, Warrants, Surveys, 1748–1763, Pasquotank County, Ma through Rowan, Hu (microform); Secretary of State, NC, Granville Land Grants, Box 118-B (microform); and Rowan County, NC, Record of Deeds, Book 4, pp. 781–783 (microform).

Rankin stated that there were 481 acres in the tract, but the grant itself and the subsequent sale of the land to John Chambers in 1773 establish that Flack's grant was for but 181 acres, well below the typical Granville parcel of 640. See Guilford County, NC, Record of Deeds, 1771–1784 (vols. 1–3), vol. 1, pp. 214–215 (microform).

30. Secretary of State, NC, Land Grant Office, Warrants, Plats, etc., Guilford County, shuck no. 789 (microform).

31. Rowan County, NC, Index to Real Estate Conveyances— Grantees, 1753–1921, vol. E–K, p. 573 (microform).

32. The Rev. S.M. Rankin, *History of Buffalo Presbyterian Church and Her People* (Greensboro, NC: Jos. J. Stone & Company, nd), p. 35.

33. Rankin, pp. 10–11, 14–15, 38, 113–114. For information on David Caldwell, see also Ethel Stephens Arnett, *David Caldwell* (Greensboro, NC: Media, Inc., Printers and Publishers, 1976); and Eli W. Caruthers, *A Sketch of the Life and Character of the Rev. David Caldwell, D.D.* (Greensborough, NC: Swaim and Sherwood, 1842).

34. Leona Bean McQuiston, compiler, *The McQuiston, McCuiston and McQuesten Families, 1620–1937* (Louisville, KY: The Standard Press, 1937), pp. 176–177.

35. See Dr. Albert H. Gerberich and Dr. Gaius M. Brumbaugh, *Lancaster County, Pennsylvania, Tax Lists, 1751, 1756, 1757, 1758* (Washington, DC: The National Genealogical Society, 1933), p. 17; Gary T. Hawbaker and Clyde L. Goff, *A New Index: Lancaster County, Pennsylvania, Before the Federal Census, vol. I, Index to the 1780 Tax Records* (Hershey, PA: n.p., 1981), pp. 21–22; Gary T. Hawbaker and Clyde L. Goff, *A New Index: Lancaster County, Pennsylvania, Before the Federal Census, vol. II, Index to the 1780 Tax Records* (Hershey, PA: n.p., 1982), p. 23; Gary T. Hawbaker and Clyde L. Goff, *A New Index: Lancaster County, Pennsylvania, Before the Federal Census, vol. III, Index to the 1750 Tax Records* (Hershey, PA: n.p., 1982), p. 32; and Gary T. Hawbaker and Clyde L. Goff, *A New Index: Lancaster County, Pennsylvania, Before the Federal Census, vol. V, Index to the 1770 Tax Records* (Hershey, PA: n.p., 1989), p. 52.

36. Lancaster County Land Warrant Map, photocopy showing location of the lands of John Fleck in Drumore Township (Lancaster County Historical Society); Lancaster County, Pennsylvania, Deed Book WW, p. 237.

37. Lancaster County, Pennsylvania, Drumore Township Tax Lists, 1757–1780; Hawbaker and Goff, vol. III, p. 32; and Gerberich and Brumbaugh, p. 17.

38. Lancaster County, Pennsylvania, Drumore Tax List, 1757; Gerberich and Brumbaugh, p. 17.

39. Op. cit., Lancaster County Land Warrant Map, showing location of the lands of John Fleck and James Porter in Drumore Township (Lancaster County Historical Society).

40. Lancaster County, Pennsylvania, Drumore Township Tax List, 1759.

41. Op. cit., Lancaster County, Pennsylvania, Deed Book WW, pp. 236–238.

42. Ramsey, see map opposite p. 28.

43. McQuiston, pp. 318–330.

44. Ibid., pp. 323–324.

45. Gary T. Hawbaker, editor, *Lancaster County, Pennsylvania Quarter Sessions Abstracts (1729–1742), Book 1* (Hershey, PA: the author, 1986), p. 40.

46. Little Britain was created from Drumore in 1738. See map in R. Thomas Mayhill, compiler, *Lancaster County Pennsylvania Deed Abstracts & Revolutionary War Oaths of Allegiance*, rev. and enlarged ed., Deed Books A through M, 1729 through c1770 with adjoining Landowners & Witnesses (Knightstown, Ind.: The Bookmark, 1988), p. ix.

47. Hawbaker, *Lancaster Quarter Sessions*, p. 90.
48. McQuiston, pp. 178–180.
49. Ibid., pp. 178–179.
50. Ibid., p. 180.
51. Ibid., p. 182.
52. For example, see Powell's *North Carolina Through Four Centuries*, p. 156, for a brief treatment of the Fanning episode.
53. William L. Saunders, ed., *The Colonial Records of North Carolina, vol. VIII, 1769 to 1771* (Raleigh, NC: Josephus Daniels, Printer to the State, 1890), p. 260.
54. Ibid., pp. 521–522.
55. Thomas Flack is named in E.O. Jones' "'List of Participants in the Battle of Alamance' from 'The War of the Regulators, It's Place in History,'" Thesis, University of North Carolina 1942, p. 6.
56. See Fred Hughes, *Guilford County: A Map Supplement* (Jamestown, NC: The Custom House, 1988), pp. 110–111; and Haun, *Journal "A"*, pp. 63–77.
57. Haun, op. cit. Charles D. Rodenbough, writing on Col. Martin, stated, "[The] Guilford troops arrived at Moore's Creek after the battle and were involved only in rounding up prisoners." See William S. Powell, ed., *Dictionary of North Carolina Biography*, vol. 4, L–O (Chapel Hill, NC: The University of North Carolina Press, 1991), p. 226. However, Moss says "[Martin's] name appears on Caswell's list as a *participant* in the battle of Moores Creek Bridge." See Bobby Gilmer Moss, *Roster of the Patriots in the Battle of Moores Creek Bridge* (Blacksburg, SC: Scotia-Hibernia Press, 1992), p. 135, emphasis added.
58. Robert Wilson Account Books, #1896, series 1, vol. 1, pp. 302, 328, 331, 345, 349, 363, 396, 413, 436; and vol. 2, p. 190 (Southern Historical Collection, Wilson Library, University of North Carolina at Chapel Hill).
59. Ibid., vol. 2, p. 190.
60. Op. cit., Guilford shuck no. 789. Thomas Flack's original Granville application had been for 700 acres, and yet he received only 181 (see note 29), perhaps because of conflicting claims. The Granville land grant office closed at the death of the second Lord Granville in 1763 (and was still closed at the time he sold the original tract in 1773). I think it is probable that the mill was established (and Flack lived) upon lands which were applied for but not received as part of the original grant and remained either unclaimed or in dispute. The State confiscated the Granville lands in 1776, and soon after the State land offices opened in 1778 Thomas Flack's widow claimed the land.

61. Guilford Deeds, vol. 3, pp. 121–122. It's also quite possible that Thomas Flack lost his life in Griffith Rutherford's expedition against the Cherokee during the summer of 1776. Col. James Martin, Flack's commander, raised a militia force of some 4000 men for this purpose. See op. cit., *North Carolina Biography*, p. 226. In addition, there were Tory disturbances in Guilford in 1776 and 1777. See Earl Milton Wheeler, "The Role of the North Carolina Militia in the Beginning of the American Revolution," Diss. Tulane University 1969, p. 198; and Mary Elinor Lazenby, comp., *Catawba Frontier, 1775–1781: Memories of Pensioners* (Washington, DC: the author, 1950), p. 74.
62. Guilford Deeds, vol. 1, pp. 214–215. Ramsey (p. 125) identifies the fairly common Scots-Irish name of Chambers with Derry Township, Lancaster County, Pennsylvania. It's also worth noting that the 1764 will of one John Chambers of Orange County, New York, was witnessed by "John Flack of Orange Co., labourer" and a Sarah Flack. See Berthold Fernow, compiler and editor, *Calender of Wills [of the State of New York]: On File and Recorded in the Offices of the Clerk of the Court of Appeals, of the County Clerk at Albany, and of the Secretary of State* (Baltimore: Clearfield Company, Inc., 1999), p. 72. There were significant Scots-Irish settlements in Ulster and Orange counties by the mid-18th century, and records there need to be researched for evidence of Flacks—especially in light of the Crawford tradition that a Flack cousin went to New York.
63. Rankin, p. 35.
64. Guilford Deeds, vol. 1, pp. 121–122.
65. Dr. A.B. Pruitt, *Abstracts of Land Entrys (sic): Guilford Co., NC, 1779–1796, and Rockingham Co., NC, 1790–1795* (N.p.: n.p., 1987), p. 7.
66. Tryon Deeds, vol. 1, pp. 119–120. The purchase from Givens was preceded by an application for a grant which was never issued. See note 1. This transaction is included in Brent Holcomb, *Deed Abstracts of Tryon, Lincoln, & Rutherford Counties, N.C.: 1769–1786, and, Tryon County, N.C. Wills & Estates* (Greenville, SC: Southern Historical Press, Inc., 1997), p. 49.
67. Secretary of State, NC, Land Grant Record Books, vol. 26, p. 197 (microform). Descendants of William Flack still possess the original grant, which was reproduced in facsimile in Ivarea Flack, facing p. 112.
68. Rutherford County, NC, Minutes, Court of Pleas & Quarter Sessions, October Court, 1792, unpag.
69. Ralph R. Flack Papers, Box VIII, Book 47; Ivarea Flack, p. 118.

70. The Draper Manuscripts, King's Mountain Papers, Series DD, vol. 7, #108, W.L. Twitty to Lyman Draper, 3 February 1881 (microform).

71. Weynette Parks Haun, *North Carolina Revolutionary Army Accounts, Book A [Treasurer, State] [Part XII]* (Durham, NC: the author, 1999), p. 1667.

72. In the 1800 Rutherford census the household of William Flack has one male in the 45 and over category—it is my assumption that this is the "brother" of John Flack. There is no William Flack household in the 1810 census.

73. Tryon Deeds, vol. 1, pp. 103–105. Also in Holcomb, *Deed Abstracts*, p. 88. John Flack's tract was originally granted to a John Bennit or Bennet in 1768. A beautiful plat of this tract survives in op. cit., Mecklenburg shuck no. 2546.

74. In his excellent study, Dr. Horace E. Flack (pp. 4–5) stated, "John Flack, evidently received a grant of land on Camp Creek, possibly at the same time his brother, William, did, for there is on record in the Register of Deeds office of Rutherford County two deeds from John Flack, December 15, 1784, to John Anderson, of Guilford County, conveying two tracts of land on the South fork of Camp Creek, containing 250 and 100 acres respectively ... though there is apparently no record in the Register of Deeds office here showing where or how he acquired said lands." The Anderson deeds can be found in Rutherford County, NC, Record of Deeds, 1779–1793, vol. C, pp. 315–316 (microform).

However, Horace Flack erred in his assertion that there was no record of the purchase of these lands in the Register of Deeds office, for these are clearly the same two tracts which Flack had bought barely a year earlier (December, 1783) from William Dunn of Georgia. Flack's error is all the more puzzling because he was aware of the Dunn tracts and even used them (again, erroneously) in an effort to show that John Flack had received a grant on Camp Creek prior to his purchase of the Catheys Creek tract in 1778. "There is ample confirmation for this," he wrote (p. 4) "in a deed from William Dunn of Georgia, dated December 10, 1783, of a tract of land containing 100 acres ... the said tract beginning at the West side of his own (John Flack's) line. But "his own" refers to the grantor (i.e., Dunn), not the grantee (Flack). The Dunn conveyances can be found in Rutherford Deeds, vol. 4–6, pp. 74–75. The Dunn tracts probably were near those of William Flack, however, because a William Dunn was a chainbearer for the 224 acre tract surveyed for William Flack in 1774. See Tryon shuck no. 1245.

Nonetheless, Horace Flack wrote (p. 4) that he "remember[ed] distinctly having seen [grants to John Flack] with wax seals attached," but that they were either lost or destroyed after being given to attorneys, and before entirely dismissing a man of such renown brilliance (a Johns Hopkins educated political scientist of some note), I would be remiss if I did not acknowledge one piece of inconclusive evidence for John Flack in Tryon County before 1778. This also is contained in the 1774 survey for the 224 acre tract awarded to William Flack. Therein the surveyor refers to "a stake in Givens line thence with *his* line and Flack's line (emphasis added)." Now, when the surveyor used the term *his*, did he mean Givens or William Flack? He clearly did use the adjective *his* to refer to William Flack when he alluded to "his own improvement," and if he also meant William Flack in the former quote, then "Flack's line" must refer to the property of another Flack—almost certainly John Flack. However, I am by no means convinced that the surveyor was consistent in his usage.

75. Jo White Linn, transcriber, *Rowan County, North Carolina, Tax Lists, 1757–1800: Annotated Transcriptions* (Salisbury, NC: published privately, 1995), p. 97. In his valuable *Revolutionary Incidents: and Sketches of Character, Chiefly in the "Old North State"* (Philadelphia: Hayes & Zell, 1854), p. 371, the Rev. E.W. Caruthers writes of "Samuel Clarke, whose sons appear to have been all decided Whigs ... and located himself on Deep river, a few miles above Bell's mill." This is certainly the same household in which we find John "Fleck" in 1768. In Rutherford records, there are several instances where John Flack's surname is spelled Fleck.

76. The Granville Grants of both Flack and Clark or Clarke are identified on Fred Hughes' "historical" map of Guilford County, though Thomas Flack is misidentified as William Flack. There is no evidence that anyone named William Flack received a grant from Lord Granville or lived in Guilford County in the 18th century. See Fred Hughes, *Guilford County, North Carolina, Historical Documentation [Hughes map]* (N.p.: Fred Hughes, 1980), sec. C4.

77. Horace Flack, pp. 4–5; Ivarea Flack, p. [1]. These conveyances consisted of two tracts, one of 250 acres, the other of 100 acres, and are discussed in note 74. See Rutherford Deeds, vol. C, pp. 315–316; and Holcomb, *Deed Abstracts*, p. 156.

78. The marriage between John Anderson and Sarah Flack is listed in *Pennsylvania Marriages Prior to 1790: Names of Persons for Whom Marriage Licenses Were Issued in the Province of Pennsylvania Previous to 1790* (Baltimore: Genealogical Publishing Company, 1968), p. 89. In

fact, the wife of "John Anderson of Guilford" may well have been named Martha. See Guilford Deeds, vol. 3, pp. 199–200.

79. Rowan County, NC, Marriage Bonds, 1753–1868, vol. C (microform).

80. Holcomb, *Deed Abstracts*, p. 39.

81. Ibid., p. 148.

82. Rutherford Deeds, vol. C, pp. 315–316. Also see note 74.

83. Op. cit., Rowan Marriages.

84. Rutherford County, NC, Record of Wills, 1782–1868, vol. B, pp. 86–87.

85. Lancaster County, PA, Drumore Township, Tax List, 1763.

86. Mayhill, p. 178.

87. Ibid., p. 143.

88. Holcomb, *Deed Abstracts*, pp. 39, 105.

89. *Commemorative Biographical Record of Washington County, Pennsylvania, Containing Biographical Sketches of Prominent and Representative Citizens, and of Many of the Early Settled Families* (Chicago: J.H. Beers & Co., 1893), p. 458.

90. Boyd Crumrine, *History of Washington County, Pennsylvania, with Biographical Sketches of Many of Its Pioneers and Prominent Men* (Philadelphia: L.H. Leverts & Co., 1882), pp. 673–686 and 811–824.

91. Ibid.

92. Op. cit., Beers.

93. Rankin, p. 151.

94. Ibid., pp. 32, 123; op. cit., *[Hughes map]*, sec. C5; Secretary of State, NC, Granville Land Grants, Box 83-E (microform).

95. Rankin, pp. 32, 151.

96. Rankin, pp. 32, 123, 133.

97. Though I should note that Rankin indicates (pp. 123, 133) John Anderson (d. 1794) remained in Guilford where he served as a ruling elder of Buffalo Presbyterian (1773–1794).

98. It seems likely that James Finley and wife removed with or followed Robert McQuiston to Rowan/Guilford since we find a "Jas. Finley" near the McQuistons in a 1768 Rowan tax list for a part of that county which would later become Guilford; and because John Gilkey in his communications with Robert L. Twitty preserved a tradition that his family lived in Guilford County — I think that it may not have been Robert Gilkey, his father, who lived in Guilford (though this is what Twitty wrote), but rather his mother, the first wife of James Finley. In the letter of 3 February 1881, Twitty wrote, "Mr. Gilkey has these facts from his mother (nee Jane McQueston of Carlisle, Penn.)." See Linn, *Rowan Tax Lists*, p. 73; op. cit., Twitty to Draper, 3 February 1881; The Draper Manuscripts, King's Mountain Papers, Series DD, vol. 7, #117, W.L. Twitty to Lyman Draper, 14 March 1881 (microform).

99. Holcomb, *Deed Abstracts*, p. 40.

100. Brent Holcomb, *Tryon County North Carolina Minutes of the Court of Pleas and Quarter Sessions, 1769–1779* (Columbia, SC: SCMAR, 1994), pp. 151, 157.

101. *The Mountain Banner* (Rutherfordton), 14 April 1882, p. 2; op. cit., Twitty to Draper, 3 February 1881; McQuiston, p. 289. Ms. McQuiston erroneously gives "John" Gilkey as Jean McQuiston's second husband. The marriage bond and date of marriage are lost.

102. Holcomb, *Deed Abstracts*, p. 168.

103. Rutherford Wills, vol. B, pp. 86–87.

104. Op. cit., Twitty to Draper, 3 February 1881. Also see note 98.

105. Robert, Walter and William Gilkey can be found in a 1753 Sadsbury tax list. See J. Smith Futhey and Gilbert Cope, *History of Chester County, Pennsylvania, with Genealogical and Biographical Sketches* (Philadelphia: Louis H. Everts, 1881), p. 204. The will of a Walter Gilkey of Sadsbury with sons William, Samuel and Jonathan, and grandson Walter, was probated in Chester in 1768. See Jacob Martin, abstractor, *Wills of Chester County, Pennsylvania, 1766–1778* (Westminster, MD: Willow Bend Books, 1999), p. 15. There were Gilkeys in Sadsbury (Jonathan?), West Nantmill (William) and West Caln (Robert) townships, Chester County, PA, in 1768. See *Tax List of Chester County, 1768* (Westminster, MD: Family Line Publications, 1998), pp. 15, 71, 83. Early Chester deed books also document land transactions naming William (1752, 1753) and Walter Gilkey (1743, 1745, 1748) in Sadsbury. See Carol Bryant, abstractor, *Abstracts of Chester County, Pennsylvania Land Records, vol. 2, 1729–1745* (Westminster, MD: Willow Bend Books, 1999), pp. 163, 186; *Abstracts of Chester County, Pennsylvania Land Records, vol. 3, 1745–1753* (Westminster, MD: Willow Bend Books, 2000), p. 101; and *Abstracts of Chester County, Pennsylvania Land Records, vol. 4, 1753–1758* (Westminster, MD: Willow Bend Books, 1999), pp. 12, 39. A Walter Gilkey obtained a land patent in Sadsbury in 1732. See Chester County Genealogy, post by Marion L. Sohn. http://www.techcrafters.net/Gen/Chester/scripts/queries.asp?ST=14 (1 May 2002).

106. Grace Turner and Miles S. Philbeck, Jr., compilers, *Rutherford County, North Carolina, Will Abstracts, 1779–1910* (Chapel Hill: the authors, 1982), unpag. [#46]. The George Black will is not in Rutherford will books, but a copy is filed with loose Rutherford estates papers at the State Archives.

107. See *[Hughes map]*, sec. C4.

108. Rowan Deeds, vol. 6, pp. 374–375.
109. Op. cit., Mecklenburg shuck no. 2539.
110. Griffin, *History*, p. 125.
111. For example, see Griffin, *History*, pp. 17–19; and Jo. Seawell Jones, *A Defense of the Revolutionary History of the State of North Carolina from the Aspersions of Mr. Jefferson* (Raleigh, NC: Turner & Hughes, 1834), pp. 181–182.
112. Griffin, *History*, p. 83.
113. Ibid., p. 57; Lyman C. Draper, *King's Mountain and Its Heroes: History of the Battle of King's Mountain, October 7th, 1780, and the Events Which Led to It* (Cincinnati: Peter G. Thompson, Publisher, 1881), pp. 153–156.
114. There is a photocopy of this inventory in the Ralph R. Flack Papers in the possession of Helen Flack Cole. It is my assumption that the original is owned by a descendant — I could not find it in Rutherford's loose estates papers at the State Archives. Horace E. Flack (p. 7) had access to the same inventory, which he noted was actually a copy made for John Flack's son, George, in 1806.
115. Op. cit., Haun, *Revolutionary Army Accounts, Book A*, pp. 1644, 1663, 1668.
116. Op. cit., Twitty to Draper, 3 February 1881.
117. For example, see entry #803 in Dr. A.B. Pruitt's *Abstracts of Land Entries: Rutherford Co., NC, 1779–1795* (N.p.: the author, 1989), p. 65, which refers to "Squire Flack's land" on Mountain Creek; and also Hedy Hughes Newton, compiler and editor, *Rutherford County North Carolina Abstracts of Minutes Court of Pleas and Quarter Sessions, 1779–1786* (Ellenboro, NC: the author, 1974), pp. 8 ff.
118. In addition to the 300 acre tract on Catheys Creek purchased in 1778, John Flack obtained a grant for an additional 80 acres there in 1782. See op. cit., Tryon shuck no. 1623; Land Grant Record Books, vol. 41, p. 235; and Rutherford Deeds, vol. A–D, p. 258. To this he added the 200 acre Mountain Creek tract shortly before he died. See Secretary of State, NC, Land Grant Office, Warrants, Plats, etc., Rutherford County, shuck no. 627; and Rutherford Deeds, vol. J, pp. 16–17. These 580 acres were divided among the sons of the first and second marriages when the committee charged with the division of the estate rendered their decision in 1797. See Rutherford Wills, vol. B, pp. 86–87.
119. The number of Negroes owned by Flack was five, both at the time of the 1790 census and at his death. See op. cit., *First Census of the United States*, p. 118; and the estate inventory in the Ralph R. Flack Papers (HFC).
120. The silver plate is noted in the estate inventory, as well as in Rutherford Court of Pleas & Quarter Sessions, October, 1792, unpag.; and April, 1796, p. 168.
121. Draper, pp. 474–475; Griffin, p. 89.
122. Draper, pp. 153–156; Griffin, pp. 57–58, 73.
123. Tryon Deeds, vol. 1, pp. 238–240; and Holcomb, *Deed Abstracts*, p. 94.
124. Griffin, *History*, p. 21. See also his *Revolutionary Service of Col. John Walker and Family and Memoirs of Hon. Felix Walker* (Forest City, NC: The Forest City Courier, 1930).
125. Op. cit., Haun, *North Carolina Revolutionary Army Accounts, Book A*, p. 1667; and Weynette Parks Haun, *North Carolina Revolutionary Army Accounts [Treasurer's and Comptroller's Papers] Volume XII* (Durham, NC: the author, 1999), p. 1457.
126. Draper, p. 265.
127. Ibid., p. 475. Griffin observed (*History*, p. 72) that Col. William Porter, whom he believed to have been of Irish parentage from Pennsylvania, served in the North Carolina Senate and House almost continuously from 1789–1816, and represented Rutherford at the State conventions at Hillsborough (1788) and Fayetteville (1789) which at first rejected, then ratified, the U.S. Constitution. Following Draper, Griffin also states that Porter was killed by a lightning strike.
128. Ibid.; and Griffin, *History*, pp. 72–73. Griffin says that court records indicate James Porter died in Rutherford in 1784, while Draper states that he later removed to Greenville, SC, where he died an old man. But Philbeck found that he died in Dallas County, Alabama, in 1840. See Miles Philbeck, "Porter of Rowan and Rutherford," *Bulletin of The Genealogical Society of Old Tryon County*, 26 (Nov. 1998), p. 179.
129. Philbeck's recent research, pp. 178–179, uncovered a petition to the North Carolina General Assembly which indicates that Maj. James Porter of Rutherford was wounded at the Battle of Ramsour's Mill (fought on the outskirts of what is now Lincolnton) on June 20th, 1780.
130. Draper, p. 475.
131. Op. cit., Rutherford Court of Pleas and Quarter Sessions, October, 1792, unpag. Also see note 127.
132. Ivarea Flack, p. 2.
133. Philbeck, p. 183.
134. Andrew Flack's birth (ca. 1775) is proven by a court record indicating that he reached his majority (age twenty-one) in 1796. See op. cit., Rutherford Court of Pleas and Quarter Sessions, October, 1796, unpag.
135. Ivarea Flack, p. 2. Once again, I can find no documentation to support Ms. Flack.

136. Ramsey, p. 120.
137. Philbeck, pp. 175 ff.
138. Griffin, *History*, p. 88.
139. The Draper Manuscripts, King's Mountain Papers, Series DD, vol. 7, # 107, W.L. Twitty to Lyman Draper, 8 January 1881 (microform).
140. Rutherford County, NC, Marriage Bonds, 1779–1868, vol. F (microform); and Holcomb, *Marriages*, p. 43.
141. James E. and Vivian Wooley, *Rutherford County, North Carolina, Wills and Miscellaneous Records, 1783–1868* (Easley, SC: Southern Historical Press, Inc., 1984), p. 42.
142. A Robert "Parter" or Porter (b. ca. 1750) of White County, Illinois, formerly of Rutherford, a cousin of Maj. James and William Porter and also a commissioned major, applied for a Revolutionary War pension in 1820. See Bobby Gilmer Moss, *The Patriots at Kings Mountain* (Blacksburg, SC: Scotia-Hibernia Press, 1990), p. 207; and Vigil D. White, abstractor, *Genealogical Abstracts of Revolutionary War Pension Files*, vol. III: N–Z (Waynesboro, TN: The National Historical Publishing Company, 1991), p. 2611. Of course, even if Robert Porter of Catheys Creek was not the officer-cousin of William and James Porter of Revolutionary War fame, the possibility of a relationship is not necessarily precluded.
143. Philbeck, p. 177.
144. Ramsey, p. 120.
145. Mayhill, pp. 164–165.
146. Historical Society of Pennsylvania, *Abstracts of Lancaster County Pennsylvania Wills, 1732–1785* (Westminster, MD: Family Line Publications, 1995), p. 176.
147. Ibid., p. 179.
148. Ibid., p. 184.
149. Historical Society of Pennsylvania, *Abstracts of Lancaster County Pennsylvania Wills, 1786–1820* (Westminster, MD: Family Line Publications, 1995), p. 181.
150. Op. cit., Rutherford Wills, vol. B, pp. 18, 86–87; see also the records of the estate scattered through the minutes of the Rutherford Court of Pleas and Quarter Sessions, 1792–98. The administrators at first attempted to settle the estate without selling the Negroes and silver plate, but this proved impossible and the court ordered them sold in 1796 (see Rutherford Court of Pleas and Quarter Sessions, April, 1796, p. 168). As well, some of the men who served as security for Mary Flack (in her administration of the estate, and for the guardianship of her children) withdrew, though it is unclear why (see Rutherford Court of Pleas and Quarter Sessions, October, 1794, p. 49; July, 1795, p. 110; October, 1796, p. 216; and January, 1798, p.

316). It is beyond my scope to recapitulate the estate settlement, though I have examined these records as well as others relating to Mary Flack and the children of the first and second marriages for clues to Flack origins. The fate of Mary Flack and "her own children" (William, John and Mary), and their association with the McLains/McLeans of Rutherford, remains a muddle for me, which I will refrain from addressing herein.

But I cannot resist noting that my examination of the records of the second generation has led me to an important correction to Flack genealogy. It has been the contention of a number of researchers (perhaps traceable to Dr. Robertson) that John Flack, Jr., the son of John Flack by his second wife, Mary, left Rutherford and settled in Perry County, Illinois, ca. 1800. I can say, with near certainty, that John Flack of Perry County, Ill., was not the son of John Flack of Rutherford. The John Flack who went to Illinois was from Iredell County, North Carolina, and was the son of a *Michael* Flack. John and Michael Flack were among the early settlers of the Stony Point area, located near the present day Alexander County-Iredell County line, and where they owned tracts adjacent to a Fergus Milligan. The wife of John Flack of Perry County was a Sarah Milligan. The parentage of John Flack is established by a land claim made by him in 1792. In that year he entered land in Iredell County; however, the land had still not been surveyed some seven years later, and, in December, 1799, he assigned the claim to his father. On the back of a warrant for this survey can be found the following: "I John Flack do by these presents assign over to my father Michael Flack all my title and claim to the within warrant for value received. Witness my hand and seal the 5th of December 1799 — John Flack seal / Test Wm. Sharpe."

Quoted from Secretary of State, NC, Land Grant Office, Warrants, Plats, etc., Iredell County, shuck no. 347. See also The Genealogical Society of Iredell County, *The Heritage of Iredell County 1980* (Statesville, NC: The Genealogical Society of Iredell County, 1980), pp. 25–27; and Dr. Robert Crawford Robertson, *Pioneer and Related Families of Randolph and Perry Counties Illinois* (Chattanooga, TN: The author, 1960), pp. 11–12, 18.

151. Veterans Records Pension File # S15430, James Flack, Revolutionary War (National Archives, Washington, DC); Vigil D. White, abstractor, *Genealogical Abstracts of Revolutionary War Pension Files*, vol. II: F–M (Waynesboro, TN: The National Historical Publishing Company, 1991), p. 1210; and Horace Flack, pp.

2–3. I think it is also possible that this James Flack is the "cousin" who went to Pennsylvania in the Crawford tradition, though John Flack of Washington County, Pennsylvania, may be another candidate.

152. I located this information during a search of the Lancaster County, Pennsylvania GenWeb site. http://www.getafix.mathcs.wilkes.edu/lancaster/ppl/g/glenn/glenn001.html (11 November 2000).

153. Quoted in Horace Flack, p. 3. See also Pension File # S15430; and White, vol. II, p. 1210.

154. Emphasis added. See Pension File # S15430; and White, vol. II, p. 1210.

155. Guilford Deeds, vol. 2, p. 133.

156. Rockingham County, NC, Record of Deeds, No. L, 1803–1804, pp. 23–24, 28–29 (microform).

157. The source cited in note 152 indicates that Hugh Glenn, the father of James Flack's wife, died in Madison County, Kentucky, in 1807.

158. Third Census of the United States, 1810: Madison County, KY, Population Schedule, p. 207 (microform).

159. Pension File # S15340; and White, vol. II, p. 1210.

160. The 1800 census clearly establishes the presence of two different James Flacks, one in Guilford, the other in Rockingham. See the Second Census of the United States, 1800: Guilford County, NC, Population Schedule, p. 660; and Rockingham County, NC, Population Schedule, p. 438.

161. Op. cit., Haun, *North Carolina Revolutionary Army Accounts ... Journal "A"*, pp. 63–77; Hughes, *Map Supplement*, pp. 110–111.

162. Pension File # S15340; White, vol. II, p. 1210; and Horace Flack, pp. 1–2.

163. Guilford Deeds, vol. 3, p. 122.

164. Ruth F. Thompson and Louise J. Hartgrove, compilers, *Vol. I, Abstracts of the Marriage Bonds and Additional Data, Guilford County, North Carolina, 1771–1840* (Greensboro, NC: The Guilford County Genealogical Society, 1981), p. 57.

165. Guilford Deeds, vol. 11, pp. 124–125.

166. White, vol. II, p. 1207.

167. Ivarea Flack (p. 113) maintained that William Flack "helped to organize Brittain Church and is buried there, without a grave marker." The grave of his son, also named William Flack (1763–1854), is identified by a conspicuous marker in the Brittain cemetery. Ms. Flack (p. 2) also held that John Flack assisted in the organization of Brittain Presbyterian and that he and his first wife Jane were buried there in unmarked graves.

Clarence Griffin numbered the Flacks among the founding families of the church as well. He wrote, "Tacked in front of the Bible of William Flack, there was found a pastoral letter from the [Presbyterian] Synod of New York and Philadelphia, addressed to the congregations under their care, to be read from the pulpits on Thursday, June 29, 1775, ... Mr. Flack was a member of Brittain Church, and it is probable that this letter was read to the Brittain congregation on the day appointed." See Griffin's *History*, pp. 585–586.

168. Information in a letter to Ms. Rush H. (Helen Flack) Cole from Capt. T. Stuart Davidson (1 November 1978).

169. George F. Black, *The Surnames of Scotland: Their Origin, Meaning, and History* (New York: The New York Public Library, 1962), pp. 267–268.

170. Edward MacLysaght, *The Surnames of Ireland*, 6th ed. (Dublin: Irish Academic Press, 1985), p. 110.

171. Black, p. 267.

172. The Rev. Henry Barber, *British Family Names, Their Origin and Meaning with Lists of Scandinavian, Frisian, Anglo-Saxon and Norman Names*, 2nd ed., enlarged (Baltimore: Genealogical Publishing Company, 1968), p. 143.

173. Patrick Hanks and Flaviq Hodges, *A Dictionary of Surnames* (New York: Oxford University Press, 1988), p. 185.

174. Barber, p. 143; and Henry Harrison, *Surnames of the United Kingdom: A Concise Etymological Dictionary* (Baltimore: Genealogical Publishing Company, 1969), p. 149.

175. See Flack Family Genealogy Forum, post by Thomas Flack (and followups). http://genforum.genealogy.com/flack/messages/338.html (1 May 2002).

176. Information in a letter to Ms. Helen Flack Cole from Mr. Charles Z. Flack, Sr. (6 February 1980); Waldo Chamberlain Sprague, "Cotton Flack of Boston, Mass.," in the *American Genealogist*, 36 (October 1960), pp. 223–228. Sprague identified both a Richard and a Thomas Flack, both of whom resided in Saffron Walden, Co. of Essex, in the late 1500s, and noted that "[the] surname Flack is quite common in co. Essex, especially in the northwest part around Saffron Walden." In *Essex Wills (England), Vol. 1, 1558–1565*, abstracted and edited by F.G. Emmison (N.p.: National Genealogical Society of America, 1982), pp. 29, 54, there are Essex wills which name a Richard Flacke.

177. Information in a letter to Ms. Helen Flack Cole from Mr. Charles Z. Flack, Sr. (6 February 1980).

178. Sprague, p. 224.
179. I have an undocumented internet source, a post to a query on the origins of the name Flack, from a Brian Flack whose "paternal family are from Essex UK." He indicates that this is "the part of England in which the majority of Flacks are found ... and we have found Flacks in the UK as far back as the 1300s."
180. Based upon LDS files, Flacks do seem comparatively more numerous in these counties. However, I have also found them in Huntingdon, Kent, Gloucester, Lancashire, Coventry, Surrey, Nottingham, Hampshire, Northumberland and Yorkshire. See FamilySearch (Church of Jesus Christ of Latter-day Saints). http://www.familysearch.org/ (1 May 2002).
181. Hanks and Hodges, p. 185.
182. Charles Wareing Bardsley, *A Dictionary of Irish and Welsh Surnames with Special American Instances*, rev. for the press by his widow (Baltimore: Genealogical Publishing Company, 1980), p. 291.
183. P.H. Reaney and R.M. Wilson, *A Dictionary of English Surnames*, 3rd ed. with corrections and additions by R.M. Wilson (London: Routledge, 1991), p. 171.
184. James G. Leyburn, *The Scotch-Irish: A Social History* (Chapel Hill: The University of North Carolina Press, 1962), p. 89.
185. Ibid., p. 91.
186. Ibid., p. 127.
187. Ibid., p. 88.
188. Ibid., p. 93.
189. Horace Flack, p. 3.
190. Robertson, p. 11; manuscript note in the Ralph R. Flack Papers (HFC). In my opinion, Legrand A. Flack and Dr. Glenn were probably following Robertson.
191. W.P.W. Phillimore and Gertrude Thrift, eds., *Indexes to Irish Wills*, 5 vols. in one (Baltimore: Genealogical Publishing Company, 1997), vol. II, pp. 40–41.
192. P. Beryl Eustace, *Registry of Deeds, Dublin, Abstracts of Wills, vol. 1, 1708–1745* (Baltimore: Clearfield Co., Inc., 1996), p. 301; and Sir Arthur Vicars, ed., *Index to the Prerogative Wills of Ireland, 1536–1810* (Baltimore: Genealogical Publishing Company, 1989), p. 172.
193. Sir Robert E. Matheson, *Special Report on Surnames in Ireland [Together With] Varieties and Synonymes of Surnames and Christian Names in Ireland* (Baltimore: Genealogical Publishing Company, 1994), p. 48.
194. I found a record for this tree in the Public Record Office of Northern Ireland search engine. http://www.proni.nics.gov.uk/index (11 November 2002).
195. Charles A. Hanna, *The Scotch-Irish or the Scot in North Britain, North Ireland, and North America* (Baltimore: Genealogical Publishing Company, 1968), p. 532.
196. Op. cit., Flack Genealogy Forum, Marie Forehan post (1 May 2002).
197. Op. cit., Beers, p. 848.
198. Op. cit., http://www.familysearch.org (1 May 2002).
199. Ibid.
200. R.S.J. Clarke, compiler, *Gravestone Inscriptions, County Down, vol. 19: Donaghcloney, Dromara, Dromore, Garvaghy and Magheralin* (Belfast: Ulster Historical Foundation, 1983), p. 101.
201. Pension File # S15340.
202. Miss I. Embleton, Secretary, Ulster-Scot Historical Society to Ralph R. Flack, 9 August 1968. Ralph R. Flack Papers (HFC).
203. Ramsey, p. 202.
204. Ibid., pp. 17–20.

Appendix VII. Plato Durham

1. *Shotwell Papers*, vol. II, pp. 346, 351, 358–361.
2. Hamilton, *Reconstruction*, p. 480.
3. Jolly, "The Ku Klux Klan in Rutherford County," pp. 21–23, 26, 28, 32, 37, 41–42.
4. Escott, p. 156.
5. Trelease, *White Terror*, p. 339.
6. John Hope Franklin, "Counter Reconstruction," in *Reconstruction in the South*, 2nd ed. (Lexington, Mass.: D.C. Heath and Company, 1972), pp. 206–207. Franklin characterized Nathan Bedford Forrest's "dissolution order" as a tactical maneuver to take the Ku Klux underground.
7. Ibid., p. 214.
8. *Legislative Biographical Sketchbook, Session 1887, North Carolina* (Raleigh: Edwards, Broughton & Co., 1887), p. 15; Twelfth Census of the United States, 1900: Rutherford County, NC, Population Schedule, enumeration district 133, sheet 1, line 67 (microform).
9. George G. Eaves, "Autobiography of the Eaves-Baxter Families," part 1, *Forest City Courier*, 2 April 1931, p. 9.
10. Mrs. Eaves' obituary may be found in the *West-Carolina Record* (Rutherfordton), 28 June 1873, p. 3.
11. Griffin, *History*, p. 318.
12. This can be extrapolated from the U.S. Census. In 1840, we find Spencer Eaves' household in Spartanburg, but by 1850 the family had returned to Rutherford. See the Sixth Census of the United States, 1840: Spartanburg County,

SC, Population Schedule, p. 70 (microform); and the Seventh Census of the United States, 1850: Rutherford County, NC, Population Schedule, p. 357 (microform).

13. This house stood until it was destroyed by fire on Sept. 5th, 1948. See the *Forest City Courier*, 9 September 1948, p. 1.

14. Court records indicate that William Baxter, Sr. gave Spencer Eaves "a certain portion of property" and that Eaves "borrowed money at several times" from old man Baxter. Baxter also once entrusted Eaves with the task of taking a "considerable amount of Alabama money" from Rutherford to Augusta, Georgia, to exchange. See North Carolina Supreme Court, case file #6863, William Costin, et al. vs. William Baxter, Sr. (1849) (NC Office of Archives and History, Raleigh, NC). Eaves shared business interests with the Baxters in Spartanburg County, SC, Rutherfordton, NC, and possibly also Murray County, Georgia, in the 1840s. See note #20 and Murray County, GA, Minutes, Superior Court 1846–1851, p. 297, microfilm roll no. RHS 4078 Georgia (State Archives of Georgia, Atlanta, GA).

15. *The News* (Rutherfordton), 23 December 1926, p. __ (unpag. clipping from the Genealogical Society of Old Tryon County "Baxter" family file).

16. William S. Powell, ed., *Dictionary of North Carolina Biography*, vol. 1, A–C (Chapel Hill: The University of North Carolina Press, 1979), p. 121.

17. Ibid., pp. 120–121.

18. Lefler and Newsome, p. 329.

19. Griffin, *History*, p. 237.

20. Spencer Eaves operated a store in Spartanburg with John Baxter about the time J.B. Eaves was born. See *The Carolina Spartan* (Spartanburg, SC), 14 April 1886, p. 2, and part 1 of George G. Eaves' "Autobiography." See also Elisha Baxter's biography in the e-text version of Goodspeed's *History of Northeast Arkansas*, http://fly.hiwaay.net/dmglenn/ inda_c.htm (10 September 2002), which states Baxter was briefly engaged in the mercantile business in Rutherfordton with Spencer Eaves about 1848–50.

21. William Baxter, Sr. owned thirty-four slaves in 1830; Spencer Eaves had sixteen in 1860. See Fifth Census of the United States, 1830: Rutherford County, NC, Population Schedule, p. 483 (microform); and Eighth Census of the United States, 1860: Rutherford County, NC, Slave Schedule, p. 51 (microform).

22. The 20 February 1890 *Asheville Democrat*, p. 6, still described the region thus: "This was a strong Union section during the rebellion, and of the loyal white stock and their descendants many are quite active Republicans." Spencer and John Baxter Eaves could probably be characterized in like terms.

Spencer Eaves ran as a Republican for Clerk of Superior Court in 1874. See the *Rutherford Star and West-Carolina Record*, 11 July 1874, p. 2. In his testimony before Congress, James M. Justice described the elder Eaves as "a republican, and a very decided one." See *Testimony Taken by the Joint Select Committee to Inquire into the Condition of Affairs in the Late Insurrectionary States* (hereafter *Testimony*), North Carolina (Washington, DC: Government Printing Office, 1872), p. 148.

23. Griffin, *History*, pp. 253–254.

24. Ruth Moore, "Plato Durham, Hero, Idol of Reconstruction Days," *The Charlotte Observer*, 26 March 1933, sec. three, p. 2.

25. Griffin, *History*, pp. 253–254.

26. Moore, p. 2; Robert Lee Durham, *Since I Was Born*, ed. by Marshall William Fishwick (Richmond, VA: Whittet & Shepperson, 1953), p. 36.

27. Eaves, part 1, op. cit.

28. Weymouth T. Jordan, Jr., compiler, *North Carolina Troops 1861–1865 A Roster*, unit histories by Louis H. Manarin, vol. VI, Infantry, 16th–18th and 20th–21st Regiments (Raleigh, NC: Division of Archives and History, 1977), p. 359.

29. Moore, p. 6; *Dictionary of North Carolina Biography*, vol. 2, p. 126.

30. Durham, pp. 30–36.

31. Weymouth T. Jordan, Jr., compiler, *North Carolina Troops 1861–1865 A Roster*, unit histories by Louis H. Manarin, vol. V, Infantry, 11th–15th Regiments (Raleigh, NC: Division of Archives and History, 1975), p. 174.

32. *The War of the Rebellion: A Compilation of the Official Records of the Union and Confederate Armies*, prepared under the direction of Lt. Col. Robert N. Scott, series I, vol. XXIX, part II, correspondence, etc. (Washington, DC: Government Printing Office, 1890), p. 769.

33. Durham, p. 36.

34. Moore, p. 2.

35. *Dictionary of North Carolina Biography*, vol. 2, p. 126.

36. Moore, p. 2.

37. Durham, p. 37; Moore, p. 2.

38. Moore, p. 2.

39. Durham, p. 43.

40. Ibid., p. 37.

41. Eaves, part 1.

42. Griffin, *History*, p. 241; *Knoxville Daily Journal*, 11 February 1890, p. 3.

43. Ibid.

44. *Knoxville Daily Journal*, 11 February 1890 p. 3; *North Carolina Troops*, vol. VI, p. 10.

45. See History of First National Bank. http://www.ibankatfnb.com/site/home-history.html (2 September 2002).
46. The Shelby Daily Star, *Our Heritage: A History of Cleveland County* (Shelby, NC: The Shelby Daily Star, 1976, pp. 243, 246.
47. Eaves, part 1.
48. Griffin, *History*, p. 318; J.S. Tomlinson, *Assembly Sketch Book, Session 1883, North Carolina*, vol. 2 (Raleigh, NC: Edwards, Broughton & Co., 1883), p. 27; J.S. Tomlinson, *Tar Heel Sketch-Book, A Brief Biographical Sketch of the Life and Public Acts of the Members of the General Assembly of North Carolina, Session of 1879* (Raleigh, NC: Raleigh News Steam Book and Job Print, 1879), p. 46.
49. George G. Eaves, "Autobiography of the Eaves-Baxter Families," part 2, *The Forest City Courier*, 9 April 1931, p. 10.
50. Griffin, *History*, p. 318.
51. Eighth Census of the United States, 1860: Rutherford County, NC, Population Schedule, p. 390 (microform).
52. Eaves, part 2.
53. Ibid.
54. Weymouth T. Jordan, Jr., compiler, *North Carolina Troops 1861–1865 A Roster*, unit histories by the same, vol. XII, Infantry, 49th–52nd Regiments (Raleigh, NC: Division of Archives and History, 1990), p. 235.
55. Kinchen Jahu Carpenter, *War Diary of Kinchen Jahu Carpenter, Confederate Soldier, May, 1862–May, 1865* (Rutherfordton, NC: Mrs. Julie Carpenter Williams, 1955), pp. 6 ff.
56. Tomlinson (1879), p. 46; Tomlinson (1883), p. 27; *Legislative Biographical Sketch Book*, p. 15; Griffin, *History*, p. 318.
57. *North Carolina Troops*, vol. XII, p. 235.
58. Griffin, *History*, pp. 253, 308, 311.
59. Holcomb, *Marriages*, p. 39.
60. Griffin, *History*, p. 227; Jolley, "The Ku Klux Klan in Rutherford County," pp. 4–9. Jolley gives a good account of Logan's war-time Unionist sympathies.
61. Griffin, *History*, p. 347. George G. Eaves stated that Eaves defeated Thomas Dixon's father in the Senate race. See part 2 of his "Autobiography."
62. *Shotwell Papers*, vol. II, p. 392; *Testimony*, p. 336.
63. Sketched in Griffin, *History*, p. 254.
64. Sketched in Ibid., pp. 354–355.
65. *The Rutherford Star*, 5 September 1868, p. 2.
66. *Testimony*, p. 141.
67. Griffin, *History*, p. 314.
68. *Testimony*, p. 141.
69. Griffin, *History*, p. 319.

70. *The Rutherford Star*, 19 September 1868, p. 2.
71. Rutherford County, NC, Record of Deeds, vol. 49, pp. 51–52 (microform).
72. Griffin, *History*, p. 318.
73. For Eaves' record in the North Carolina Senate during this period see *Journal of the Senate of The General Assembly of the State of North Carolina, at Its Session of 1868–'69* (Raleigh: M.S. Littlefield, State Printer & Binder, 1869), pp. 4 ff.
74. *The Rutherford Star*, 4 December 1869, p. 2.
75. *Senate Journal*, pp. 93, 209, 237, 250, 417.
76. *The Rutherford Star*, 22 July 1869, p. 2.
77. Ibid.; *The Rutherford Star*, 19 August 1869, p. 2.
78. *The Rutherford Star*, 12 August 1869, p. 2.
79. Hamilton, *Reconstruction*, p. 395; *The Rutherford Star*, 4 September 1869, p. 2. See Allen Trelease's detailed account in *The North Carolina Railroad, 1849–1871, and the Modernization of North Carolina* (Chapel Hill: The University of North Carolina Press, 1991), pp. 291–293.
80. *The Rutherford Star*, 27 November 1869, p. 3.
81. Griffin, *History*, p. 313.
82. Hamilton, *Reconstruction*, p. 453.
83. Holden's reactionary use of Kirk's militia had as much to do with the unraveling of Republican control in North Carolina as Klan violence and intimidation. See Eric Foner, *Reconstruction: America's Unfinished Revolution, 1863–1877* (New York: Harper & Row, 1988), pp. 440–441.
84. *The Rutherford Star*, 31 October 1868, p. 2.
85. *Senate Reports*, 42nd Congress, 1st Session, No. 1, p. 129.
86. Hamilton, *Reconstruction*, pp. 253 ff., 271n, 286.
87. *Testimony*, pp. 310, 312, 317–318.
88. See Daniel W. Jolley, "The Ku Klux Klan in Western North Carolina, 1870–1871." http://www.geocities.com/darkgenius.geo/klanruth.html (27 June 2002). This seems to be a revision of Jolley's UNC–Chapel Hill master's thesis.
89. *The Rutherford Star*, 28 November 1868, p. 2. It is interesting to note that even at this early date, Durham and McAfee, on the stump in Haywood County, employed "red shirts" at a campaign rally in order to intimidate their Republican opponents. See *The Rutherford Star*, 31 October 1868, p. 2.
90. *The Rutherford Star*, 20 February 1869, p. 2.

91. Hamilton, *Reconstruction*, pp. 374–375.
92. *The Rutherford Star*, 30 July 1870, p. 2.
93. In PBS's American Experience documentary "Nixon," (1998), Roger Morris used these words to describe Richard Nixon's reaction to alleged fraud in Texas and Illinois in the 1960 presidential election.
94. Trelease, *White Terror*, p. 13.
95. *Testimony*, pp. 317–318.
96. Franklin, p. 197 ff.
97. *North Carolina Troops*, vol. V, p. 174.
98. Ibid.
99. Ibid., vol. VI, p. 10.
100. Ibid., vol. XII, p. 26. In addition to his military service, Leroy M. McAfee (1836–1873) was an 1859 graduate of the University of North Carolina. He represented Cleveland County in the State House in 1870–71. See *The Daily Sentinel* (Raleigh), 1 October 1873.
101. *North Carolina Troops*, vol. V, p. 535.
102. *Our Heritage*, p. 129.
103. *Testimony*, pp. 139, 144, 203, 208–209, 221, 316–317, 322; *Senate Reports*, p. 187.
104. Ibid., p. 319.
105. *The Rutherford Star*, 23 October 1869, p. 2.
106. *Testimony*, p. 140.
107. *The Rutherford Star*, 27 August 1870, p. 2.
108. Ibid., 10 December 1870, p. 2; *Testimony*, p. 108. Col. Logan was a brother of Judge Logan. See R.W. Logan's testimony in *Senate Reports*, pp. 127–128, in which he describes the raiding of his uncle in Cleveland County.
109. *The Rutherford Star*, 17 December 1870, p. 2.
110. *Senate Reports*, pp. 127, 187.
111. *The Rutherford Star*, 25 December 1869, p. 2; *Testimony*, p. 137.
112. *Testimony*, pp. 137, 175, 179.
113. *The Rutherford Star*, 16 October 1869, p. 2.
114. *Testimony*, pp. 103, 105, 151, 153, 229.
115. Ibid., pp. 166, 199, 223. Within the umbrella of a County Klan organization there were typically a number of "dens." Membership in a den could vary greatly, "from fewer than a dozen to nearly a hundred members." See Trelease, *White Terror*, p. 59.
116. *The Rutherford Star*, 9 April 1870, p. 2.
117. *Testimony*, pp. 22, 105, 151, 165–166, 305–308, 473, 483.
118. Ibid., p. 367. See also *The Rutherford Star*, 26 February 1870, p. 2; and 22 July 1871, p. 2.
119. *The Western Vindicator* (Rutherfordton), 26 June 1871, p. 1.
120. *Testimony*, pp. 21, 112, 146, 161, 170–171, 223.
121. Ibid., p. 337. The case was still pending in McDowell court in July, 1871. See *The Rutherford Star*, 22 July 1871, p. 2.
122. *The Rutherford Star*, 12 March 1870, p. 2; 19 March 1870, p. 3; 2 April 1870, p. 2; and 9 April 1870, p. 2.
123. Ibid., 11 June 1870, p. 3.
124. Ibid., 9 April 1870, p. 2.
125. Rutherford County, NC, Minutes, Superior Court, 1869–1876 (vol. 1), p. 142 (microform); *Testimony*, p. 22.
126. *Testimony*, pp. 213, 227.
127. Ibid., pp. 171, 189, 252, 307–308, 313–314. Eaves testified that "from the time of the outrage upon McGahey up to November or December, with the exception of right along the South Carolina line, in our county things were comparatively quiet." See Ibid., p. 169. In late December, 1870, Judge Logan wrote Governor Caldwell that Ku Klux activity had "commenced anew" in Cleveland County, and opined that "the only force to be effective [against them] must be *blue coats*." "When the ball opens," added the Judge, "it may be one of some dimensions." See George W. Logan to Gov. Todd R. Caldwell, 27 December 1870, Governors' Letterbooks #62, p. 36 (NC Office of Archives and History, Raleigh, NC).
A man named Hawkins (in Cleveland County) was also raided for helping McGaughey. See *Testimony*, p. 223.
128. *Testimony*, p. 443. Owens was among the "original" Cherry Mountain Klansmen which also included William DePriest and others who were indicted for the McGaughey raid. However, I believe this original Cherry Mountain den was "reorganized" under the leadership of John C. Withrow (who fought in a Cleveland regiment under McAfee) during the Spring of 1871, just before the Biggerstaff raid. See note 145.
129. Melvin L. White, *A History of the Life of Amos Owens, The Noted Blockader, of Cherry Mountain, N.C.* (Shelby, NC: Cleveland Star Job Print, 1901), p. 22.
130. Ibid., pp. 13–14; *North Carolina Troops*, vol. V, p. 43; and Weymouth T. Jordan, Jr., compiler, *North Carolina Troops 1861–1865 A Roster*, vol. XIII, 53rd–56th Regiments (Raleigh, NC: Division of Archives and History, 1975), p. 688.
131. *Testimony*, pp. 21, 146, 170–171, 222, 234, 367, 443. In his testimony, Schenck claimed the feud originated with neighbors in the Cherry Mountain section "report[ing] on each other."
132. Ibid., pp. 20, 23, 26, 29, 109, 163–164, 166, 173–175, 209. Rutherford den leaders probably were: Capt. John Lafayette Eaves; William

Edgerton; Jesse R. DePriest; John C. Withrow; Matt McBrayer; Adin Rucker; William Webster; and Ladson Mills, Jr. See *Testimony*, passim.

133. Ibid., pp. 29, 161, 180, 191–194, 200, 307, 484–485.

134. Ibid., pp. 24, 207–208.

135. *The Rutherford Star*, 8 April 1871, p. 3.

136. *Testimony*, pp. 110, 181, 207; *Shotwell Papers*, vol. II, pp. 326–327.

137. *The Rutherford Star*, 8 April 1871, p. 3.

138. *Shotwell Papers*, vol. II, pp. 344–350; *Testimony*, p. 147. Shotwell wrote, on p. 346: "'Of course you are one of us Shotwell'—said D[urham] with a significant gesture [or Ku Klux sign], which I caught, and returned."

139. Trelease, *White Terror*, p. 339; *Shotwell Papers*, vol. II, pp. 72, 100–202, 300–310, 404–406; Jolly, pp. 12 ff.; Griffin, pp. 342–344.

140. *Testimony*, pp. 470, 472, 475, 488.

141. Ibid., pp. 189, 194, 211, 214, 224, 397, 406, 410, 493–494, 537–538, 540, 545, 579–580, 583, 585.

142. *Carolina Era* (Raleigh), 12 October 1871, p. 1.

143. *Testimony*, pp. 378, 397.

144. Ibid., pp. 112–113, 470–473, 484–485, 504, 541, 579.

145. Ibid., pp. 189–190, 194, 211, 214, 224, 447, 493–495, 537–538, 540, 545–546, 579–580, 583, 585. The testimony of Alvin Johnson (pp. 545–546) indicates that the Cherry Mountain den was "organized" (probably reorganized) under Withrow in the Spring of 1871—around the time of the initiations at Spring court and the first Biggerstaff raid. While this is all very speculative, it goes to the heart of the problem of Cleveland involvement. Does it not stand to reason that the lawyer-politicians of Cleveland would have appointed a man with whom they were familiar (Withrow) to command the "unruly" Cherry Mountain den—much as they appointed Shotwell as County Chief of Rutherford?

146. Eighth Census of the United States, 1860: Rutherford County, NC, Population Schedule, p. 594 (microform); Ninth Census of the United States, 1870: Rutherford County, NC, Population Schedule, p. 66 (microform); *North Carolina Troops*, vol. V, p. 543; *North Carolina Troops*, vol. XII, p. 54.

147. *Testimony*, pp. 30, 410.

148. Ibid., pp. 111, 153, 169, 190, 402–403.

149. Ibid., pp. 369, 401–402; David Schenck Papers, #652, diaries, vols. 5 & 6 in one (typed manuscript), pp. 216–217 (Southern Historical Collection, Wilson Library, University of North Carolina at Chapel Hill).

150. *The Rutherford Star*, 29 April 1871, p. 2; George W. Logan to Gov. Todd R. Caldwell, 9 April 1871, Governors' Papers, box #227 (NC Office of Archives and History, Raleigh, NC); also in Governors' Letterbooks #62, p. 81. Judge Logan had used similar language to describe conditions in Cleveland as early as February, before the Biggerstaff raid. See *Senate Reports*, pp. 186–188.

151. *Testimony*, pp. 53–54, 190, 252, 315, 369–370, 401–402; Schenck diary, vols. 5 & 6 in one, pp. 221–230.

152. Ibid., pp. 132–133, 148–149, 186–187. This is of course a very famous Rutherford murder case. The case was moved to Henderson County where the Adairs and Baynard were found guilty and sentenced to be hanged. After an N.C. Supreme Court appeal, the Adairs were executed on the 12th of July, 1872. Baynard's hanging was scheduled for October 18th, but, granted a final conjugal visit with his wife on the night before he was to be hung, he miraculously escaped by dressing in his wife's clothing (which included a large bonnet and a handkerchief which he held close to his "sobbing" face as he left the jail). See Henderson County, NC, Superior Court, Criminal Action Papers, 50.326.31 (NC Office of Archives and History, Raleigh, NC); *North Carolina Reports: Cases Argued and Determined in the Supreme Court of North Carolina*, vol. 66, January Term, 1872, rep. by W.M. Shipp & annotated by Walter Clark ([Raleigh]: E.M. Uzzell & Co., State Printers & Binders, 1908), pp. 213–219; *Carolina Era* (Raleigh), 18 November 1871, p. 2; *The Charlotte Democrat*, 30 July 1872, p. 1; and 12 November 1872, p. 1; *The Southern Home* (Charlotte), 28 October 1872, p. 3; *The Western Vindicator* (Rutherfordton), 12 January 1899, p. 1.

Jesse Parker Bogue, Jr., in his "Violence and Oppression in North Carolina During Reconstruction 1865–1873," PhD. Diss., The University of Maryland, 1973, p. 262, attributed the murders to "[a] party of Ku Klux." Though most are in agreement that these murders had nothing to do with the Klan, the unscrupulous Adair brothers did apparently implicate Ladson Mills, Jr. (village chief of Rutherfordton) and a few other Rutherford men before their execution. See *The Charlotte Democrat*, 30 July 1872, p. 1; *The Western Vindicator* (Rutherfordton), 22 July 1872, p. 2.

153. *Testimony*, pp. 112–113, 171–172.

154. Ibid., pp. 112–113, 453–455, 457.

155. Ibid., pp. 171–172. Affidavits from Biggerstaff and his daughter, Mary Ann Norville, were forwarded to Governor Caldwell with a May 14th letter from J.B. Carpenter, Eaves and

Jim Justice. See J.B. Carpenter, John B. Eaves and James M. Justice to Gov. Todd R. Caldwell, 14 May 1871, Governors' Papers, box #227 (NC Office of Archives and History, Raleigh, NC). Writing back to Carpenter, Caldwell expressed frustration that Biggerstaff had not named his attackers. See Gov. Todd R. Caldwell to J.B. Carpenter, 22 May 1871, Governors' Letterbooks #62, p. 89 (NC Office of Archives and History, Raleigh, NC).

156. *Testimony*, pp. 224, 463–464. The second Biggerstaff or Grassy Branch raid is also discussed in *The Western Vindicator* (Rutherfordton), 26 June 1871, p. 1; and *The Rutherford Star*, 27 May 1871, pp. 2, 4.

157. Ibid., pp. 184–185; George W. Logan to Gov. Todd R. Caldwell, 5 May 1871, Governors' Papers, box #227 (NC Office of Archives and History, Raleigh, NC).

158. *Testimony*, pp. 20, 24–25, 29, 148, 216, 219, 445.

159. Ibid., pp. 114–115, 159, 178; op. cit., Carpenter, Eaves and Justice to Caldwell.

160. *Testimony*, p. 128.

161. Ibid., pp. 156, 159, 228; *Shotwell Papers*, vol. II, pp. 390–392.

162. *Testimony*, p. 115.

163. Ibid., pp. 117, 119, 156, 200.

164. *Shotwell Papers*, vol. II, pp. 393–396.

165. *Testimony*, pp. 157, 432, 434, 445; *Shotwell Papers*, vol. II, p. 396.

166. *Testimony*, pp. 445, 451.

167. *The Raleigh News*, 16 April 1878, p. 1.

168. *Testimony*, pp. 147, 225; 429 431, 435, 442, 433, 435; also see the affidavits of participants in *The Raleigh News*, 23 August 1878, p. 1.

169. *Shotwell Papers*, vol. II, p. 411.

170. Ibid., p. 406; *Testimony*, p. 219.

171. *Testimony*, pp. 206, 220, 429, 434. It should be noted that Randolph Shotwell *may* have had *personal* reasons for targeting Justice, dating back to his *North Carolina Citizen* days in Asheville. In response to Shotwell's allegation that Justice was a Confederate deserter (apparently published in *The Citizen*), Justice retorted in a letter to *The Star* that Shotwell was "a public liar and a drunken slanderer." See *The Rutherford Star*, 2 July 1870, p. 3. The prose in the Shotwell diaries is exceptionally vindictive with respect to Justice.

172. If not the leader, Lyle was almost certainly involved. The Congressional testimony (South Carolina) includes the following statement: "[M]y information from Washington is that the Ku Klux in Rutherford County, who are confessing, have given the information that Mr. Lyle was in council with the commanders of the Klan, who planned and carried out the raid on Rutherfordton...." See *Testimony Taken By the Joint Select Committee to Inquire into the Condition of Affairs in the Late Insurrectionary States, South Carolina* (hereafter *SC Testimony*), vol. II (Washington, DC: Government Printing Office, 1872), p. 788. Also see the same volume, pp. 878–879. Justice testified that he believed the leader "was a South Carolina chief." See *Testimony*, p. 158. Following his arrest, Shotwell referred to his ability to make a jail break from the Rutherfordton gaol "should I send word to Capt. Jim _____, and the _____ at L____." See the *Shotwell Papers*, vol. II, p. 504.

Capt. Lyle served in the 5th SC Infantry. See Jane B. Hewett, ed., *The Roster of Confederate Soldiers 1861–1865*, vol. X, Loflan, F.B. to McMillark, A.M. (Wilmington, NC: Broadfoot Publishing Co., 1996), p. 88.

173. Trelease, *White Terror*, pp. 353, 358–359, 413–414; also see *SC Testimony*, vol. II, pp. 897–898, for a long list of Limestone Springs victims.

174. Quoted from *SC Testimony*, vol. III, p. 1613; also see Trelease, *White Terror*, p. 353. Interstate cooperation is perhaps also suggested by the testimony of a member of Horse Creek den who stated that he was initiated by Col. McAfee. See *Testimony*, p. 431.

175. Trelease, *White Terror*, p. 353. Trelease probably inferred Lyle's roll as "Grand Klan chief" from a *New-York Tribune* article which described the Grand Klan as "a sort of congress of the Order" for Spartanburg's seventy-seven dens—but not as a multi-county, inter-state organization. In my opinion, and if the findings of the Columbia grand jury were accurate, Lyle would have likely functioned as an *equal* with other upcountry and North Carolina county chiefs. See the *New-York Tribune*, 24 November 1871, p. 2.

176. *Testimony*, pp. 118, 213; James M. Justice to Gov. Todd R. Caldwell, 12 June 1871, Governors' Papers, box #228 (NC Office of Archives and History, Raleigh, NC); *Shotwell Papers*, vol. II, pp. 395, 419; and *The Rutherford Star*, 28 June 1871, p. 2.

177. *Testimony*, p. 176.

178. In addition to Durham and Lee, Eaves' "Klan relations" included his uncle, Guilford Eaves, and cousin, Capt. Lafayette Eaves. See *Testimony*, pp. 30, 147, 220.

179. *Testimony*, pp. 176–177.

180. J.G. de Roulhac Hamilton, with the collaboration of Rebecca Cameron, *The Papers of Randolph Shotwell* (Raleigh: The North Carolina Historical Commission, 1936), Vol. III, p. 451.

181. I differ here with Bogue, p. 258.
182. *North Carolina Troops*, vol. XII, p. 239.
183. Ibid., vol. VI, p. 67; *Testimony*, pp. 202, 422. DePriest's den seems to have been associated with the Burnt Chimney section and was called the Burnt Chimney den as well as Den No. 3 (but see note 192).
184. *Testimony*, pp. 438–439.
185. *Shotwell Papers*, vol. II, pp. 425–427.
186. *The Raleigh News*, 16 April 1878, p. 1.
187. *Testimony*, pp. 130–131, 155, 182, 437, 439.
188. Ibid., p. 176.
189. *North Carolina Troops*, vol. XII, p. 245.
190. *Testimony*, p. 206
191. *Shotwell Papers*, vol. II, p. 350.
192. *Testimony*, pp. 218, 444, 498. Part of DePriest's den (including Harrill) withdrew and formed their own (*also* known as Burnt Chimney den). The leader of this group of "young bloods" was eighteen year-old Matt McBrayer (1852–1922), who would later be a prominent Forest City and Rutherfordton attorney. See Griffin, *History*, pp. 409–410. Helen Flack Cole recalled (personal communication) that McBrayer's son, Dr. Matt McBrayer (1886–1964), a Rutherfordton dentist, was active in the revived Klan, ca. 1930.
193. *North Carolina Troops*, vol. XII, p. 241.
194. *Testimony*, pp. 125, 130.
195. Ibid., pp. 131, 215, 316; *Shotwell Papers*, vol. II, p. 404.
196. *Shotwell Papers*, vol. II, pp. 350–351, 403–404; *Testimony*, p. 316.
197. *Testimony*, p. 200.
198. Following the Rutherfordton raid, Judge J.M. Cloud was sent to Rutherford by Caldwell (along with William Preston Bynum). He "found a bad condition of things," noted that as many as fifty affidavits had been taken by Judge Logan, issued eleven warrants himself, then turned that matter over to U.S. Commissioner Scoggins. See Judge J.M. Cloud to Gov. Todd R. Caldwell, 12 July 1871, Governors' Papers, box #228 (NC Office of Archives and History, Raleigh, NC).
Scoggins wrote Caldwell a week later that the Commissioner's court had tried thirty cases over three weeks for Ku Kluxing. Of these, twenty-one had failed to give bail and were confined in the village jail (including Shotwell). Sixty to seventy had made affidavits before Judge Logan and had given the names of between 150 and 200 engaged in raiding. Comm. Nathan Scoggins to Gov. Todd R. Caldwell, 19 July 1871, Governors' Papers, box #228 (NC Office of Archives and History, Raleigh, NC).

199. *The Rutherford Star*, 13 August 1871, p. 2.
200. *Testimony*, p. 447; Trelease, *White Terror*, p. 404.
201. Durham, p. 44.
202. *Testimony*, pp. 143, 344.
203. *Shotwell Papers*, vol. III, pp. 75–76.
204. Rutherford County, NC, Record of Deeds, vol. 50, pp. 328–329 (microform).
205. *The Rutherford Star*, 11 November 1871, p.3; and 18 November 1871, p. 3; *The Daily Sentinel* (Raleigh), 13 September 1871, p. 2; and 3 October 1871, p. 2; *Carolina Era* (Raleigh), 14 September 1871, p. 2; 12 October 1871, p. 1; and 16 November 1871, p. 3.
206. *The Rutherford Star*, 28 October 1871, p. 2.
207. Schenck diary, vols. 5 & 6 in one, p. 246. See also *The Rutherford Star*, 21 October 1871, p. 1.
208. See Durham, pp. 44–45.
209. *Weekly Pioneer* (Asheville), 1 August 1874, p. 2.
210. *Carolina Era* (Raleigh), 28 October 1872, p. 2.
211. *Yorkville (SC) Enquirer*, 25 September 1873, p. 2; *The Southern Home* (Charlotte), 29 September 1873, p. 2; *The Daily Sentinel* (Raleigh), 1 October 1873, p. 1.
212. *Our Heritage*, p. 315.
213. Major Erwin originally opposed secession. See Griffin, *History*, p. 296.
214. *Testimony*, p. 591.
215. *Greensboro Patriot*, 31 July 1872, p. 3; Schenck diary, vols. 5 & 6 in one, pp. 271–272.
216. Durham, pp. 44–45.
217. *Carolina Era* (Raleigh), 4 November 1872, p. 1.
218. *Greensboro Patriot*, 30 October 1872, p. 2.
219. Schenck diary, vol. 7, pp. 18–19; *The Southern Home* (Charlotte) 24 March 1873, p. 3; *The Southern Home* (Charlotte) 21 April 1873, p. 3; *Carolina Watchman* (Salisbury), 24 April 1873, p. 2; *The Daily Sentinel* (Raleigh), 29 April 1873, p. 1.
220. *Shelby Banner*, 8 April 1875, p. 3.
221. *Carolina Era* (Raleigh), 28 October 1872, p. 2.
222. *Shotwell Papers*, vol. III, p. 449.
223. Ibid., pp. 73–74.
224. Shotwell's language. Ibid., p. 449.
225. *The Southern Home* (Charlotte), 15 November 1875, p. 3.
226. *The Rutherford Star and West-Carolina Record*, 20 June 1874, pp. 2–3.
227. *Weekly Pioneer* (Asheville), 22 August 1874, p. 2.

228. *The Rutherford Star and West-Carolina Record*, 18 July 1874, p. 2.
229. Durham, p. 48.
230. *The Southern Home* (Charlotte), 15 November 1875, p. 3.
231. Ibid.
232. *The Daily Sentinel* (Raleigh), 11 November 1875, p. 2.
233. *The Daily News* (Raleigh), 12 November 1875, p. 2.
234. Griffin, *History*, p. 318; Ninth Census of the United States, 1870: Rutherford County, NC, Population Schedule, p. 151 (microform); Tomlinson (1879), p. 46; Tomlinson (1883), p. 27.
235. Tenth Census of the United States, 1880: Rutherford County, NC, Population Schedule, ed 168, sheet 1, line 12 (microform).
236. *The Mountain Banner* (Rutherfordton), 14 April 1882, p. 3.
237. Ibid., 26 January 1883, p. 3.
238. Ibid., 11 April 1884, p. 2.
239. Rutherford County, NC, Record of Deeds, General Indices, Grantor, letter E, p. 1; and Grantee, letter E, pp. 15–16 (microform).
240. Griffin, *History*, p. 340.
241. Ibid.; *Shotwell Papers*, vol. III, p. 452; *The Raleigh News*, 16 August 1878, p. 1. An undated clipping in the Shotwell Papers stated that Justice, who had only recently moved to Hendersonville, "was attending superior court in [Columbus, Polk] county, before which he had several important causes…. It was noticeable during the afternoon that he was drinking heavily, and at an early hour in the night he walked off the second story balcony of Hill's Hotel, sustaining injuries which rendered him insensible from the time of his accident to his death, which occurred on the 19th [of September, 1877]." See the Randolph Abbott Shotwell Papers, P.C. 243.8, diaries, vol. #9, unpag. (NC Office of Archives and History, Raleigh, NC).
242. Griffin, *History*, p. 254.
243. Ibid., pp. 319–320.
244. Ibid., pp. 351–352.
245. Ibid., p. 318.
246. Ibid., p. 319.
247. Capt. John Edwards (34th NC, Co. B), Capt. Francis Twitty (34th NC, Co. C) and Col. Champ Davis (16th NC, Co. G) were killed; Maj. H.D. Lee (16th NC, Co. D) moved to Shelby; Capt. Lawson Harrill (50th NC, Co. I), Capt. Thompson J. Wood (34th NC, Co. I) and Capt. George Andrews (50th NC, Co. G) also left Rutherford soon after the War. Brig. Gen. Collet Leventhorpe, the County's most distinguished veteran, moved to the Happy Valley section of Caldwell County sometime in the 1870s.

There were of course, in addition to Eaves, prominent ex–Confederates who remained in postbellum Rutherford. These included Capt. M.O. Dickerson, Sr. (34th NC, Co. C), Maj. L.P. Erwin (16th NC, Co. G), Capt. Joseph Walker (56th NC, Co. B), T.B. Twitty (34th NC), Capt. John Y. McEntire (16th NC, Co. G), Capt. Samuel Wilkins (50th NC, Co. K), Capt. Joseph Creighton Byers (34th NC, Co. B), Capt. W.L. Twitty (1st Bat., Co. C), Capt. J.L. McDowell (34th NC, Co. I) and Lt. George H. Mills (16th NC, Co. G). See Griffin, *History*, pp. 226–227, 244–245, 273, 293–298, 300, 302, 304. But few of these men held company commands which were comparable to Eaves' in length.

248. *New Era* (Shelby), 2 June 1888, p. 3; *Union Republican* (Winston), 31 May 1888, p. 1; Gordon B. McKinney, *Southern Mountain Republicans 1865–1900: Politics and the Appalachian Community* (Chapel Hill: The University of North Carolina Press, 1978), p. 159.

249. Benjamin Harrison Papers, Republican State Executive Committee circulars dated 29 October 1888 & 31 October 1888, Series 2, October 21, 1888 to November 2, 1888, reel #57 (microform); *The Landmark* (Statesville), 1 November 1888, p. 2; *The News and Observer* (Raleigh), 30 October 1888, p. 1; *Charlotte Chronicle*, 2 November 1888, pp. 1, 2; 3 November 1888, pp. 1, 2; and 5 November 1888, p. 1.

There were at least two circulars, both of which are preserved in the Benjamin Harrison Papers. One, sent to Democratic registrars, reminded them that it would "give us … pleasure to introduce a lot of ballot-box thieves to the inside of Albany Penitentiary"—a reminder of the fate of Shotwell and the Rutherford Ku Kluxers. The other circular recruited "reliable" Republicans to act as poll watchers. During the controversy over Eaves' appointment as Revenue Collector, the former circular seems to have been derisively referred to as the "Not Afraid of the Devil" circular. See the *Asheville Democrat*, 29 February 1890, p. 6; 10 April 1890, p. 4; and 24 April 1890, p. 5; *Charlotte Chronicle*, 13 April 1890, p. 1; and *The Landmark* (Statesville), 17 April 1890, p. 3.

250. *The Daily News* (Charlotte), 2 March 1889, p. 4.

251. *Journal of the Proceedings of the Senate of the United States of America from March 5, 1889, to March 3, 1891, Inclusive*, vol. XXVII (Washington, DC: Government Printing Office, 1901), p. 250.

252. McKinney, pp. 63 ff.
253. *Charlotte Chronicle*, 25 June 1890, p. 4.
254. McKinney, p. 159.
255. Ibid.; *Charlotte Chronicle*, 25 June 1890,

p. 4; James Howard Hershman, Jr., "The North Carolina Republican Party: The Years of Revitalization, 1888–1892," M.A. Thesis, Dept. of History, Wake Forest University, 1971, pp. 73–74.

256. Benjamin Harrison Papers, Dr. John J. Mott to Pres. Benjamin Harrison, 7 April 1890, Series 1, March 1, 1890 to April 28, 1890, reel #26 (microform).

257. *Senate Proceedings*, pp. 668–669.

258. Jeter Pritchard nominated Eaves and the enthusiasm for the Rutherford man was described thus: "Cries of 'acclamation!' were heard all over the hall, and the question was at once put. A resounding 'aye went up that shook the walls, which was followed by the most uproarious applause and shouting heard at any time during the convention." *Union Republican* (Winston), 4 September 1890, p. 1.

259. Ibid., 11 September 1890, p. 2; McKinney, p. 159.

260. *The Asheville Citizen*, 29 August 1890, p. 1.

261. See the biographical sketch of Harris in William S. Powell, ed., *The Dictionary of North Carolina Biography*, vol. 3, H–K (Chapel Hill: The University of North Carolina Press, 1988), pp. 53–54.

262. *The Landmark* (Statesville), 12 February 1891, p. 1.

263. McKinney, p. 160.

264. Ibid.; *Union Republican* (Winston), 4 June 1891, p. 2; and 11 June 1891, p. 2.

265. Benjamin R. Justesen, *George Henry White: An Even Chance in the Race of Life* (Baton Rouge: Louisiana State University Press, 2001), p. 172.

266. During the White Supremacy campaign of 1898, Eaves stated: "I am not in favor of putting negroes in office over white men.... [But] I do not want to be understood as being opposed to negroes holding offices which they are competent to fill and where they do not come into social conflict with white people. The negroes themselves do not really want such offices." From *The Charlotte Daily Observer*, 4 October 1898, p. 8.

267. *Union Republican* (Winston), 11 June 1891, p. 2.

268. Joseph F. Steelman, "Vicissitudes of Republican Party Politics: The Campaign of 1892 in North Carolina," *The North Carolina Historical Review*, vol. XLIII, no. 4 (Autumn 1966), pp. 430–436.

269. *Union Republican* (Winston), 4 June 1891, p. 2.

270. Steelman, "Campaign of 1892," p. 433.

271. Ibid., p. 434.

272. Justesen, pp. 171–176.

273. Ibid., pp. 175–176.

274. Benjamin Harrison Papers, John Baxter Eaves to Pres. Benjamin Harrison, 2 July 1892, Series 2, June 13, 1892 to July 22, 1892, reel #83 (microform).

275. Justesen, p. 177.

276. Steelman, "Republican Party Strategists," p. 245; Justesen, p. 177.

277. Steelman, "Issue of Fusion," p. 252.

278. Ibid., p. 245.

279. Ibid., p. 248.

280. McKinney, p. 163; Steelman, "Issue of Fusion," pp. 258–260.

281. Steelman, "Issue of Fusion," pp. 254–255; *The Charlotte Daily Observer*, 31 August 1894, p. 1.

282. McKinney, p. 164; *The Charlotte Daily Observer*, 31 August 1894, p. 1.

283. *The Charlotte Daily Observer*, 4 October 1898, p. 8.

Bibliography

Arnett, Ethel Stephens. *David Caldwell*. Greensboro, NC: Media, Inc., Printers and Publishers, 1976.
The Asheville Citizen (Asheville, NC).
Asheville Daily Gazette (Asheville, NC).
Asheville Democrat (Asheville, NC).
Ayers, Edward L. *The Promise of the New South*. New York: Oxford University Press, 1992.
_____. *Vengeance & Justice: Crime and Punishment in the 19th-Century American South*. New York: Oxford University Press, 1984.
Barber, The Rev. Henry. *British Family Names, Their Origin and Meaning with Lists of Scandinavian, Frisian, Anglo-Saxon and Norman Names*, 2nd ed., enlarged. Baltimore: Genealogical Publishing Company, 1968.
Bardsley, Charles Wareing. *A Dictionary of Irish and Welsh Surnames with Special American Instances*, rev. for the press by his widow. Baltimore: Genealogical Publishing Company, 1980.
Black, George F. *The Surnames of Scotland: Their Origin, Meaning and History*. New York: The New York Public Library, 1962.
Bogue, Jesse Parker, Jr. "Violence and Oppression in North North Carolina During Reconstruction 1865–1873." PhD. Diss., University of Maryland, 1973.
Bradley, Stephen E., abs. *North Carolina Confederate Militia and Home Guard Records*. Volumes 1–3. Virginia Beach, VA: the author, 1995.
_____, ed. *North Carolina Confederate Militia Officers Roster as Contained in the Adjutant-General's Officers Roster*. Wilmington, NC: Broadfoot Publishing Company, 1992.
Bruce, Dickson D., Jr. *Violence and Culture in the Antebellum South*. Austin, TX: University of Texas Press, 1979.
Brundage, W. Fitzhugh. *Lynching in the New South: Georgia and Virginia, 1880–1930*. Urbana: University of Illinois Press, 1993.
_____, ed. *Under Sentence of Death: Lynching in the South*. Chapel Hill: The University of North Carolina Press, 1997.
Bryant, Carol, abstractor. *Abstracts of Chester County, Pennsylvania Land Records*, vols. 2–4. Westminster, MD: Willow Bend Books, 1999–2000.
The Burke County News (Morganton, NC).
Butler, Marion, Papers of, #114 (Southern Historical Collection, Wilson Library, University of North Carolina at Chapel Hill).
Carlton, David. *Mill and Town in South Carolina, 1880–1920*. Baton Rouge: Louisiana State University Press, 1982.
Carolina Era (Raleigh, NC).

Bibliography

The Carolina Spartan (Spartanburg, SC).
Carolina Watchman (Salisbury, NC).
Carpenter, Kinchen Jahu. *War Diary of Kinchen Jahu Carpenter, Confederate Soldier, May, 1862–May, 1865*. Rutherfordton, NC: Mrs. Julie Carpenter Williams, 1955.
Caruthers, Eli W. *A Sketch of the Life and Character of the Rev. David Caldwell, D.D.* Greensborough, NC: Swaim and Sherwood, 1842.
_____. *Revolutionary Incidents: and Sketches of Character, Chiefly in the "Old North State."* Philadelphia: Hayes & Zell, 1854.
Cash, Wilbur Joseph. *The Mind of the South*. New York: Alfred A. Knopf, 1941.
Casstevens, Frances H. *The Civil War and Yadkin County, North Carolina: A History*. Jefferson, NC: McFarland & Co., Inc., Publishers, 1997.
The Caucasian (Raleigh, NC).
Cecelski, David S., and Timothy B. Tyson, eds. *Democracy Betrayed: The Wilmington Race Riot of 1898 and Its Legacy*. Chapel Hill: The University of North Carolina Press, 1998.
Charlotte Chronicle (Charlotte, NC).
The Charlotte Democrat (Charlotte, NC).
The Charlotte News (Charlotte, NC).
Chester County Genealogy. http://www.techcrafters.net/Gen/ Chester/scripts/queries. asp?ST=14 (1 May 2002).
Clarke, R.S.J., compiler. *Gravestone Inscriptions, County Down, vol. 19: Donaghcloney, Dromara, Dromore, Garvaghy and Magheralin*. Belfast: Ulster Historical Foundation, 1983.
Clark, Walter, collector and editor. *The State Records of North Carolina*, vols. XI, XIII, XXII. Wilmington, NC: Broadfoot Publishing Company, 1993–94.
Cleveland County, NC, Minutes, Superior Court, Criminal, 1900–1906, vol. 4 (microform).
Cole, Helen Flack. Interview on 1 April 1998 in Lenoir, NC.
Collins & Goodwin. *Biographical Sketches of the Members of the General Assembly of North Carolina, 1895*. Raleigh, NC: Edwards & Broughton, 1895.
Commemorative Biographical Record of Washington County, Pennsylvania, Containing Biographical Sketches of Prominent and Representative Citizens, and Many of the Early Settled Families. Chicago: J.H. Beers & Co., 1893.
The Concord Times (Concord, NC).
Confederate Widows, North Carolina, Pension Records, 1900 (NC Office of Archives and History, Raleigh, NC).
Conner, R.D.W. *The Life and Speeches of Charles Brantley Aycock*. Garden City, NY: Doubleday, Page & Co., 1912.
Cook, Gerald Wilson. *The Last Tarheel Militia 1861–1865*. Winston-Salem, NC: the author, 1987.
Crow, Jeffery J., and Robert F. Durden. *Maverick Republican in the Old North State: A Political Biography of Daniel L. Russell*. Baton Rouge: Louisiana State University Press, 1977.
Crumrine, Boyd. *History of Washington County, Pennsylvania, with Biographical Sketches of Many of Its Pioneers and Prominent Men*. Philadelphia: L.H. Leverts & Co., 1882.
Cutler, James Elbert. *Lynch-Law*. New York: Longmans, Green, and Co., 1905.
The Daily Charlotte Observer or *Charlotte Daily Observer* (Charlotte, NC).
The Daily News (Raleigh, NC).
The Daily Sentinel (Raleigh, NC).
Daniels, Josephus. *Editor in Politics*. Chapel Hill: The University of North Carolina Press, 1941.
Davidson, Capt. T. Stuart. Letter to Mrs. Rush H. (Helen Flack) Cole on 1 November 1978.
Department of Commerce and Labor, Bureau of the Census. *Heads of Families at the First Census of the United States Taken in the Year 1790, North Carolina* Washington, DC: Government Printing Office, 1908.
_____. *Thirteenth Census of the United States, Taken in the Year 1910, Abstract of the Census, Statistics of Population, Agriculture, Manufactures, and Mining for the United States, the States, and Principal Cities, with Supplement for North Carolina, Containing Statistics for the State, Counties, Cities, and Other Divisions*. Washington, D.C.: Government Printing Office, 1913.
Dickey, James. *Deliverance*. Boston: Houghton Mifflin Company, 1970.
Dowd, Clement. *Life of Zebulon Vance*. Charlotte, NC: Observer Printing & Publishing House, 1897.
Draper, Lyman C. *King's Mountain and Its Heroes: History of the Battle of King's Mountain, October 7th, 1780, and the Events which Led to It*. Cincinnati: Peter G. Thompson, Publisher, 1881.
The Draper Manuscripts. King's Mountain Papers, Series DD (microform).

Durham, Robert Lee. *Since I Was Born*, ed. by Marshall William Fishwick. Richmond, VA: Whittet & Shepperson, 1953.
Eaves, George G. "Autobiography of the Eaves-Baxter Families," part 1, *The Forest City Courier*, 2 April 1931, p. 9; and part 2, *The Forest City Courier*, 9 April 1931, p. 10.
Edmonds, Helen G. *The Negro and Fusion Politics in North Carolina, 1894–1901*. Chapel Hill: The University of North Carolina Press, 1951.
Eighth Census of the United States, 1860: Rutherford County, NC, Slave Schedule (microform).
Emmison, F.G., abstractor and editor. *Essex Wills (England), Vol. 1, 1558–1565*. N.p.: National Genealogical Society of America, 1982.
Escott, Paul D. *Many Excellent People: Power and Privilege in North Carolina, 1850–1900*. Chapel Hill: The University of North Carolina Press, 1985.
Eustace, P. Beryl. *Registry of Deeds, Dublin, Abstracts of Wills, vol. 1, 1708–1745*. Baltimore: Clearfield Company, Inc., 1996.
FamilySearch (Church of Jesus Christ of Latter-day Saints). http://www.familysearch.org (1 May 2002).
Faulkner, William. *Intruder in the Dust*. New York: Signet Books, 1958.
Fernow, Berthold, compiler and editor. *Calender of Wills [of the State of New York]: On File and Recorded in the Offices of the Clerk of the Court of Appeals, of the County Clerk at Albany, and of the Secretary of State*. Baltimore: Clearfield Company, Inc., 1999.
Fifth Census of the United States, 1830: Rutherford County, NC, Population Schedule (microform).
Flack, Charles Z., Sr. Letter to Ms. Helen Flack Cole on 6 February 1980 (HFC). Grandson of Mills Flack.
_____. Letter to Ms. Helen Flack Cole on 23 April 1985 (HFC). Grandson of Mills Flack.
_____. Unpublished manuscript, ca. 1985 (HFC).
Flack Family Genealogy Forum. http://www.genforum.genealogy.com/flack/messages (1 May 2002).
Flack, Horace E. *The Flack Family*. [Lenoir, NC]: Helen Flack Cole, 1972.
Flack, Ivarea. *Flack Family Heritage 1975*. Rutherfordton, NC: Liberty Press, 1975.
Flack, Ralph R. *Memories*. Ed. Helen Flack Cole. [Lenoir, NC]: n.p., 1978.
_____. Papers of (HFC).
_____. Papers of (ICC).
_____. Unpublished manuscript, 1968 (HFC).
Foner, Eric. *Reconstruction: America's Unfinished Revolution, 1863–1877*. New York: Harper & Row, 1988.
Forest City Courier (Forest City, NC).
Forest City, NC, Records of the First Baptist Church, 1888–1991, 10 vols. (microform, Baptist Historical Archives, Wake Forest University).
Foucault, Michel. *Discipline and Punish: The Birth of the Prison*, trans. by Alan Sheridan. New York: Vintage Books, 1979.
Franklin, John Hope. "Counter Reconstruction," in *Reconstruction in the South*, 2nd ed. Lexington, Mass.: D.C. Heath and Company, 1972.
Futhey, J. Smith, and Gilbert Cope. *History of Chester County, Pennsylvania, with Genealogical and Biographical Sketches*. Philadelphia: Louis H. Everts, 1881.
The Genealogical Society of Iredell County. *The Heritage of Iredell County 1980*. Statesville, NC: The Genealogical Society of Iredell County, 1980.
Genealogical Society of Old Tryon County. *The Heritage of Rutherford County, North Carolina, Volume I, 1984*. Winston-Salem, NC: Hunter Publishing Co., 1984.
"George Flack Family Bible." *Bulletin of the Genealogical Society of Old Tryon County, North Carolina*, 1 (August 1973), pp. 26–28.
Gerberich, Dr. Albert H., and Dr. Gaius M. Brumbaugh. *Lancaster County, Pennsylvania, Tax Lists, 1751, 1756, 1757, 1758*. Washington, DC: The National Genealogical Society, 1933.
Gilmore, Glenda Elizabeth. *Gender & Jim Crow: Women and the Politics of White Supremacy in North Carolina, 1896–1920*. Chapel Hill: The University of North Carolina Press, 1996.
Goodspeed's *History of Northeast Arkansas*. http://fly.hiwaay.net/dmglenn/inda_c.htm (10 September 2002).
Goodwyn, Lawrence. *The Populist Moment: A Short History of the Agrarian Revolt in America*. New York: Oxford University Press, 1978.
Governors' Letterbooks #62 (NC Office of Archives and History, Raleigh, NC).
Governors' Papers, box #s 227 & 228 (NC Office of Archives and History, Raleigh, NC).

Bibliography

Greensboro Patriot (Greensboro, NC).
Griffin, Clarence W. *Essays on North Carolina History*. Forest City, NC: The Forest City Courier, 1951.
____. *The First Baptist Church of Forest City, N.C*. Forest City, NC: The Forest City Courier, 1939.
____. *The History of Old Tryon and Rutherford Counties*. Asheville, NC: The Miller Printing Company, 1937.
____. *Revolutionary Service of Col. John Walker and Family and Memoirs of Hon. Felix Walker*. Forest City, NC: The Forest City Courier, 1930.
Guilford County, NC, Record of Deeds, vols. 1–3, 11 (micro-form).
____, Record of Wills, vol. A (microform).
Hair, William Ivy. *Carnival of Fury: Robert Charles and the New Orleans Race Riot of 1900*. Baton Rouge: Louisiana State University Press, 1976.
Hall, Jacquelyn Dowd. *Revolt Against Chivalry: Jessie Daniel Ames and the Women's Campaign Against Lynching*. New York: Columbia University Press, 1979.
Hamilton, J.G. de Roulhac, ed., with the collaboration of Rebecca Cameron. *The Papers of Randolph Shotwell*, vols. II, III. Raleigh, NC: The North Carolina Historical Commission, 1931–36.
____. *Reconstruction in North Carolina*. Gloucester, Mass.: Peter Smith, 1964, a rpt. of the Columbia University ed. of 1914.
Hanks, Patrick, and Flaviq Hodges. *A Dictionary of Surnames*. New York: Oxford University Press, 1988.
Hanna, Charles A. *The Scotch-Irish or the Scot in North Britain, North Ireland, and North America*. Baltimore: Genealogical Publishing Company, 1968.
Harrison, Benjamin, Papers (microform).
Harrison, Henry. *Surnames of the United Kingdom: A Concise Etymological Dictionary*. Baltimore: Genealogical Publishing Company, 1969.
Haun, Weynette Parks. *Johnston County, North Carolina Land Warrants, Surveys & Miscellaneous Land Papers (Secretary of State Papers), 1737–1899*. Durham, NC: the author, 1993.
____. *North Carolina Revolutionary Army Accounts, Book A [Treasurer, State] [Part XII]*. Durham, NC: the author, 1999.
____. *North Carolina Revolutionary Army Accounts: Secretary of State, Treasurer's & Comptroller's Papers, Journal "A", (Public Accounts) 1775–1776*. Durham, NC: the author, 1988.
Hawbaker, Gary T., Editor. *Lancaster County, Pennsylvania Quarter Sessions Abstracts (1729–1742), Book 1*. Hershey, PA: self published, 1986.
____, and Clyde L. Goff. *A New Index: Lancaster County, Pennsylvania, Before the Federal Census*, vols. I–III, V. Hershey, PA: n.p., 1981–82, 1989.
Haynes, Mrs. Grover C., Sr. *Raleigh Rutherford Haynes: A History of His Life and Achievements*. Asheville, NC: Miller Printing Company, 1954.
Hemphill Family Committee. *Hemphills in North Carolina*. Collegedale, TN: The College Press, 1981.
Henderson County, NC, Superior Court, Criminal Action Papers, 50.326.31 (NC Office of Archives and History, Raleigh, NC)
Hendrick, Burton J. *Statesmen of the Lost Cause*. New York: The Literary Guild of America, 1939.
Hershman, James Howard, Jr. "The North Carolina Republican Party: The Years of Revitalization, 1888–1892." M.A. Thesis, Dept. of History, Wake Forest University, 1971.
Hewett, Jane B., ed. *The Roster of Confederate Soldiers 1861–1865*, vol. X, Loflan, F.B. to McMillark, A.M. Wilmington, NC: Broadfoot Publishing Co., 1996.
Historical Society of Pennsylvania. *Abstracts Of Lancaster County Pennsylvania Wills*, 2 vols. Westminster, MD: Family Line Publications, 1995.
History of North Carolina: North Carolina Biography, vol. VI. Chicago: The Lewis Publishing Company, 1919.
History of the First National Bank (Shelby, NC). http://www.ibankatfnb.com/site/home-history.html (2 September 2002).
History of the General Assembly of North Carolina, January 9–March 13, 1895, Inclusive. Raleigh, NC: E.M. Uzzell, Printer and Binder, 1895.
Hoffman, Margaret M. *The Granville District of North Carolina: Abstracts of Miscellaneous Land Office Records*, vol. 5. N.p.: the author, 1995.
Hofstadter, Richard. *The Age of Reform: From Bryan to F.D.R*. New York: Vintage Books, 1955/1960.
Holcomb, Brent H. *Anson County, NC Deed Abstracts, vol. II: 1757–1766 & 1763 Tax List*. [Clinton, SC]: self published, 1975.

_____. *Deed Abstracts of Tryon, Lincoln, & Rutherford Counties, N.C.: 1769–1786, and, Tryon County, N.C. Wills & Estates*. Greenville, SC: Southern Historical Press, Inc., 1997.
_____, compiler. *Marriages of Rutherford County, North Carolina, 1779–1868*. Baltimore: Genealogical Publishing Company, 1986.
_____. *Tryon County North Carolina Minutes of the Court of Pleas and Quarter Sessions, 1769–1779*. Columbia, SC: SCMAR, 1994.
Huber, Patrick J. "'Caught up in the Violent Whirlwind of Lynching': The 1885 Quadruple Lynching in Chatham County, North Carolina." *The North Carolina Historical Review*, 75 (April 1998), pp. 135–160.
Hughes, Fred. *Guilford County: A Map Supplement*. Jamestown, NC: The Custom House, 1988.
_____. *Guilford County, North Carolina, Historical Documentation [Hughes Map]*. N.p.: Fred Hughes, 1980.
Inscoe, John C., and Gordon B. McKinney. *The Heart of Confederate Appalachia: Western North Carolina in the Civil War*. Chapel Hill: The University of North Carolina Press, 2000.
Inverarity, James M. "Populism and Lynching in Louisiana, 1889–1896." *American Sociological Review*, 41 (April 1976), pp. 262–280.
Jolley, Daniel Wayne. "The Ku Klux Klan in Rutherford County, North Carolina, 1870–1871." M.A. Thesis, University of North Carolina, 1994.
_____. The Ku Klux Klan in Western North Carolina, 1870–1871. http://www.geocities.com/ darkgenius.geo/klanruth.html (27 June 2002).
Jones, E.O. "'List of Participants in the Battle of Alamance' from 'The War of the Regulators, It's Place in History.'" Thesis, University of North Carolina 1942.
Jones, May F., ed. *Memoirs and Speeches of Locke Craig, Governor of North Carolina, 1913–1917: A History—Political and Otherwise from Scrapbooks and Old Manuscripts*. Asheville, NC: Hackney and Moale Company, 1923.
Jones, Jo. Seawell. *A Defense of the Revolutionary History of the State of North Carolina from the Aspersions of Mr. Jefferson*. Raleigh, NC: Turner & Hughes, 1834.
Jordan, Weymouth T., Jr., compiler. *North Carolina Troops 1861–1865 A Roster*, vols. V–VI, XII–XIII. Raleigh, NC: Division of Archives and History, 1975–1990.
The Journal or *Winston-Salem Journal* (Winston-Salem, NC).
Journal of the House of Representatives of the General Assembly of the State of North Carolina, at its Session of 1895. Winston, NC: M.I. & J.C. Stewart, Public Printers and Binders, 1895.
Journal of the Proceedings of the Senate of the United States of America from March 5, 1889, to March 3, 1891, Inclusive, vol. XXVII. Washington, DC: Government Printing Office, 1901.
Journal of the Senate of the General Assembly of the State of North Carolina, at Its Session of 1868–'69. Raleigh, NC: M.S. Littlefield, State Printer & Binder, 1869.
Justesen, Benjamin R. *George Henry White: An Even Chance in the Race of Life*. Baton Rouge: Louisiana State University Press, 2001.
Knoxville Daily Journal (Knoxville, TN).
Lancaster County, Pennsylvania, Deed Book WW.
_____, Genweb. http://getafix. mathcs.wilkes.edu/lancaster/ppl/g/glenn/glenn001.html (11 November 2000).
_____, Land Warrant Map (photocopy from the collection of the Lancaster County Historical Society).
_____, Tax Lists, Drumore Township, 1757–1780.
The Landmark (Statesville, NC).
Lazenby, Mary Elinor, compiler. *Catawba Frontier, 1775–1781: Memories of Pensioners*. Washington, DC: the author, 1950.
Lefler, Hugh Talmage, and Albert Ray Newsome. *North Carolina: The History of a Southern State*. Chapel Hill: The University of North Carolina Press, 1954.
Legislative Biographical Scrapbook, Session 1887, North Carolina. Raleigh, NC: Edwards, Broughton & Co., 1887.
Leyburn, James G. *The Scotch-Irish: A Social History*. Chapel Hill: The University of North Carolina Press, 1962.
Linn, Jo White, transcriber. *Rowan County, North Carolina, Tax Lists, 1757–1800: Annotated Transcriptions*. Salisbury, NC: published privately, 1995.
Litwack, Leon. *Trouble in Mind: Black Southerners in the Age of Jim Crow*. New York: Alfred A. Knopf, 1998.

Lockhart, Walter Samuel, III. "Lynching in North Carolina: 1888–1906." M.A. Thesis, University of North Carolina 1972.
Lu, Helen Mason, and Gwen Blomquist Neumann, compilers. *North Carolina Spectator and Western Advertiser (1830–1835) Rutherford County, North Carolina Abstracts.* Dallas, TX: the authors, 1982.
MacLysaght, Edward. *The Surnames of Ireland*, 6th ed. Dublin: Irish Academic Press, 1985.
Martin, Jacob, abstractor. *Wills of Chester County, Pennsylvania, 1766–1778.* Westminster, MD: Willow Bend Books, 1999.
Matheson, Sir Robert E. *Special Report on Surnames in Ireland [Together With] Varieties and Synonymes of Surnames and Christian Names in Ireland.* Baltimore: Genealogical Publishing Company, 1994.
Matthews, Donald G. "The Southern Rite of Human Sacrifice." *The Journal of Southern Religion,* vol. III (2000). http://jsr.as.wvu.edu/mathews.htm (19 July 2001).
Maurice, Caroline Parker. *The Hampton Family: The History and Genealogy of Some of the Descendants of the Immigrant John Hamton who Migrated From New Jersey to Maryland to North Carolina to Kentucky to Illinois to Kansas to Indian Territory, Oklahoma.* Placitas, New Mexico: the author, 1993.
Maxwell, Nelda. Letter to author on 25 April, 1998. Granddaughter of Mills Flack.
_____. Letter to Ms. Helen Flack Cole on 10 May 1985 (HFC); and on 12 September 1989 (HFC).
Mayhill, R. Thomas, Compiler. *Lancaster County Pennsylvania Deed Abstracts & Revolutionary War Oaths of Allegiance,* rev. and enlarged ed., Deed Books A through M, 1729 through c1770 with adjoining Landowners & Witnesses Knightstown, Ind.: The Bookmark, 1988.
McBee, May Wilson. *Anson County, North Carolina, Abstracts of Early Records, vol. 1.* N.p.: the author, 1950.
McKinney, Gordon B. *Southern Appalachian Republicans 1865–1900: Politics and the Appalachian Community.* Chapel Hill: The University of North Carolina Press, 1978.
McMath, Robert C., Jr. *Populist Vanguard: A History of the Southern Farmers' Alliance.* New York: W.W. Norton & Company, 1977.
McNealy, Terry A., and Francis Wise Waite, compilers. *Bucks County Tax Records 1693–1778.* Doylestown, PA: Bucks County Genealogical Society, 1982.
McQuiston, Leona Bean, compiler. *The McQuiston, McCuiston, McQuesten Families, 1620–1937.* Louisville, KY: The Standard Press, 1937.
Mitchell, Theodore. *Political Education in the Southern Farmers' Alliance, 1887–1900.* Madison, Wis.: The University of Wisconsin Press, 1987.
Moore, Ruth. "Plato Durham, Hero, Idol of Reconstruction Days." *The Charlotte Observer,* 26 March 1933, sec. three, pp. 2, 6.
Morrow, D.F. *Then and Now: Reminiscences and Historical Romance, 1856–1865.* Macon, GA: J.W. Burke Co., 1926.
Moss, Bobby Gilmer. *The Patriots at King's Mountain.* Blacksburg, SC: Scotia-Hibernia Press, 1990.
_____. *Roster of the Patriots in the Battle of Moore's Creek Bridge.* Blacksburg, SC: Scotia-Hibernia Press, 1992.
The Mountain Banner (Rutherfordton, NC).
Murray County, GA, Minutes, Superior Court, 1846–1851 (State Archives of Georgia, Atlanta, GA).
The New Era (Shelby, NC).
New-York Tribune (New York, NY).
The News (Rutherfordton, NC).
News and Observer (Raleigh, NC).
Newton, Hedy Hughes, compiler and editor. *Rutherford County North Carolina Abstracts of Minutes Court of Pleas and Quarter Sessions, 1779–1786.* Ellenboro, NC: the author, 1974.
Ninth Census of the United States, 1870: Rutherford County, NC, Agricultural Schedule (microform).
Ninth Census of the United States, 1870: Rutherford County, NC, Population Schedule (microform).
"Nixon." American Experience, PBS (1998).
Noblin, Stuart. *Leonidas LaFayette Polk: Agrarian Crusader.* Chapel Hill: The University of North Carolina Press, 1949.
North Carolina: Rebuilding an Ancient Commonwealth, vol. III. New York: The American Historical Society, Inc., 1928.
North Carolina Reports: Cases Argued and Determined in the Supreme Court of North Carolina, vol.

66, January Term, 1872, rep. by W.M. Shipp & annotated by Walter Clark. [Raleigh, NC]: E.M. Uzzell & Co., State Printers & Binders, 1908.

North Carolina State Farmer's Alliance, Records of (NC Office of Archives and History, Raleigh, NC).

North Carolina Supreme Court, case file #6863, William Costin, et al. vs. William Baxter, Sr. (1849) (NC Office of Archives and History, Raleigh, NC).

Olzack, Susan. "The Political Context of Competition: Lynching and Urban Racial Violence, 1886–1914." *Social Forces*, 69 (December 1990), pp. 395–421.

Orr, Oliver H., Jr. *Charles Brantley Aycock*. Chapel Hill: The University of North Carolina Press, 1961.

Palmer, Bruce. *"Man Over Money": The Southern Populist Critique of American Capitalism*. Chapel Hill: The University of North Carolina Press, 1980.

Pardons, Daniel L. Russell to Charles B. Aycock, 1899–1902, G.O. 48 (NC Office of Archives and History, Raleigh, NC).

Pardons, Reasons for, Charles B. Aycock to Robert B. Glenn, 1901–1907, G.O. 53 (NC Office of Archives and History, Raleigh, NC).

Pennsylvania, Historical Society of. *Abstracts of Bucks County, Pennsylvania Wills, 1785–1825*. Westminster, MD: Family Line Publications, 1998.

Pennsylvania Marriages Prior to 1790: Names of Persons for Whom Marriage Licenses Were Issued in the Province of Pennsylvania Previous to 1790. Baltimore: Genealogical Publishing Company, 1968.

Philbeck, Miles, "Porter of Rowan and Rutherford," *Bulletin of the Genealogical Society of Old Tryon County*, 26 (November 1998), pp. 175–185.

Phillimore, W.P.W., and Gertrude Thrift, eds. *Indexes to Irish Wills*, 5 vols. in one. Baltimore: Genealogical Publishing Company, 1997.

Powell, William S., ed. *Dictionary of North Carolina Biography*, vols. 1–4. Chapel Hill: The University of North Carolina Press, 1979–91.

_____. *North Carolina Through Four Centuries*. Chapel Hill: The University of North Carolina Press, 1989.

Prather, H. Leon. *We Have Taken a City: Wilmington Racial Massacre and Coupe of 1898*. Cranbury, NJ: Associated University Presses, 1984.

Price, R.E. *Rutherford County: Economic and Social*. Durham, NC: The Seeman Printery, 1918.

The Progressive Farmer (Raleigh, NC).

Pruitt, Dr. A.B. *Abstracts of Land Entrys (sic): Guilford Co., NC, 1779–1796, and Rockingham Co., NC, 1790–1795*. N.P.: n.p., 1987.

_____. *Abstracts of Land Entries: Rutherford Co., NC, 1779–1795*. N.p.: the author, 1974.

The Public Record Office of Northern Ireland. http:// proni.nics.gov.uk/index.htm (11 November 2000).

The Raleigh News (Raleigh, NC).

Ramsey, Robert W. *Carolina Cradle: Settlement of the Northwest Carolina Frontier, 1747–1762*. Chapel Hill: The University of North Carolina Press, 1964.

Rankin, the Rev. S.M. *History of Buffalo Presbyterian Church and Her People*. Greensboro, NC: Joseph J. Stone & Company, nd.

Reaney, P.H., and R.M. Wilson. *A Dictionary of English Surnames*, 3rd with corrections and additions by R.M. Wilson. London: Routledge, 1991.

Robertson, Dr. Robert Crawford. *Pioneer and Related Families of Randolph and Perry Counties Illinois*. Chattanooga, TN: the author, 1960.

Rockingham County, NC, Record of Deeds, No. L (microform).

Rowan County, NC, Index to Real Estate Conveyances—Grantees, 1753–1921 (microform).

_____, Marriage Bonds, 1753–1868, vol. C (microform).

_____, Record of Deeds, Book 4 (microform).

The Rutherford County News (Rutherfordton, NC).

Rutherford County, NC, Bastardy Bonds, 1872–1878, 1 vol. (microform).

_____, Criminal Action Papers, 086.326.1 (NC Office of Archives and History, Raleigh, NC).

_____, Marriage Bonds, 1779–1868, vol. F (microform).

_____, Minutes, Board of County Commissioners, 1900–1901 (microform).

_____, Minutes, Court of Pleas & Quarter Sessions, 1779–1798, unpag.; 1850–1868, 2 vols. (microform).

_____, Minutes, Superior Court, 1869–1876, vol. 1; and 1894–1902, 2 vols. (microform).

Bibliography

———, Record of Administrators, 1896–1913, vol. 1 (microform).
———, Record of Deeds, vols. A–D, C, J, 4–6, 49–50, 58, 62–63, 67, 71 and 100 (original court ledgers and microform).
———, Record of Deeds, General Indices, Grantor and Grantee (microform).
———, Record of Estate Settlements, 1868–1920, vol. A (microform).
———, Record of Widow's Yearly Allowance, 1889–1962, vols. A–L (microform).
———, Record of Wills, 1791–1813, vol. B; and 1782–1868, vol. E (microform).
———, Special Proceedings, 1901–1914, vol. C (microform).
The Rutherford Star (Rutherfordton, NC).
The Rutherford Star and Western-Carolina Record (Rutherfordton, NC).
The Rutherfordton Tribune (Rutherfordton, NC).
Saunders, William L., ed. *The Colonial Records of North Carolina, vol. VIII, 1769 to 1771*. Raleigh, NC: Josephus Daniels, Printer to the State, 1890.
Schenck, David, Papers of #652 (Southern Historical Collection, Wilson Library, University of North Carolina at Chapel Hill).
Seawell, Joseph Lacy. *The First Lynching was the First Overt Act for American Liberty*, revised and reprinted from *Wayside Tales from Carolina*. N.p.: n.p., July, 1927.
Second Census of the United States, 1800: Guilford County, NC, Population Schedule (microform).
Second Census of the United States, 1800: Rockingham County, NC, Population Schedule (microform).
Secretary of State, NC, Granville Land Grants (microform).
———, Granville Proprietary Land Office, Warrants, Surveys (microform).
———, Land Grant Office, Warrants, Plats, etc., Guilford, Iredell, Mecklenburg, Rutherford & Tryon counties (microform).
———, Land Grant Record Books, vols. 26, 41 (microform).
Senate Reports, 42nd Congress, 1st Session, No. 1.
1755 Granville County, North Carolina Tax List, North Carolina Tax Series. Signal Mountain, TN: Mountain Press, nd.
1763 Anson County, North Carolina Tax List, North Carolina Tax Series. Signal Mountain, TN: Mountain Press, nd.
Seventh Census of the United States, 1850: Rutherford County, NC, Agricultural Schedule (microform).
Seventh Census of the United States, 1850: Rutherford County, NC, Population Schedule (microform).
Seventh Census of the United States, 1850: Rutherford County, NC, Slave Schedule (microform).
Shelby Banner (Shelby, NC).
The Shelby Daily Star. *Our Heritage: A History of Cleveland County*. Shelby, NC: The Shelby Daily Star, 1976.
Shotwell, Randolph Abbott, Papers, P.C. 243 (NC Office of Archives and History, Raleigh, NC).
Sixth Census of the United States, 1840: Spartanburg County, SC, Population Schedule (microform).
Smith, Gen. William Alexander, and W. Thomas Smith, compilers. *Family Tree Book Genealogical and Biographical: Listing the Relatives of General William Alexander Smith and W. Thomas Smith*. Data for the Flake Tables gathered by Mrs. Julia Flake Burns and Osmer D. Flake. Los Angeles: W. Thomas Smith, 1922.
Soule, Sarah A. "Populism and Black Lynching in Georgia, 1890–1900." *Social Forces*, 71 (December 1992), pp. 431–449.
The Southern Home (Charlotte, NC).
Sprague, Waldo Chamberlain. "Cotton Flack of Boston, Mass." *American Genealogist*, 36 (October 1960), pp. 223–228.
Steelman, Joseph F. "Republican Party Strategists and the Issue of Fusion with Populists in North Carolina, 1893–1894." *The North Carolina Historical Review*, 47 (July 1970), pp. 244–269.
———. "Vicissitudes of Republican party Politics: The Campaign of 1892 in North Carolina." *The North Carolina Historical Review*, 43 (Autumn 1966), pp. 430–442.
The Sun (Rutherfordton, NC).
Tax List of Chester County, 1768. Westminster, MD: Family Line Publications, 1998.
Tenth Census of the United States, 1880: Rutherford County, NC, Agricultural Schedule (microform).
Tenth Census of the United States, 1880: Rutherford County, NC, Population Schedule (microform).

Testimony Taken by the Joint Select Committee to Inquire into the Condition of Affairs in the Late Insurrectionary States, North Carolina; and *South Carolina*, vols. II–III. Washington, DC: Government Printing Office, 1872.
Third Census of the United States, 1810: Madison County, KY, Population Schedule (microform).
Thirteenth Census of the United States, 1910: Rutherford County, NC, Population Schedule (microform).
Thompson, Ruth F., and Louise J. Hartgrove, compilers. *Vol. I, Abstracts of the Marriage Bonds and Additional Data, Guilford County, North Carolina, 1771–1840*. Greensboro, NC: The Guilford County Genealogical Society, 1981.
Tolnay, Stewart E., and E.M. Beck. *A Festival of Violence: An Analysis of Southern Lynchings, 1882–1930*. Urbana, Ill.: University of Illinois Press, 1995.
Tomlinson, J.S. *Assembly Sketch Book, Session 1883, North Carolina*, vol. 2. Raleigh, NC: Edwards, Broughton & Co., 1883.
_____. *Tar Heel Sketch-Book, A Brief Biographical Sketch of the Life and Public Acts of the Members of the General Assembly of North Carolina, Session of 1879*. Raleigh, NC: Raleigh News Steam Book and Job Print, 1879.
Trelease, Allen. *The North Carolina Railroad, 1849–1871, and the Modernization of North Carolina*. Chapel Hill: The University of North Carolina Press, 1991.
_____. *White Terror: The Ku Klux Klan Conspiracy and Southern Reconstruction*. New York: Harper & Row, Publishers, 1971.
Tryon County, NC, Record of Deeds, vol. 1 (microform).
Turner, Grace, and Miles S. Philbeck, Jr., compilers. *Rutherford County, North Carolina, Will Abstracts, 1779–1910*. Chapel Hill: the authors, 1982.
Twelfth Census of the United States, 1900: Cleveland County, NC, Population Schedule (microform).
Twelfth Census of the United States, 1900: Rutherford County, NC, Population Schedule (microform).
The Union Republican (Winston-Salem, NC).
Vance, Zebulon B., Papers of, #3952 (Southern Historical Collection, Wilson Library, University of North Carolina at Chapel Hill).
Veterans Records Pension Files (National Archives, Washington, DC).
Vicars, Sir Arthur, ed. *Index to the Perogative Wills of Ireland, 1536–1810*. Baltimore: Genealogical Publishing Company, 1989.
von Franz, Marie-Louise. *C.G. Jung: His Myth in Our Time*. New York: G.P. Putnam's Sons, 1975.
Waddell, Alfred Moore. *Some Memories of My Life*. Raleigh, NC: Edwards & Broughton, 1908.
The War of the Rebellion: A Compilation of the Official Records of the Union and Confederate Armies, prepared under the direction of Lt. Col. Robert N. Scott, series I, vol. XXIX, part II, correspondence, etc. Washington, DC: Government Printing Office, 1890.
Washburn, Benjamin E. *Rutherford County and Its Hospital*. Spindale, NC: The Spindale Press, 1960.
_____. *To Everything a Season: Rutherfordton Long, Long Ago*. Spindale, NC: The Spindale Press, nd.
Weekly Pioneer (Asheville, NC).
West-Carolina Record (Rutherfordton, NC).
The Western Vindicator (Rutherfordton, NC).
Wheeler, Earl Milton. "The Role of the North Carolina Militia in the Beginning of the American Revolution." PhD. Diss., Tulane University 1969.
White, Melvin L. *A History of the Life of Amos Owens, The Noted Blockader, of Cherry Mountain, N.C.* Shelby, NC: Cleveland Star Job Print, 1901.
White, Virgil D., abstractor. *Genealogical Abstracts of Revolutionary War Pension Files*, vols. II–III. Waynesboro, TN: The National Historical Publishing Company, 1991.
White, Walter. *Rope & Faggot: A Biography of Judge Lynch*. New York: Alfred A. Knopf, 1929.
Williamson, Joel. *The Crucible of Race: Black-White Relations in the American South Since Emancipation* New York: Oxford University Press, 1984.
Wilson, Charles Reagan, et al., eds. *The Encyclopedia of Southern Culture*. Chapel Hill: The University of North Carolina Press, 1989.
Wilson, Robert, Account Books, #1896 (Southern Historical Collection, Wilson Library, University of North Carolina at Chapel Hill).
Woodward, C. Vann. *Origins of the New South, 1877–1913*. Baton Rouge: Louisiana State University Press, 1971.
_____. *The Strange Career of Jim Crow*, 3rd revised ed. New York: Oxford University Press, 1974.

Bibliography

_____. *Tom Watson: Agrarian Rebel.* New York: Oxford University Press, 1963.
Wooley, James E. and Vivian. *Rutherford County, North Carolina, Wills and Miscellaneous Records, 1783–1868.* Easley, SC: Southern Historical Press, Inc., 1984.
Wyatt-Brown, Bertram. *Honor and Violence in the Old South*, abridged ed. New York: Oxford University Press, 1986.
Yates, Richard E. *The Confederacy and Zeb Vance.* Confederate Centennial Studies, 8. Tuscaloosa, AL: Confederate Publishing Co., Inc., 1958.
Yorkville Enquirer (Yorkville, SC).

Index

*Numbers in **boldface** refer to pages with photographs.*

Abernathy, W.L. 36
Adair, Columbus 133
Adair, Govan 133
Alamance, Battle of 107
Anderson, John (of Guilford) 109–110, 164–165n
Anderson, John, the Rev. (of Washington Co., PA) 110
Anderson, William, Jr. 110
Anderson, William, Sr. 110
Andrews, Capt. George 176n
Averasboro, Battle of 123
Aycock, Gov. Charles B. 9, 17, 52–53, 56–58, **59**, 61, 153n; opposition to lynching 19–20, 78–81, 83–84; pardon of Raney Mills 78–81, 83–84

Baber, William O. 35–36, 153n
Banker's House 122–123
Barber (Baber?), B.A. 35, 151n
Baxter, Catherine Lee 122
Baxter, Elisha 120, 170n
Baxter, Ester McDowell *see* Durham, Ester McDowell Baxter
Baxter, John 120, 122
Baxter, William, Sr. 120, 170n
Baynard (Benard?) Martin 133, 173n
Beatty's Ford 110
Bentonville, Battle of 123
Big Troublesome Creek 113
Biggerstaff, Aaron V. 127–135, 139, 174n
Biggerstaff, Samuel 127–129
Biggerstaff raids *see* Ku Klux Klan
Biggerstaff's Old Fields 11

Birge, Nelson 127
Black, George 110–111
"Blanton old precinct" 126–127
Boggs, George 55
Brittain Presbyterian Church 24, 114, 149n, 168n
Brooks, Elizabeth 136
Brown, Joseph E. 25
Bryan, Nelson 124
Bryan, William Jennings 48, 72, 157n
Bryan House 135
Bruce, Alonzo 28
Bruce, Samuel J. 28, 150n
Bruce, Sarah Elizabeth 28, 150n
Bryant, H.E.C. "Red Buck" 53, 57–58
"Bucks County theory" 104
Buffalo Creek 106
Buffalo Presbyterian Church (Guilford) 106, 108
Burns, Julia Flake 106
Burnt Chimney, NC 5, 24, 29, 120–121, 175n
Butler, Marion 38, 40, 42, **43**, 47, 54
Byers, Capt. John Creighton 176n
Bynum, William Preston 175n

Cabiness, Harvey 124, 126
Caldwell, the Rev. David 106, 110
Caldwell, Joseph P. 10
Caldwell, Gov. Todd R. 133, 175n
Camp Creek 104, 108, 164n
Camp Creek Township 55
Cane Creek 110
Caroleen, NC 53
Carpenter, J.B. 123, 129, 136, 141

Index

Carrier, John V. 51
Carson, Olin O. 128
Caswell, Gov. Richard 106
Catawba River 109–110
Catheys Creek 23–24, 28, 104, 109–112, 149n, 164n, 166–167n
Caviness, D.N. 34
Cedar Creek 149n
Central Hotel 51
Chambers, John (of Guilford) 162n
Chambers, John (of Orange Co., NY) 163n
Charles, Robert 60, 155n
Cherokee County, NC 27
Cherokee Expedition 163n
Cherry, David 109
Cherry, Robert 109–110
Cherry Mountain *see* Ku Klux Klan
Chester County, PA 110
Chimney Rock, NC 123
Clark (Clarke?) Samuel 109, 164n
class conflict 33–34, 45–46, 78–79, 83–84, 151n
Cleveland Banner 138, 140
Cloud, J.M., Judge 175n
Cole, Helen Flack 1, 82, 158n, 166n, 175n
Colored Alliance 7
Conscription Act (CSA) 25–26
Constitutional Convention of 1868 125
Cool Springs Baptist Church 24, 29–30, 150n
Cool Springs Cemetery 73
Cool Springs Township 5, 28
Cove Creek 24–25, 27–28, 30–31, 149n
Cox, Edward V. 46
Cox's Shop 135
Craig, Locke 9–10
Crawford, Dudley W. 104–105, 114
Crawford, W.T. 55
"Crawford tradition" 104–105
Cross Creek Expeditions 106, 108
Cumberland County, PA 107, 110

Daniels, Josephus 9, 52
Davis, Col. Champ 176n
Davis, J.S. 37
Deep River 109
Denny, Ann 107
Denny, Walter 107
Denny family 110
DePriest, Decatur 127–129, 131–132, 139
DePriest, Jesse R. 136–137, 173n, 175n
DePriest, William 128, 172n
Derry Township (Lancaster Co., PA) 163n
Dickerson, M.O., Jr. 3, 44, 153n
Dickerson, Capt. M.O., Sr. 176n
Dixon, Thomas, Jr. 126
Dixon, Thomas, Sr. 171n
Dixon's Store 44
Downey, Thomas J. 134, 136–137

Drumore Township (Lancaster Co., PA) 106–107, 109, 113, 162n
Dunn, William 164n
Durham, Catherine Lenora Tracy 122
Durham, Ester McDowell Baxter 121
Durham, L.N. 37
Durham, Micajah 121, 135
Durham, Capt. Plato 4, 118–122, **121**, 125–126, 128–129, 132, 134–135, 137–141, 171n, 173–174n

Eaves, Andrew 120
Eaves, George G. 121
Eaves, Guilford 174n
Eaves, Jane Baxter 120
Eaves, Capt. John Baxter 3–4, 43, 53–54, 56, **120**–121, 123–125, 127, 129, 133–134, 136–137, 141–144, 153n, 170–171n, 173–174n, 176–177n
Eaves, Capt. John Lafayette 172n, 174n
Eaves, Johnnie Amelia Logan 123–124
Eaves, Spencer 120–121, 134, 170n
Eaves House 120, 134, 170n
Edgerton, William 172–173n
Edwards, Capt. John 176n
Ellenboro, NC 52, 154n
Erwin, Maj. Lawson P. 10, 54, 146n, 176n
Erwin, Marcus 137–138
Erwin, O. Carson 3, 68, 157n
Essex, County of, UK 114–115, 168–169n
Ewart, H.G. 46–47, 142, 153n
exemptions, military (CSA) 26
Exum, Wyatt P. 40, 153n

Fanning Edmund 107
Faulkner, William 11
Felton, Rebecca Latimer 16
Finch, Harriet 77
Finley, James 110, 165n
First Baptist Church (Forest City) 24, 29–30, **32**, 38
First Baptist Church (Rutherfordton) 1
Flack, Andrew (of Guilford) 105, 161n
Flack, Andrew Braxton 27, 32, 82, 85, 156n, 158n
Flack, Andrew, Jr. 23–25, 149n
Flack, Andrew, Sr. 23–24, 105, 112–113, 161n, 166n
Flack, Charles Z., Jr. 2
Flack, Charles Z., Sr. 2, 74, 82, 85, 103, 114, 158n
Flack, Christopher Jason 105
Flack, Effie 28
Flack, Elisha 161n
Flack, Emma Harrill 82, 158n
Flack, Fergus 116
Flack, George 23–25, 105, 112, 149n, 166n
Flack, George Andrew 105

Index

Flack, Dr. Horace E. 103–105, 109, 113, 115, 164n, 166n
Flack, Ivarea 103–104, 109, 112, 166n, 168n
Flack, J. Mills 105
Flack, James (of Bucks) 104
Flack, James (of County Cork) 115
Flack, James (of Dublin) 116
Flack, James (of Guilford/Rockingham) 104, 113–114, 116–117, 168n
Flack, James (of Rowan/Guilford) 114, 168n
Flack, James Ewell 27
Flack, Jane or Jean McQuiston (of Lancaster/Rowan/Guilford) 107–108, 114, 161n
Flack, Jean Glenn (of Lancaster/Guilford/Rockingham) 113
Flack, "Jefferson" 104, 161n
Flack, John (of Bucks) 104
Flack, John (of County Down) 116
Flack, John (of Iredell/Perry) 167n
Flack, John (of Lancaster) 106–107, 116
Flack, John (of Tryon/Rutherford) 4, 23–24, 103–106, 108–113, 116, 160–161n, 164n, 166–168n
Flack, John (of Washington) 109–110
Flack, John Buford 27
Flack, John Jefferson 161n
Flack, John, Jr. 167n
Flack, Joseph F. 105
Flack, Katie Harrill 28–30, **29**, 63, 82, 149n, 159n
Flack, Leander or Lee Roswell 19, 25, 158n
Flack, Legrand A. 115, 161n
Flack, "Major" John 24, 28
Flack, Margaret Alvira Hemphill **25**, 27–28
Flack, Mary (wife of John) 112–113
Flack, Mary Lenora 28
Flack, Mays Cleveland 156n
Flack, Michael 167n
Flack, Millard B. 105
Flack, Mills Higgins **36, 45**; Alliance membership 34, 37–38; ancestry 3–4, 23–24, 103–117, 160–169n; anti–Semitism 38; Bruce affair 28, 150n; candidacy for Clerk of Court (1898) 50, 55; candidacy for State House (1892) 40–41; candidacy for State House (1894) 43–44; class, views on 37–38; Cove Creek farm 25, 27–28, 30–31, 151n; debts 30–31, 75; education 24; farmer 25, 27–28, 30–32, 75; Forest City farm 28–29; Hamilton Quarters farm 28–29, 75, 150n; and honor 63–65, 67, 72–73, 82–85; legislative service 45–47, 154n; marriages 25, 28; memory of 84–85; military service 25–27; "murder" of 63–67; political ideas 37–38, 45–47; religion 24, 29–30, 150–151n
Flack, name origins 114–115
Flack, Otho Gerod Remus 28, 63–67, **66**, 74–75, 82–83, 156n, 158n

Flack, Polly Porter 112
Flack, Posey Maggie 27, 74, **75**, 150n, 158n
Flack, Ralph R. 1, 28, 31, 82, 84–85, 103, 105, 115, 156n, 159n
Flack, Richard 168n
Flack, Robert 116
Flack, Samuel Mills 27, 75, 159n
Flack, Sarah 109
Flack, Thomas (of County Cork) 115–116
Flack, Thomas (of County Down) 116
Flack, Thomas (of Rowan/Guilford) 104–111, 113–114, 116–117, 162–164n
Flack, Thomas (of Saffron Walden) 168n
Flack, Thomas Millard 19, 27, 32
Flack, William (of Bucks) 104
Flack, William (of Mecklenburg/Tryon/Rutherford) 103–105, 108, 111, 113, 116, 160n, 164n, 168n
Flack family 30; children of M.H. Flack 25, 27–28; lynching of Avery Mills 74–75, 82–85, 158–159n; slaveholdings 24–25
Flack-Wilson, Lalla Chinara 28, 75, 82, 158n
Flacke, Richard 168n
"Flaick," Samuel 105
"Flaick," Thomas 105
Flake, John 106
Flake, Osmer D. 106
Flake, Samuel 105, 117
Flake, Thomas 106
Flake, William 106
Fleck, John (of Little Milton) 114
"Fleck," John (of Rowan/Guilford) 109, 164n
Fleck, Robert 114
Fleck, William 114
Flecke, Andro 114
Flek, Patryk 114
Fleming, Thomas 111
Florence Mill 6, 29, **31**
Floyd's Creek community 120
Forest City sub-alliance 36
Forrest, Nathan Bedford 169n
Fortune, Julius 128
Fourth Creek 112
Fowler, Leonard 40
Fredericksburg, Battle of 122
"free silver" 47–48, 154n
Freeman, Francis 54
"Fusion" 8–11, 21, 42–61; Legislature of 1895 44–47; in Rutherford County 40, 43–44, 48–51, 54–55

Gettysburg, Battle of 131
Gilkey, Jane or Jean McQuiston 110, 165n
Gilkey, John 110–112, 165n
Gilkey, Jonathan 165n
Gilkey, Robert 110, 165n
Gilkey, Samuel 165n
Gilkey, Walter 165n

Index

Gilkey, William 110, 165n
Gilkey family 110
Givens, Samuel 108
Glenn, Dr. Charles Foster 115
Glenn, Hugh 113, 168n
Golden Grove Seminary 24
Golden Valley 158n
Grace Cotton Mill 1
"grandfather clause" 56–57, 80
Grant, Ulysses S. 137, 140
Granville land grant office 163n
Grassy Branch 133, 139
Gray's Chapel sub-alliance 36
Greeley, Horace 137, 140
Green, L.E. 52, 154n
Greene, J. Cicero 68, 156–157n
Guion, H.W. 128

H.D. Lee & Company, Bankers 123
Hamilton, Lafayette 51
Hampton, Col. Andrew 105, 111, 161n
Hampton, Jonathan 111, 161n
Hamrick, Sam 68–69, 157n
Hardin, L.C. 36, 151n
Hardin, William C. 68, 157n
Harper, James C. 140
Harrill, Alfred W. 28, 137
Harrill, Housen D. 29–30, 150n
Harrill, John B. 129, 132, 135, 137, **138**
Harrill, Katie see Flack, Katie Harrill
Harrill, Capt. Lawson 176n
Harrill, Martin J. 150n
Harrill, S.F. 44
Harrill, Ursula 28
Harrill family 28–30, 150n
Harris, Col. Ceburn L. 26–27, 44, 123–125, 141, 143, 149n
Harris, J.C.L. 143–144
Harrison, Benjamin 142–143
Haw River Presbyterian Church 108
Haynes, Raleigh Rutherford 6
Hays, Henry 109
Hemphill, John 25
Hemphill, Margaret Alvira see Flack, Margaret Alvira Hemphill
Hemphill family 24
Hemphill family cemetery 28
Henrietta Mill No. 1 29
Henrietta Mill No. 2 29
Hester, Joseph G. 133
Hicks, Dr. Oliver 39, 55, 152n
Higgins, Alvira 24
Higgins, Mills 148n
High Shoals community 120–122
Holden, Gov. William W. 123–126, 171n
Holland, William 128, 133
Home Guard (CSA) 3, 25–27
honor, southern code of 17–20, 72–73, 83–85

Horde, Martin 132
Howe, Lt. Albion 138
Hunting Creek 110

illegal distilling 46, 118, 128–129, 172n
individuation/alienation 18–19, 83; of the "New Negro" 62
"Irish" settlement 112

Jenkins, Ibbey 127
Jones, A.H. 125
Justice, James D. 68–69, 157n
Justice, James M. 119, 123–124, 126, 128–129, 134–137, 141, 174n, 176n
Justice, Michael Hoke 3, 40, 48, 58–61, **60**, 152–153n
Justice, T.B. 152n
Justice, W.D. 136
"jute bag" cartel 8, 35, 145n

Kenady Creek 110
"Killserl" (Killeysorrell?) Ireland 113, 116
King's Mountain, Battle of 10–11, 23, 105, 110–112
Kitchen, William W. 16
Knoxville, TN 120–122
Ku Klux Klan 4, 12, 73; arrests, indictments and trials 133–134, 136–138, 140; Bald Rock Den 135; Biggerstaff raid (1st) 131–133, 139; Biggerstaff raid (2nd) 133–134; Burnt Chimney den 134–135, 137, 175n; Cherry Mountain den 118, 127–129, 131–135, 139, 172–173n; Cleveland involvement in Rutherford 129, 131–133; defined 125–126; "dens" 172n; "dissolution order" 169n; ex-Confederates in 119, 126, 139; "Grand Klan" 135, 174n; Horse Creek den 135, 174n; illegal distilling 128–129, 172n; informers 136–137; initiations in Rutherfordton 129, 131; leaders in Cleveland 125–126, 137–140; McGaughey raid 127–129, 132, 172n; purposes of raids 129; raids in Cleveland 126–127; raids in Rutherford 127–129, 131–136, 139, 172–175n; raids near SC line 129, 134–135; Rutherfordton raid 134–136; Spartanburg County 135, 174n; Weston murders 133, 173n

Lancaster County, PA 103, 106–107, 109–110, 112–114, 116–117
Lane, E. 44
Ledbetter Road 2, 5, 69
Lee, Maj. Herbert D. 122–123, 126, 128–129, 134, 137, 139–140, 174n, 176n
Lee, Gen. Robert E. 122
Leventhorpe, Brig. Gen. Collet 176n
Lewis, Jane Flack 28
Lewis, Joe 60

Index

Limestone Springs, SC 135
Little Britain Township (Lancaster Co., PA) 106–107, 162n
Logan, B.F. 126, 133, 137–138
Logan, George W. 27, 119, 123–126, 128, 131–133, 136–137, 139, 141, 172–173n, 175n
Logan, Col. John 127, 172n
Logan, Robert W. 123, 136
Logan, William 53
Lowman, Adam 108
Lusk, Virgil S. 131
Lyle, Capt. J. Banks 135–137, 174n
"lynch law" 11
lynching(s): Forest City, explanations of 70–73; "mass mob" 72–73; Polk County, NC (1900) 60; racial, origins of 11–21, 147–148n; Salisbury, NC (1906) 20; Shelby, NC (ca. 1870) 125

Macune, Charles 35, 39, 152n
Manly, Alexander 55–56, 147n, 155n
Marion, NC 76, 159n
Martin, Elijah A. 68–69, 157n, 159n
Martin, Col. James 107, 163n
Martin, Richard 137
Maxwell, Nelda 75, 158n
McAfee, Col. Leroy M. 119, 126, **127**, 129, 133, 137–139, 171–172n, 174n
McArthur House 5
McBrayer, Matt 137, 173n, 175n
McBrayer, Dr. Matt 175n
McBrayer, Ned 127
McCall, J.D. 45
McDowell, Col. John L. 34, 151n
McDowell, Louis 124
McDowell County, NC 159n
McEntire, Capt. John Y. 176n
McEntire, R.A. 128
McFarland, J.V. 49–50, 154n
McGaughey, James 127–129, 132, 172n
McKesson, Charles 51
McQuiston, James 107
McQuiston, Jean *see* Flack, Jane; Gilkey, Jane
McQuiston, Robert 107, 109–110, 165n
McQuiston, Sarah 109
Michael, John 152n
militia, Rutherford (CSA) 26–27
Miller, C.L. 154n
Miller, Martin 53
Miller, William 123
Miller & Eaves, Rutherfordton 123
Mills, Avery 2, 5, 14–21, 62–74, **70**, 83–86, 156n, 158n
Mills, Ladson, Jr. 135, 173n
Mills, Massey 62
Mills, Raney 18–20, 62–63, 66, 68–69, 76–81, 84–85, 156n, 159n
Montford Cove Baptist Church 24, 150n

Montford Cove community 25, 28
Moore, Franklin 153n
Moore, Logan ("Log") A. 158n
Moore's Creek, Battle of 108, 163n
Morgan, A.F. 154n
Morgan, J.P. 38
Morrow, D.F. 27
Mott, Dr. John J. 142–144
Mountain Creek 111, 166n
Mountain Creek Baptist Church 24, 149n

National Farmers' Alliance & Industrial Union 7–8, 13, 33–37; anti-Semitism in 88; biblical imagery in 38; congresses 35–36; cooperative exchanges 35–36; lecturing system 36–37; "producerist" ideology 7, 33, 36
Negro militias 125, 133
Negro Republicans (Rutherford Co.) 50–54
New Bern, NC 52
New Hanover County, NC 52
New Orleans, LA, race riot 60, 72, 155n
Normal and Industrial School (UNC–Greensboro) 45–46, 153n
The North Carolina Citizen 131
North Carolina Farmers' Association 34
Norville, Mary Ann 132, 173n
Nottingham Colony 106, 110

Ocala demands 39
Octoraro Creek 107, 110
Orange County, NY 163n
Owens, Almon 127
Owens, Amos 46, 118, 128–132, 137, 139, 153n, 172n

Palmer, Gen. William J. 128
patrols, slave 11–12
Pea Ridge sub-alliance 36, 39
Pearson, Rep. Richmond 44, 55
Pearson, Judge Richmond M. 25–26, 122
Polk, Leonidas L. 34, 38–39, **40**, 45–46, 151–152n
Polk County, NC 27, 60
Ponder, John 60
Populist (or People's) Party 8–11, 14–17, 21, 33, 38–41, 42–61
Porter, James (of Lancaster) 107, 113
Porter, Capt. James (of Rowan?) 107
Porter, Maj. James (of Tryon/Rutherford) 112–113, 166–167n
Porter, Jane 112
Porter, Robert (of Tryon/Rutherford) 112, 167n
Porter, Col. Robert (of Tryon/Rutherford) 112
Porter, Samuel 109
Porter, Thomas 109, 113
Porter, William (of Lancaster) 113

Index

Porter, Col. William (of Tryon/Rutherford) 110–112, 166–167n
Porter family 112–113
Pritchard, Jeter 48–50, 52, 143–144
Protective Tarriff League 143
Purgason, Lindsay 48, 50, 154n
Putnam, Bush 127

railroads (of Forest City) 29
Ramsey, A. 128
Ramsour's Mill, Battle of 166n
"rape complex" 12–15
Red Shirts 146n, 171n
Red Tavern 120, 134
Reedy Fork Creek 106–108, 110, 114
Regulation, War of 107
Republican Party (NC) 8–10, 42–43, 45–48, 57, 79, 142–144
Republican Party (Rutherford Co.): post–War/Reconstruction era 119, 121, 123–125, 128–129, 131–132; post–Reconstruction/Fusion era 40, 43–44, 48–55, 141–142, 170n
Robertson, William 111
Robinson, William S.O"B. **78**, 159n
Rock Springs Campground 127
Ross, Nancy 114
Roswell, Lee *see* Flack, Leander
Rountree, George 55
Rucker, Adin 172n
Russell, Daniel 144, 153n
Rutherford, Griffith 163n
Rutherford & Spartanburg Railroad Commission 141
Rutherford Farmers' Alliance 34–41
Rutherford Press, threats against 84, 156n
Rutherford Railway Construction Co. 29, 141
The Rutherford Star 123, 136
Rutherfordton Academy 123

Saffron Walden, Village of, UK 114–115
Sampson, Adm. William Thomas 154n
Sandy Run section 127
Schenck, David 132–133, 141, 172n
Scoggins, Nathan 123, 154n, 175n
Seaboard Airline Railway 29; depot of 68
Second Creek 112
Shaw, Thomas J. 74, 77, 158n
Shelby, NC 77, 125
Shotwell, Addison 135
Shotwell, Randolph A. 12, 118, 129, 131, 135–137, 140, 173–174n
Simmons, Furnifold M. 9, 11, 17, 19–20, 52, 56
Southern Railway 29
Spartanburg County, SC 120, 135
Spindale, NC 21, 24
Spurlin, Wiley 53

Statesville, NC 76, 142
Steadman, Polly 133
Stoneman's Raid 128
"subtreasury plan" 8, 146n
Sunshine sub–alliance 35

Tanner, Simpson Bobo 6
Tate, John, store ledger of 108
tenant farming 32–33
textile mills (in Forest City) 6, 29
Third Creek Presbyterian Church 112
Thomason, Levi 60
Thompson, Cyrus 52–53, 58, 153n
Tillman, Benjamin 10, 46, 80
Toney, Webb 128
"Trading Camp" settlement 112
Trout, Gaither 137
Tryon Association 110
Twitty, Capt. Francis 176n
Twitty, T.B. 141, 176n
Twitty, Capt. W.L. 110–111, 176n

Union Mills, NC 133
Upper Buffalo Presbyterian Church (Washington Co., PA) 110

Vance, Robert B. 140
Vance, Zebulon B. 25–26, 39, 140, 152n
Village Hotel 123

Waddell, Alfred Moore 16, 55–56, 58–**59**, 87
Wade, Capt. Thomas 106
Walker, Col. John 111
Walker, Capt. Joseph 176n
Wall, S.F. 154n
Wallace, Alphonso DeKalb 3, 44, 47–48, 52–53, 58, 153n, 155n
Walnut Branch (of Guilford) 106, 108–109, 162n
Walnut Branch (of Rowan) 112
Washington County, PA 109–110, 117
Watson, W.P. 154n
Weaver, Gen. James B. 40
Webster, William 134–135, 173n
Wells, J.R. 154n
The Western Vindicator 131
Weston, Silas 133
Weston murders 133, 173n
Wetmore, L.B. 51
Whig Party 120–121
White, M.L. "Corn Cracker" 58, 128
White, R.S. 45–46
White Supremacy Clubs 10, 146n
Whiteside, Jacob 50–51
Wilderness, Battle of 122, 135
Wiley, John 132
Wilkins, Samuel, Capt. 176n

Index

Wilmington, NC 52; race riot of 1898 55–56, 59, 72
Wilson, Chinara Flack *see* Flack, Lalla Chinara
Wilson, Frank I. 123
Wilson, Capt. George 106
Withrow, John C. 132–135, 139, 172–173n

Wood, Capt. Thompson J. 176n
Wright, Uncle Simon 152n

Yell County, AR 28
Yorkville, SC 138
Young, William 112

www.ingramcontent.com/pod-product-compliance
Ingram Content Group UK Ltd.
Pitfield, Milton Keynes, MK11 3LW, UK
UKHW042010140426
5217IPUK00015B/1087